GRADUATE STEM EDUCATION FOR THE 21ST CENTURY

Alan Leshner and Layne Scherer, *Editors*

Committee on Revitalizing Graduate STEM Education
for the 21st Century

Board on Higher Education and Workforce

Policy and Global Affairs

A Consensus Study Report of

The National Academies of
SCIENCES · ENGINEERING · MEDICINE

THE NATIONAL ACADEMIES PRESS
Washington, DC
www.nap.edu

THE NATIONAL ACADEMIES PRESS   500 Fifth Street, NW   Washington, DC 20001

This activity was supported by contracts between the National Academy of Sciences, the National Science Foundation (1642408), the Institute of Education Sciences (R305U160001), the Burroughs Wellcome Fund (103932-4031), and the Spencer Foundation. Any opinions, findings, conclusions, or recommendations expressed in this publication do not necessarily reflect the views of any organization or agency that provided support for the project.

International Standard Book Number-13:   978-0-309-47273-9
International Standard Book Number-10:   0-309-47273-3
Library of Congress Control Number: 2018941720
Digital Object Identifier: https://doi.org/10.17226/25038

Additional copies of this publication are available for sale from the National Academies Press, 500 Fifth Street, NW, Keck 360, Washington, DC 20001; (800) 624-6242 or (202) 334-3313; http://www.nap.edu.

Suggested citation: National Academies of Sciences, Engineering, and Medicine. 2018. *Graduate STEM Education for the 21st Century*. Washington, DC: The National Academies Press. doi: https://doi.org/10.17226/25038.

The National Academies of
SCIENCES · ENGINEERING · MEDICINE

The **National Academy of Sciences** was established in 1863 by an Act of Congress, signed by President Lincoln, as a private, nongovernmental institution to advise the nation on issues related to science and technology. Members are elected by their peers for outstanding contributions to research. Dr. Marcia McNutt is president.

The **National Academy of Engineering** was established in 1964 under the charter of the National Academy of Sciences to bring the practices of engineering to advising the nation. Members are elected by their peers for extraordinary contributions to engineering. Dr. C. D. Mote, Jr., is president.

The **National Academy of Medicine** (formerly the Institute of Medicine) was established in 1970 under the charter of the National Academy of Sciences to advise the nation on medical and health issues. Members are elected by their peers for distinguished contributions to medicine and health. Dr. Victor J. Dzau is president.

The three Academies work together as the **National Academies of Sciences, Engineering, and Medicine** to provide independent, objective analysis and advice to the nation and conduct other activities to solve complex problems and inform public policy decisions. The National Academies also encourage education and research, recognize outstanding contributions to knowledge, and increase public understanding in matters of science, engineering, and medicine.

Learn more about the National Academies of Sciences, Engineering, and Medicine at **www.nationalacademies.org**.

The National Academies of
SCIENCES · ENGINEERING · MEDICINE

Consensus Study Reports published by the National Academies of Sciences, Engineering, and Medicine document the evidence-based consensus on the study's statement of task by an authoring committee of experts. Reports typically include findings, conclusions, and recommendations based on information gathered by the committee and the committee's deliberations. Each report has been subjected to a rigorous and independent peer-review process and it represents the position of the National Academies on the statement of task.

Proceedings published by the National Academies of Sciences, Engineering, and Medicine chronicle the presentations and discussions at a workshop, symposium, or other event convened by the National Academies. The statements and opinions contained in proceedings are those of the participants and are not endorsed by other participants, the planning committee, or the National Academies.

For information about other products and activities of the National Academies, please visit www.nationalacademies.org/about/whatwedo.

COMMITTEE ON REVITALIZING GRADUATE STEM EDUCATION FOR THE 21ST CENTURY

Members

ALAN LESHNER (*Chair*) [NAM], Chief Executive Officer, Emeritus, American Association for the Advancement of Science

SHERILYNN BLACK, Assistant Professor of the Practice, Medical Education; Associate Vice Provost for Faculty Advancement; and Co-Principal Investigator, Duke University BioCoRE Program, Duke University

MARY SUE COLEMAN [NAM], President, Association of American Universities

JAIME CURTIS-FISK, Scientist and STEM Education Advocate, Dow Chemical Company

KENNETH GIBBS, JR., Program Director, National Institute of General Medical Sciences

MAUREEN GRASSO, Professor of Textile Sciences and Former Graduate School Dean, North Carolina State University

SALLY F. MASON, President Emerita, University of Iowa

MARY MAXON, Associate Laboratory Director for Biosciences, Lawrence Berkeley National Laboratory

SUZANNE ORTEGA, President, Council of Graduate Schools

CHRISTINE ORTIZ, Morris Cohen Professor of Materials Science and Engineering, Massachusetts Institute of Technology, and Founder, Station1

MELANIE ROBERTS, Director of State and Regional Affairs, Pacific Northwest National Laboratory

HENRY SAUERMANN, Associate Professor of Strategy and Peter Pühringer Chair in Entrepreneurship, European School of Management and Technology, Berlin; Research Associate, National Bureau of Economic Research

BARBARA ANNA SCHAAL [NAS], Dean of Arts and Sciences and Professor, Washington University in St. Louis

SUBHASH SINGHAL [NAE], Battelle Fellow and Fuel Cells Director, Pacific Northwest National Laboratory

KATE STOLL, Senior Policy Advisor, MIT Washington Office

JAMES M. TIEN [NAE], Distinguished Professor and Dean Emeritus, University of Miami College of Engineering

KEITH R. YAMAMOTO [NAM, NAS], Vice Chancellor for Science Policy and Strategy, Director of Precision Medicine, and Professor of Cellular and Molecular Pharmacology, University of California, San Francisco

Study Staff

LAYNE SCHERER, Study Director
THOMAS RUDIN, Director, Board on Higher Education and Workforce
ADRIANA NAVIA COUREMBIS, Financial Officer
TOM ARRISON, Program Director, Policy and Global Affairs
JAY LABOV, Senior Advisor for Education and Communication
BARBARA NATALIZIO, Program Officer, Board on Higher Education and Workforce
MARIA LUND DAHLBERG, Program Officer, Board on Higher Education and Workforce
YASMEEN HUSSAIN, Christine Mirzayan Science and Technology Policy Fellow and Associate Program Officer, Board on Higher Education and Workforce (*January to July 2017*)
ELIZABETH GARBEE, Christine Mirzayan Science and Technology Policy Fellow, Board on Higher Education and Workforce (*January to April 2018*)
IRENE NGUN, Research Associate
AUSTEN APPLEGATE, Senior Program Assistant
ALLISON L. BERGER, Senior Program Assistant
JAIME COLMAN, Senior Program Assistant (*through November 2017*)
FREDERIC LESTINA, Senior Program Assistant

Consultants

JOSEPH ALPER, Writer
MARGARET BLUME-KOHOUT, Visiting Professor in Economics, Colgate University
JENNIFER LEBRÓN, Doctoral Student, Higher Education and International Education, George Mason University
JESSICA ROBLES, Senior Research Associate, Research Triangle International
ROBIN WISNIEWSKI, Director of Education Systems Improvement, Research Triangle International

Acknowledgments

The Committee on Revitalizing Graduate STEM Education for the 21st Century would like to acknowledge and thank the many people who made this study possible. First, we would like to acknowledge the support of the standing National Academies Board on Higher Education and Workforce (BHEW), which offered oversight for this study. Second, we would like to acknowledge that this report was informed by the efforts of many people who shared their data, insights, ideas, enthusiasm, and expertise with the committee. We would especially like to thank the following people (in alphabetical order), who presented at the open sessions of the committee's meetings:

DAVID ASAI, Howard Hughes Medical Institute
ELIZABETH BACA, California Governor's Office of Planning and Research
PATRICK BRENNWALD, University of North Carolina at Chapel Hill
THOMAS BROCK, National Center for Education Research
AMY CHANG, American Society for Microbiology
DONA CHIKARAISHI, Duke University (Emerita)
EARNESTINE PSALMONDS EASTER, National Science Foundation
DAVID FELDON, Utah State University
JOAN FERRINI-MUNDY, National Science Foundation
CHRIS GOLDE, Stanford University
CHRISTINE GRANT, North Carolina State University
JOSEPH GRAVES, North Carolina A&T University
CLAUDIA GUNSCH, Duke University
DAVE HARWELL, American Geophysical Union
SAMANTHA HINDLE, University of California, San Francisco

THEODORE HODAPP, American Physical Society
STEVEN HUNTER, IBM Fellow at North Carolina State University
YASMEEN HUSSAIN, National Academies of Sciences, Engineering, and
    Medicine
DANA (KEOKI) JACKSON, Lockheed Martin
NIMMI KANNANKUTTY, National Science Foundation
JONATHAN KERSHAW, Purdue University
TRISH LABOSKY, National Institutes of Health
JULIA LANE, New York University
MICHAEL LIPPS, LexisNexis
SEAN MCCONNELL, University of Chicago
VICTORIA MCGOVERN, Burroughs Wellcome Fund
THOMAS MILLER, North Carolina State University
BARBARA NATALIZIO, AAAS Fellow, National Science Foundation
HIRONAO OKAHANA, Council of Graduate Schools
JASON OWEN-SMITH, Institute for Research on Innovation in Science
MARINA RAMON, Cabrillo College
MICHAEL RICHEY, The Boeing Company
NANCY SCHWARTZ, University of Chicago
DAVID SHAFER, North Carolina State University
BASSAM SHAKHASHIRI, University of Wisconsin–Madison
DEBRA STEWART, NORC
LINDA STRAUSBAUGH, Professional Science Master's Association
LE TANG, ABB
CORY VALENTE, The Dow Chemical Company
KIMBERLY WEEMS, North Carolina Central University
BRUCE WEINBERG, Ohio State University
AYANNA BOYD WILLIAMS, North Carolina A&T University

The committee would like to thank the sponsors that made this study possible: the National Science Foundation (NSF), the Institute of Education Sciences, the Burroughs Wellcome Fund, and the Spencer Foundation. In addition, we would like to send our deep appreciation to our Program Officer Earnestine Easter (program director, NSF) and Joan Ferrini Mundy (assistant director for education and human resources, NSF, at the time of award and chief operating officer at time of publication).
    We would like to express our sincere gratitude to the generous hosts for the focus groups conducted by Research Triangle International: the American Indian Science and Engineering Society, Florida A&M University, South Dakota State University, Texas A&M University Corpus Christi, Texas A&M University Kingsville, and University of Northern Colorado. Additionally, we would like to thank all of the current and former participants and directors of the Institute

of Education Sciences' Predoctoral Interdisciplinary Research Training Program who contributed their responses to our researcher, Ms. Jennifer Lebrón.

The committee would also like to thank all of those who took time to provide valuable feedback to the project during the information-gathering period. This includes individuals who attended conference sessions or meetings on the topic, who hosted us at their institutions, or who responded to the committee's "Discussion Document and Call for Community Input."

We would like to send our thanks to the hosts of our two regional meetings at North Carolina State University and the University of California, San Francisco.

The committee would like to acknowledge the work of the consultants who have contributed to the report: Dr. Margaret Blume-Kohout, Ms. Jennifer Lebrón, Dr. Jessica Robles, and Dr. Robin Wisniewski. The committee would also like to thank Daniel Bearss, Senior Researcher at the National Academies, for his fact-checking and research assistance. We would like to send our deepest thanks to our report writer, Joseph Alper, for his tremendous work on this report.

This Consensus Study Report was reviewed in draft form by individuals chosen for their diverse perspectives and technical expertise. The purpose of this independent review is to provide candid and critical comments that will assist the National Academies of Sciences, Engineering, and Medicine in making each published report as sound as possible and to ensure that it meets the institutional standards for quality, objectivity, evidence, and responsiveness to the study charge. The review comments and draft manuscript remain confidential to protect the integrity of the deliberative process.

We wish to thank the following individuals for their review of this report: Dianne Chong, Boeing Research and Technology (Retired); Jingsheng Cong, University of California, Los Angeles; Peter Fiske, Lawrence Berkeley National Laboratory; Chris Golde, Stanford University; Beverly Hartline, Montana Tech; Kasia Grzebyk, University of North Carolina; Jonathan Kershaw, Purdue University; Philip Kutzko, University of Iowa; Deb Niemeier, University of California, Davis; Jennifer Pearl, American Association for the Advancement of Science; Julie Posselt, University of Southern California; Vassie Ware, Lehigh University; Hugh Welsh, DSM; and Carl Wieman, University of Colorado at Boulder.

Although the reviewers listed above provided many constructive comments and suggestions, they were not asked to endorse the conclusions or recommendations of this report nor did they see the final draft before its release. The review of this report was overseen by John Dowling, Harvard University, and Catherine Kling, Iowa State University. They were responsible for making certain that an independent examination of this report was carried out in accordance with the standards of the National Academies and that all review comments were carefully considered. Responsibility for the final content rests entirely with the authoring committee and the National Academies.

Finally, we thank the staff of this project for their valuable leadership, input, and support. Specifically, we would like to thank Program Officer and Study

Director, Layne Scherer; BHEW Director, Tom Rudin; Program Director, Tom Arrison; Senior Advisor, Jay Labov; Program Officer, Barbara Natalizio; Program Officer, Maria Dahlberg; Christine Mirzayan Science and Technology Fellow and Associate Program Officer, Yasmeen Hussain; Christine Mirzayan Science and Technology Fellow, Elizabeth Garbee; Research Associate, Irene Ngun; Senior Program Assistant, Austen Applegate; Senior Program Assistant, Allison Berger; Senior Program Assistant, Jaime Colman; and Senior Program Assistant, Frederic Lestina.

Contents

Tables and Figures

TABLES

FIGURES

Abbreviations and Acronyms

AAAS	American Association for the Advancement of Science
AAU	Association of American Universities
AGEP	Alliances for Graduate Education and the Professoriate
AIAN	American Indian and Alaska Native
BEST	Broadening Experiences in Scientific Training program
BHEW	Board on Higher Education and Workforce
BLS	Bureau of Labor Statistics
CGS	Council of Graduate Schools
COSEMPUP	Committee on Science, Engineering, Medicine, and Public Policy
GRE	Graduate Record Examinations
IES	Institute of Education Sciences
IIE	Institute of International Education
IoT	Internet of Things
IRIS	Institute for Research on Innovation and Science
LSAMP	Louis Stokes Alliances for Minority Participation program
MARC U-STAR	Maximizing Access to Research Careers Undergraduate Student Training in Academic Research

NCES	National Center for Education Statistics
NCSES	National Center for Science and Engineering Statistics
NIGMS	National Institute of General Medical Sciences
NIH	National Institutes of Health
NRSA	National Research Service Award
NSF	National Science Foundation
OPT	Optional Practical Training Extension
PREP	Postbaccalaureate Research Education Program
PSM	Professional Science Master's (degree)
RTI	Research Triangle International
S&E	science and engineering
SDR	Survey of Doctorate Recipients
SED	Survey of Earned Doctorates
SEI	Science and Engineering Indicators
STEM	science, technology, engineering, and mathematics
URM	underrepresented minority
USCIS	U.S. Citizen and Immigration Services

Summary

The U.S. system of graduate education in science, technology, engineering, and mathematics (STEM) has served the nation and its science and engineering enterprise extremely well. In many ways, it is the "gold standard" for graduate STEM education in the world as evidenced by, among other measures, the substantial number of international students coming to the United States to study. Over the course of their education, graduate students become involved in advancing the frontiers of discovery, as well as in making significant contributions to the growth of the U.S. economy, its national security, and the health and well-being of its people. However, continuous, dramatic innovations in research methods and technologies, changes in the nature and availability of work, shifts in demographics, and expansions in the scope of occupations needing STEM expertise raise questions about how well the current STEM graduate education system is meeting the full array of 21st-century needs. Indeed, recent surveys of employers and graduates and studies of graduate education suggest that many graduate programs do not adequately prepare students to translate their knowledge into impact in multiple careers.

To respond to these issues, the National Academies of Sciences, Engineering, and Medicine appointed the Committee on Revitalizing Graduate STEM Education for the 21st Century. The committee was charged with examining the state of U.S. graduate STEM education, last fully reviewed by the Academies in 1995, and how the system might best respond to ongoing developments in the conduct of research on evidence-based teaching practices[1] and in the needs and interests of its students and the broader society it seeks to serve. Over the course of 18 months, this committee examined a wide array of data about the U.S. graduate STEM education system and held focus groups and discussions with diverse stakeholders, including students, faculty, university administrators, industry leaders, and policy makers. The committee also commissioned specialized analyses to review the scholarly research on educational practices at the graduate level to help inform its work.

ABOUT THIS REPORT

This is not the first—nor will it likely be the last—report focusing on American STEM graduate education. A combination of elements, however, make it unique. First, this report calls for a systems approach to moving graduate STEM education forward. The goals laid out in this report will only be accomplished with a consistent and robust commitment from all stakeholders in the nation's scientific enterprise and in its STEM graduate education system. Chapter 6 articulates the actions needed by each stakeholder group.

Second, this report proposes an ideal graduate STEM education and then recommends action steps for each stakeholder in the system to help achieve that ideal. A central element of the strategy laid out here is to make the system more student focused while maintaining the central attributes that have made it the gold standard for the world.

A critical element is the report's articulation of the core competencies that all students who have been through U.S. graduate STEM education should acquire, at both the master's and the Ph.D. levels. While the report recommends that students be offered some supplemental coursework and training experiences, the committee feels strongly that instilling those core competencies should remain the American graduate STEM education system's primary task.

After laying out the reasons for the committee's work in Chapter 1, the report, covering both master's and doctoral STEM education, lays out its analysis of the current education system in Chapter 2. Chapters 3, 4, and 5 offer recommendations to ensure that the system remains dynamic by addressing current needs and anticipating future contexts in graduate education. Chapter 6 presents a summary of what an ideal graduate education system would be like if all the recommendations in this report were to be implemented. It also provides a listing of the committee's recommendations organized by stakeholder, to make clear what each must do to actualize the revised graduate STEM education system the committee envisions.

---

[1] The committee was unable to explore graduate-level teaching practices in STEM in great detail during the course of this study as a result of the limited available research; however, the committee did consider the translation of undergraduate STEM education practices such as the Association of American Universities framework for effective STEM teaching at the undergraduate level.

AN IDEAL GRADUATE STEM EDUCATION

Implementing the recommendations in this report would produce a U.S. graduate STEM education system that better enables graduate students of all backgrounds to meet the highest standards of excellence in 21st-century STEM fields and to use their knowledge and sophistication across the full range of occupations essential to address global societal needs using science- and technology-informed decision making. These recommendations build on the current strengths of the graduate STEM enterprise, urging careful attention to core educational elements and learning objectives—one set for the master's degree and another for the Ph.D.—that are common across all STEM fields. However, many of the recommendations in this report are also intended to stimulate review and revision of incentive and reward policies, teaching and mentoring practices, and curricular offerings. They may also lead to the expansion of career exploration mechanisms and transparency about trainee outcomes that can inform career paths for students.

Importantly, this report also calls for a shift from the current system that focuses primarily on the needs of institutions of higher education and those of the research enterprise itself to one that is *student centered*, placing greater emphasis and focus on graduate students as individuals with diverse needs and challenges. An ideal, student-centered STEM graduate education system would include several attributes that are currently lacking in many academic institutions. In an ideal STEM graduate education system:

- Prospective graduate students would be able to select their graduate program aided by fully transparent, easily accessible data about costs incurred and viable career pathways and successes of previous students, at the level of the institution and its departments.
- Students would acquire broad technical literacy coupled with deep specialization in an area of interest. They would acquire the core competencies outlined in Chapters 3 and 4. As they acquire this knowledge base, students would have multiple opportunities to understand better and to learn to consider ethical issues associated with their work, as well as the broader implications of their work for society.
- Students from all backgrounds would fully participate and achieve their greatest potential during their educational experience through transparent institutional action to enhance diversity and promote inclusive and equitable learning environments.
- Students would encounter a variety of points of view about the nature, scope, and substance of the scientific enterprise and about the relationships between science, engineering, and society, and they would be encouraged to understand and grapple with differences of opinion, experiences, and ideas as part of their graduate education and training.

- Students would have opportunities to communicate the results of their work and to understand the broader impacts of their research. This includes the ability to present their work and have exposure to audiences outside of their department, ranging from peers in other departments to the broader scientific community and nontechnical audiences. Students would also understand and learn to consider ethical and cultural issues surrounding their work, as well as the broader needs of society.
- Students would be encouraged to create their own project-based learning opportunities—ideally as a member of a team—as a means of developing transferable professional skills such as communication, collaboration, management, and entrepreneurship. Experiences where students "learn by doing," rather than simply learn by lecturing and coursework, would be the norm.
- Students would be encouraged and given time, resources, and space to explore diverse career options, perhaps through courses, seminars, internships, and other kinds of real-life experiences. While some institutions have launched such programs, they should become universal, albeit sensitive to the specific contexts of individual institutions. For example, students clearly interested in future faculty positions might have the opportunity to teach undergraduates from a variety of institutions, from community colleges to research-based universities. Those students wishing to compete for research-intensive university positions would be advised about appropriate postdoctoral positions and the track records of those universities and/or specific faculty members in placing such individuals in faculty positions. Students with potential interests in nonacademic careers would be provided with opportunities to attend workshops and seminars about jobs in a wide range of industries, nonprofit organizations, and government, together with opportunities for placements in nonacademic job settings. Internships with corporations, government agencies, or nonprofit employers during summer months or the school year would become the norm rather than the exception for graduate students seeking careers outside of academia. Institutions would seek corporate and foundation funding to support such learning experiences.
- Graduate programs and departments would develop more efficient channels for students to communicate with the administration and faculty regarding processes and decisions within the department and the graduate school that affect graduate student education. These channels would facilitate communication in both directions, offering students mechanisms to provide feedback and giving administrators and faculty a better understanding of the student perspectives on issues important to them.
- Graduate programs would develop course offerings and other tools to enable student career exploration and to expose students to career options. Faculty advisors would encourage students to explore career options

broadly and would not stigmatize those who favor careers outside of academia.

- Institutions would help students identify advisors and mentors who can best support their academic and career development.
- Institutions would provide faculty with training, resources, and time both to improve their own skills as mentors and to provide for quality mentoring and advising to the graduate students they supervise directly, as well as other students in their departments or from across the institution, as appropriate. Training would provide strategies for navigating relationships in which goals and identities (cultural or demographic differences, career aspirations) may differ between mentor and mentee, and mentoring would center on the goals set jointly by the student and mentors and provide strategies for navigating relationships in which goals may differ between supervisor and student. This training would consider the various challenges faculty face at different stages of their own careers. For example, early-career faculty who are in the process of establishing themselves in a department with a research group or laboratory may require a primer on best practices for becoming a mentor and advisor. Long-tenured faculty might benefit from periodic refreshers to explore new skills or techniques in supporting student success. Institutions would provide opportunities for students to seek and develop multiple separate mentoring and advising relationships, including those that are interdisciplinary and cross departments. Institutions would also reward faculty for their accomplishments as mentors and advisors.

DRIVING CHANGE

Seeing this vision come to fruition will require firm and commensurate commitments at all levels and from all stakeholders in the nation's STEM graduate education system. Academic institutions must provide faculty time, resources, and incentives to focus more on the totality of graduate student learning through the adoption of evidence-based teaching practices and to support the broad range of educational and career goals that students hold. At the same time, educational institutions and the state and federal agencies and other funders that support and set policies for financial support of both research and graduate students will need to adjust the incentive systems so that they reward educational as well as research accomplishments. Such a change in incentive systems will reflect the conviction that producing well-educated students is a central element of their charge.

Achieving what the committee sees as the ideal, modern graduate STEM education will require substantial cultural change throughout the system. As discussed throughout this report, the system must become more student-centric and must increase the value it places on best practices of mentorship and advising. The value placed on educating students at the master's level must be increased.

The mind-set that seems to most heavily value preparing students at the Ph.D. level for academic research careers must readjust to recognize that some of the best students will not pursue academic research but will enter careers in other sectors, such as industry or government.

These cultural changes will only come about if there are changes in the incentive system that appears to drive so much of academia. The current system is heavily weighted toward rewarding faculty for research output in the form of publications and the number of future scientists produced. It must be realigned to increase the relative rewards for effective teaching, mentoring, and advising. Unless faculty behavior can be changed—and changing the incentive system is critical in that regard—the system will not change.

The committee recognizes that these cultural changes will inevitably have costs associated with them. The committee did not provide estimates for the financial costs, including the costs of creating, supporting, and maintaining new programs for students, data collection, and staff to provide support to students, because each institution will have different existing infrastructure, constraints, local context, and other considerations to manage in the implementation of these recommendations. Beyond shifts in the budget, many of the cultural changes also pose costs related to time and human capital resources, such as the increasing expectations on faculty and the effort expended by leadership and administration to support change. However, despite any costs, the changes advocated in this report must be achieved. Without such a unified commitment to continue the legacy of excellence in the system, the United States may not unlock the full potential of discovery to power its economy, protect its national interests, and lead the world in addressing the grand challenges of the 21st century.

Federal and state funding agencies have a particularly important role to play since their funding and support policies are often cited as being critical to the overall context and climate in which academic institutions are situated. Those policies are influential in shaping the incentive systems under which research institutions operate and researchers are rewarded. In fact, many of the recommendations in this report will be impossible to implement until federal and state policy makers are willing to reaffirm the value of graduate education to our nation's intellectual, social, and economic prosperity and to formulate policies that will enhance the quality of master's and doctoral education in the United States. Since so many STEM graduate students are supported through federal programs, the funding criteria for those programs present a unique opportunity to help shape the culture of graduate education throughout the country. Even in periods of extreme fiscal constraint, the federal government should recommit to making significant, coordinated investments in higher education and research, especially at the graduate level.

With these challenges in mind, we urge all relevant stakeholders—federal and state policy makers, colleges, universities, employers, faculty and administrators, students, national scientific and educational organizations, advocacy groups, and the public who supports and benefits from advances in STEM fields—to unite behind the recommendations in this report and, going forward, continuously assess whether STEM graduate education in the United States is meeting the needs of both a fully modern STEM enterprise and the nation it serves. A renewed national commitment to modernizing STEM graduate education would surely benefit society for generations to come. Consistent with Vannevar Bush's recognition of science as the endless frontier, the nation will benefit fully from applying the power of STEM to the problems and opportunities of today and tomorrow.

RECOMMENDATIONS OF THE COMMITTEE ON REVITALIZING GRADUATE STEM EDUCATION FOR THE 21ST CENTURY

The committee's recommendations are summarized here and presented in the order in which the issues and goals are discussed in Chapters 3-5. Included as bullets are the actions the committee believes each stakeholder must take to resolve the issue or achieve the goal, particularly regarding the difficult topic of cultural change that the committee stresses is necessary to realize the vision it sets out for the ideal graduate education. The aggregated set of actions the committee recommends for each stakeholder is presented in Chapter 6. The intent of the listing in Chapter 6 is to lay out a systemwide action plan for achieving the goals outlined in this report, stipulating what each stakeholder must do to make the ideal graduate education system a reality.

Chapter 3

RECOMMENDATION 3.1—Rewarding Effective Teaching and Mentoring: Advancement procedures for faculty, including promotion and tenure policies and practices, should be restructured to strengthen recognition of contributions to graduate mentoring and education.

- Federal and state funding agencies should align their policies and award criteria to ensure that students in the programs they support experience the kind of graduate education outlined in this report and achieve the scientific and professional competencies articulated in this report, whether they are on training or research grant mechanisms.
- Institutions should increase priority and reward faculty for demonstrating high-quality teaching and inclusive mentoring practices for all graduate students, including the recognition of faculty teaching in master's degree programs, based on the results of restructured evaluations.
- Institutions should include teaching and mentoring performance as important considerations for reappointment, promotion, annual performance review, and tenure decisions. Institutions should also nominate faculty

for external awards (such as those from technical societies) that reward teaching excellence.

RECOMMENDATION 3.2—Institutional Support for Teaching and Mentoring: To improve the quality and effectiveness of faculty teaching and mentoring, institutions of higher education should provide training for new faculty and should offer regular refresher courses in teaching and mentoring for established faculty.

- Institutions should require faculty and postdoctoral researchers who have extensive contact with graduate students to learn and demonstrate evidence-based and inclusive teaching and mentoring practices.
- Graduate programs should facilitate mentor relationships between the graduate student and the primary research advisors, as well as opportunities for students to develop additional mentor or advisor relationships, including with professionals in industry, government laboratories, and technical societies.
- Graduate schools should provide extra-departmental mentoring and support programs.
- Graduate students should seek multiple mentors to meet their varied academic and career needs.

RECOMMENDATION 3.3—Comprehensive National and Institutional Data on Students and Graduates: Graduate programs should collect, update, and make freely and easily accessible to current and prospective students information about master's- and Ph.D.-level educational outcomes. In addition, to make appropriate future adjustments in the graduate education system, it is essential that comprehensive datasets about the system, its participants, and its outcomes be collected in a standard format, be fully transparent, and be easily accessible and transferable across multiple computer and statistical analysis platforms.

- Federal and state funding agencies should require institutions that receive support for graduate education to develop policies mandating that these data be collected and made widely available to qualify for traineeships, fellowships, and research assistantships.
- Institutions should develop a uniform, scalable, and sustainable model for data collection that can operate beyond the period of extramural funding. The data collection should follow standard definitions that correspond with national STEM education and workforce surveys to help inform benchmarking or higher education research.
- Departments and programs should review their own data from current students and alumni to inform curricula and professional development

offerings, and they should provide these data to current and prospective students.

- Prospective students should use these data to inform graduate program selection, educational goal development, and career exploration.

RECOMMENDATION 3.4—Funding for Research on Graduate STEM Education: The National Science Foundation, other federal and state agencies, and private funders of graduate STEM education should issue calls for proposals to better understand the graduate education system and outcomes of various interventions and policies, including but not limited to the effect of different models of graduate education on knowledge, competencies, mind-sets, and career outcomes.

- Funders should support research on the effect of different funding mechanisms on outcomes for doctoral students, including traineeships, fellowships, teaching and research assistantships; the effects of policies and procedures on degree completion, disaggregated by gender, race and ethnicity, and citizenship; and the effect of expanding eligibility of international students to be supported on federal fellowships and training grants.

RECOMMENDATION 3.5—Ensuring Diverse, Equitable, and Inclusive Environments: The graduate STEM education enterprise should enable students of all backgrounds, including but not limited to racial and ethnic background, gender, stage of life, culture, socioeconomic status, disability, sexual orientation, gender identity, and nationality, to succeed by implementing practices that create an equitable and inclusive institutional environment.

- Faculty and administrators involved in graduate education should develop, adopt, and regularly evaluate a suite of strategies to accelerate increasing diversity and improving equity and inclusion, including comprehensive recruitment, holistic review in admissions, and interventions to prevent attrition in the late stages of progress toward a degree.
- Faculty should cultivate their individual professional development skills to advance their abilities to improve educational culture and environments on behalf of students.
- Institutions, national laboratories, professional societies, and research organizations should develop comprehensive strategies that use evidence-based models and programs and include measures to evaluate outcomes to ensure a diverse, equitable, and inclusive environment.
- Institutions should develop comprehensive strategies for recruiting and retaining faculty and mentors from demographic groups historically underrepresented in academia.

- Federal and state agencies, universities, professional societies, and non-governmental organizations that rate institutions should embed diversity and inclusion metrics in their criteria.
- Federal and state funding agencies and private funders that support graduate education and training should adjust their award policies and funding criteria to include policies that incentivize diversity, equity, and inclusion and include accountability measures through reporting mechanisms.

RECOMMENDATION 3.6—A Dynamic Graduate STEM Education System: The STEM education system should develop the capabilities to adjust dynamically to continuing changes in the nature of science and engineering activity and of STEM careers. This includes mechanisms to detect and anticipate such changes, experiment with innovative approaches, implement appropriate educational methods, and support institutional mechanisms on a larger scale.

- Faculty and graduate departments and programs should periodically review and modify curricula, dissertation requirements, and capstone projects to ensure timeliness and alignment with the ways relevant work is conducted and provide students with opportunities to work in teams that promote multidisciplinary learning.
- Professional societies and nonprofit organizations should convene and lead discussions with graduate programs, employers, and other stakeholders and disseminate innovative approaches.
- Federal and state funding agencies, professional societies, and private foundations that support or conduct education research should support studies on how different STEM disciplines can integrate the changing scientific enterprise into graduate education programs and curricula.
- Graduate students should learn how to apply their expertise in a variety of professional contexts and seek guidance from faculty, research mentors, and advisors on strategies to gain work-related experience while enrolled in graduate school.

RECOMMENDATION 3.7—Stronger Support for Graduate Student Mental Health Services: Institutions should provide resources to help students manage the stresses and pressures of graduate education and maximize their success. Institutions of higher education should work with their faculty to recognize and ameliorate behaviors that exacerbate existing power differentials and create unnecessary stress for graduate students. Toward that end:

- Institutions should administer periodic climate surveys of graduate students at the departmental level to assess their well-being in the aggregate and make adjustments when problems are identified.

- Institutions should take extra steps to provide and advertise accessible mental health services, such as those already available to veterans and most undergraduate students, at no cost to graduate students.
- Institutions should develop clear policies and reporting procedures for instances of sexual harassment and bullying.
- Graduate programs should fully incorporate awareness of mental health issues into the training experience for both students and faculty and should assess services to ensure that they are meeting the needs of graduate students.
- Faculty should be regularly informed on how to support and engage with students requiring or seeking mental health services.
- Graduate programs should encourage students to engage as a group in activities and experiences outside of traditional academic settings as a means of increasing feelings of inclusion and normalizing feelings associated with negative phenomena, such as imposter syndrome, that can reduce productivity and success in the training experience and extend time to degree.
- Graduate programs should allow students to have an active and collaborative voice to proactively engage in practices that support holistic research training and diverse career outcomes and that allow students to provide feedback on their experiences.

Chapter 4

RECOMMENDATION 4.1—Core Competencies for Master's Education: Every STEM master's student should achieve the core scientific and professional competencies and learning objectives described in this report.

- Institutions should verify that every graduate program they offer provides for the master's core competencies outlined in this report and that students demonstrate that they have achieved them before receiving their degrees.
- Graduate departments should publicly post how their programs reflect the core competencies for master's students, including the milestones and metrics they use in evaluation and assessment.
- Federal and state funding agencies should adapt funding criteria for institutions to ensure that all master's students they support—regardless of mechanism of support—are in programs that ensure that they develop, measure, and report student progress toward acquiring the scientific and professional competencies outlined in this report.
- Graduate students should create an individual development plan that includes the core competencies, as outlined in this report for master's degrees, as a key feature of their own learning and career goals and that

utilizes the resources provided by their university and relevant professional societies.

- Students should provide feedback to graduate faculty and deans about how they could help students better develop these competencies.

RECOMMENDATION 4.2—Career Exploration for Master's Students: Master's students should be provided opportunities for career exploration during the course of their studies.

- Faculty, who serve as undergraduate advisors, should discuss with their students whether and how a master's degree will advance the students' long-term educational and career goals.
- Institutions should integrate professional development opportunities, including relevant course offerings and internships, into curriculum design.
- Master's students should seek information about potential career paths, talk to employers and mentors in areas of interest, and choose a master's program optimal for gaining the knowledge and competencies needed to pursue their career interests.
- Industry, nonprofit, government, and other employers should provide guidance and financial support for relevant course offerings at institutions and provide internships and other forms of professional experiences to students and recent graduates.
- Professional societies should collaborate with other sectors to create programs that help master's students make the transition into a variety of careers.

Chapter 5

RECOMMENDATION 5.1—Core Competencies for Ph.D. Education: Every STEM Ph.D. student should achieve the core scientific and professional Ph.D. competencies detailed in this report.

- Universities should verify that every graduate program that they offer provides for these competencies and that students demonstrate that they have achieved them before receiving their doctoral degrees.
- Universities should scrutinize their curricula and program requirements for features that lie outside of these core competencies and learning objectives and that may be adding time to degree without providing enough additional value to students, such as a first-author publication requirement, and eliminate those features or requirements.
- Graduate departments should publicly post how their programs reflect the core competencies for doctoral students, including the milestones

and metrics the departments and individual faculty use in evaluation and assessment.
*   Federal and state funding agencies should adapt funding criteria for institutions to ensure that all doctoral students they support—regardless of mechanism of support—are in programs that ensure that they develop, measure, and report these scientific and professional competencies.
*   Students should create an independent development plan that includes the competencies outlined in this report as a core feature of their own learning and career goals and that utilizes the resources provided by their university and relevant professional societies.
*   Students should provide feedback to the graduate faculty and deans about how they could help students better develop these competencies.

RECOMMENDATION 5.2—Career Exploration and Preparation for Ph.D. Students: Students should be provided an understanding of and opportunities to explore the variety of career opportunities and pathways afforded by STEM Ph.D. degrees.

*   Faculty who serve as undergraduate and master's advisors should discuss with their students whether and how a Ph.D. degree will advance the students' long-term educational and career goals.
*   Institutions should integrate professional development opportunities, including relevant course offerings and internships, into doctoral curriculum design.
*   Institutions, through their career counselors and career centers, should assist students in gaining an understanding of and opportunities to explore career options afforded by STEM Ph.D. degrees.
*   Students should seek information about potential career paths, talk to employers and mentors in areas of interest, and choose a doctoral program optimal for gaining the knowledge and competencies needed to pursue their career interests.
*   Every student and his or her faculty advisor should prepare an individual development plan.
*   Industry, nonprofit, government, and other employers should provide guidance and financial support for relevant course offerings at institutions and provide internships and other forms of professional experiences to students and recent graduates.
*   Federal and state agencies and private foundations that support graduate education should require STEM graduate programs to include career exploration curricular offerings and require STEM doctoral students to create and to update annually individual development plans in consultation with faculty advisors to map educational goals, career exploration, and professional development.

- Professional societies should collaborate with leaders in various sectors to create programs that help Ph.D. recipients transition into a variety of careers.

RECOMMENDATION 5.3—Structure of Doctoral Research Activities: Curricula and research projects, team projects, and dissertations should be designed to reflect the state of the art in the ways STEM research and education are conducted.

- Universities, professional societies, and higher education associations should take the lead in establishing criteria and updating characteristics of the doctoral research project and dissertation preparation and format.
- Students should seek opportunities to work in cross-disciplinary and cross-sector teams during their graduate education and via extracurricular activities and be incentivized by their departments and faculty advisors to do so.
- Graduate programs and faculty should encourage and facilitate the development of student teams within and across disciplines.

1

Introduction

For more than 70 years, the American science, technology, engineering, and mathematics (STEM) enterprise[1] has served the nation extremely well, yielding great benefits in virtually every sphere of life, including the economy, the environment, national security, and the health of the public. On the economic front, for example, nearly 8.6 million Americans were employed in STEM jobs in 2015, 93 percent of which paid better than the average national wage (Fayer et al., 2017). STEM workers are also more likely to apply for, receive, and commercialize patents (Thomasian, 2011). The STEM education enterprise has excelled at serving the nation by training generations of professionals with STEM graduate degrees who have the deep knowledge base, advanced critical thinking skills, and ability to be the independent thinkers who are most likely to produce the innovations and scientific advances that have given the United States a competitive edge in today's global economy.

However, since graduate degrees began to proliferate after World War II, and particularly in the two decades since the National Academies last reported on graduate STEM education (NAS/NAE/IOM, 1995), there have been profound developments in workforce needs, approaches to STEM research and education, demographic composition of graduate student programs, and potential societal applications of STEM expertise. Given these changes and the continuing evolution of STEM, many institutions, higher education associations, professional societies, and federal agencies have launched initiatives, conducted research, and developed strategies to ensure that graduate STEM education in the United

---

[1] This report uses the National Science Foundation's definition of STEM, which includes mathematics, natural sciences, engineering, computer and information sciences, and the social and behavioral sciences—psychology, economics, sociology, and political science (NSF, 2018).

States continues to be dynamic. These efforts have seeded interest in the graduate STEM education community for a systemic approach for national-level change. Leveraging this momentum, the Burroughs Wellcome Fund, the Institute of Education Sciences, the National Science Foundation, and the Spencer Foundation called upon the National Academies to charter a committee to conduct a comprehensive review of the U.S. graduate STEM education system and recommend adjustments to how it operates. The resulting committee also received support from the National Academy of Sciences (NAS) Kobelt Fund, the NAS Scientists and Engineers for the Future Fund, and the NAS Coca–Cola Foundation Fund. The primary question the committee addressed was: How can the U.S. system of graduate education, given the significant contextual shifts in the 21st century, best serve students and the nation both now and into the future?

By asking that question, the Committee on Revitalizing Graduate STEM Education for the 21st Century does not mean to imply that the U.S. graduate STEM education ecosystem is not preparing outstanding scientists, technologists, engineers, and mathematicians. Indeed, U.S. STEM graduate programs continue to be a magnet for the students from all over the world. However, the committee wants to ensure that the enterprise remains synchronous with the many related factors that influence its trajectory, such as the changes in the population of individuals seeking graduate degrees in STEM fields over the past decades. Increasingly, students pursue more varied career paths (St. Clair et al., 2017), and the population of students pursuing STEM degrees is itself more diverse in many dimensions, including gender (NSB, 2016a), race and ethnicity (NSB, 2016b), disability, socioeconomic background, and country of origin.

For U.S. society, the graduate STEM education system produces scientists, engineers, and research professionals by stimulating curiosity and enabling students to develop the intellectual capacity to recognize, formulate, and communicate complex problems; by helping students understand and create multidimensional, analytical approaches toward solutions; and by creating opportunities for students to discover knowledge that advances their understanding of the world around them. In addition, graduate STEM education also produces a substantial amount of the basic and applied research and development that directly and indirectly propels societal advancement, innovation, and economic growth. It achieves this through research and discovery, and by creating new products and services, spawning new start-up companies, and in partnership with government and business, developing programs that strengthen national security, protect the environment, and improve health and medical care.

THE ROLE OF GRADUATE STEM EDUCATION

Graduate STEM education plays an essential role in ensuring our nation's place as a leading force in the world's economy and in solving the most pressing problems facing the nation and the rest of the world. In many respects, the framing of graduate education from the National Academies' report *Reshaping the Graduate Education of Scientists and Engineers* (NAS/NAE/IOM, 1995, p. 1) continues to hold true:

> Graduate education is basic to the achievement of national goals in two ways. First, our universities are responsible for producing the teachers and researchers of the future — the independent investigators who will lay the groundwork for the paradigms and products of tomorrow and who will educate later generations of researchers. Second, graduate education contributes directly to the broader national goals of technological, economic, and cultural development. We increasingly depend on people with advanced scientific and technological knowledge in developing new technologies and industries, reducing environmental pollution, combating disease and hunger, developing new sources of energy, and maintaining the competitiveness of industry. Our graduate schools of science and engineering are therefore important not only as sources of future leaders in science and engineering, but also as an indispensable underpinning of national strength and prosperity — sustaining the creativity and intellectual vigor needed to address a growing range of social and economic concerns.

For both the K-12 and higher education enterprises, graduate education is the lifeblood of the instructional system. Nearly all community college instructors and university faculty as well as increasing percentages of K-12 teachers hold graduate degrees. In considering the future of U.S. competitiveness, the contributions of STEM graduate degree holders in the broader education system will only increase as the global race to invest in science, education, and innovation continues (NSB, 2015).

Perhaps the most important outcomes of graduate education, in addition to the research generated by the faculty and students, is the preparation of innovators and entrepreneurs capable of advancing the frontiers of discovery. For students, graduate STEM education provides experiential, relevant exposure to the process by which STEM professionals conduct research, make new discoveries, and foster innovation.

Our nation's future depends on a graduate education system that continues to evolve and meet its charge to create highly trained researchers, to develop future faculty and teachers responsible for the educational enterprise, and to support national economic, social, and cultural development. For the most part, graduate students and postdoctoral researchers in the life sciences, physical sciences, engineering, and behavioral and social sciences conduct a large percentage of the day-to-day research work at universities (NAS/NAE/IOM, 2014), and in doing so, are acquiring essential skills and other core principles fundamental to excellent research and contributing directly to the current research infrastructure (see Chapters 4 and 5 for more information on core competencies for the master's degree and Ph.D., respectively). Indeed, graduate students are vital to the success of the enterprise. As Vannevar Bush stated in his report to President Roosevelt, *Science: The Endless Frontier* (Bush, 1945, p. 23):

> The responsibility for the creation of new scientific knowledge—and for most of its application—rests on that small body of men and women who understand the fundamental laws of nature and are skilled in the techniques of scientific research. We shall have rapid or slow advance on any scientific frontier depending on the number of highly qualified and trained scientists exploring it.

CATALYZING CULTURAL CHANGE IN GRADUATE STEM EDUCATION

The committee recognized at the outset of its work that (1) there are components of graduate education that can be improved, and (2) implementing many of the changes suggested in this report will require attitudinal, behavioral, and organizational changes among individual and communities of stakeholders in the U.S. STEM graduate education *system*. These stakeholder communities include students and their faculty mentors; academic department chairs, deans, provosts, and even institutional boards of trustees; the state- and federal-level government agencies that control policies for STEM and education; the public and private entities that provide financial support; and the employers that hire STEM graduates. Indeed, the committee recognizes that the overarching theme of its recommendations—an increased focus on the needs of students—calls for no less than pervasive and sustained cultural changes in academia, because without these changes nothing much will happen. As described in this report, the entire graduate education system should ensure that students achieve a broad set of core competencies and that the recognition and incentive systems of institutions offering graduate STEM degrees undergo substantial modification. Unless there is a clear, common commitment from all stakeholders to make the system work better for master's and Ph.D. students themselves, the recommendations in this report will likely have no more than minimal impact, as have many previous reports on the same topic.

The committee's data-gathering activities and conversations with graduate students, faculty members, and employers outside of academia revealed numerous areas of concern. Some primary examples are: (1) there is a mismatch between the incentives that determine the professional priorities of many faculty members and universities and the diverse education and career needs of STEM graduate students, notably at the Ph.D. level; (2) graduate STEM education is not fully meeting the needs of the entire population of potential graduate students, which is increasingly diverse with respect to dimensions including but not limited to gender, race, ethnicity, visa status, or socioeconomic background at a time when the nation needs to access all available talent; and (3) although unemployment among those with STEM graduate degrees is low, demand is uneven across fields. Some graduates have difficulty identifying career opportunities and may be underemployed (Xue and Larson, 2015). The outcome of these and other concerns is that STEM graduate education in the United States is far less effective than it might be at educating graduate students prepared for the wide range of STEM careers in this century's ever-evolving work environment.

At many research-intensive universities today, STEM Ph.D. education to a large degree is intertwined completely with generating research results and publications. This integration is reinforced by the incentive systems under which institutions and their faculty operate—more research publications and research grants lead to greater rewards. The incentive structure under which faculty members operate regarding tenure, promotion, and procuring grants defines the culture of U.S. academic research institutions and deemphasizes the importance of teaching and mentoring.

Consequently, in the process of producing high-quality research, some of the educational needs of graduate students appear to be getting less attention than they require in their development. The current system therefore acts as an impediment to changes that would benefit students. Although there are institutions, departments, and individual faculty that have been able to overcome these barriers to change (some examples of which are highlighted in Chapters 3, 4, and 5), these adjustments have not been adopted evenly across the system. These incentive structure changes are essential to provide STEM graduate students with the education they need for successful careers and to address our nation's challenges.

Beyond academia, the drivers of graduate STEM education employment also have changed considerably since World War II, mostly triggered by technological progress. For example, revolutions in data science, artificial intelligence, machine learning, and automation are profoundly impacting the global workforce, and in turn, demand changes in the ways in which the leaders of the future are educated. In an environment with a steep innovation trajectory, individuals who will thrive will be those who have been prepared with life-long learning skills in digesting new content, adopting new methods, and formulating creative approaches to problem solving.

In addition, the demand for graduates with master's degrees in STEM disciplines continues to grow across sectors. The committee received comments from a range of employers, both inside and outside academia, affirming the value of the analytical, research, and critical thinking skills that STEM graduates at both the master's and Ph.D. levels bring to the workplace. However, these employers also stated that many new hires struggle with a variety of other important skills—communication, working effectively in teams with members from different cultural or disciplinary backgrounds, mentoring, networking, and leadership. In response, many universities are working to develop programs for students wishing to pursue those career paths. In some instances, universities are working with local and regional businesses to design such programs and attract students to them.

Many studies and workshops have described the desire of graduate students in STEM to be provided with opportunities for career exploration that allow them to make more informed career choices (Fuhrmann et al., 2011; Golde and Dore, 2001; NASEM, 2016; Thiry et al., 2015). Indeed, one of the consistent comments we received from both students and nonacademic employers was that STEM graduate students would benefit from exposure to more varied educational experiences, perhaps through internships and coursework outside of their disciplines, to explore career options and determine skills necessary across a range of work environments.

A 2017 report from the Council of Graduate Schools (CGS) (Denecke et al., 2017) notes that while many universities offer students the opportunity to develop capabilities in addition to those related to research and disciplinary knowledge on an ad hoc basis, Ph.D. students report having difficulty finding out about those opportunities and taking advantage of them. The CGS report also identifies several challenges and barriers that limit the effectiveness of programs for enhancing graduate student professional development. For example, the perceived level of faculty support for professional development and exploration of multiple career paths can affect students' pursuit of fields and relevant skills outside of academic research. In addition, funding for traineeships and fellowships that may promote capacity development in both research and professional skills is far outweighed by research assistantships, which lack mandates for education or familiarization with skills across a range of potential careers. Institutions, professional societies, and other organizations have developed resources to support professional and career development for students; however, many of these programs do not have the resources to support extensive evaluation, assessment, and sharing of effective practices. While federal funders have spearheaded national efforts and funded pilots to test the efficacy of these types of programs, the evaluation and assessment outcomes are not yet available. The absence of comprehensive data hampers engagement of key potential advocates including faculty, student participants, alumni, employers, funders, and senior administrators who could implement these programs.

As this report will show, there is both a demand and momentum to address these barriers, and in doing so, modernize the graduate STEM education ecosystem to reflect the ongoing changes in the conduct of science and the continued importance of STEM education to the health of the U.S. economy. The goal of such an effort is for the graduate STEM education ecosystem to become more inclusive and equitable, and to better meet the needs and interests of an increasingly diverse student body pursuing a broad spectrum of careers in a world in which labor markets, funding sources, institutional policies, and the very nature of STEM research are undergoing rapid change.

For graduate STEM education to remain aligned with broader shifts in science and engineering as well as 21st-century society, the entire system needs to undergo significant cultural change to reflect the ways in which the world and the STEM enterprise have evolved. The system needs to establish core principles and learning objectives common across STEM graduate education and recognize that STEM advanced degree holders will be increasingly needed in many occupational sectors. The system also needs to become more student-focused and develop ways to prepare students with a broader range of research and transferrable professional skills to meet their educational and career goals. Funding agencies, academic institutions, and other stakeholders that hold power in the system should revisit their incentive and reward policies to better align recognition for achievements in education and research, and to support career exploration and diversity.

The committee recognizes that this kind of cultural change will not come easily, even with the best of intent. The committee is recommending substantial changes in the roles, behavior, and resource allocations among all elements of the graduate education system, beginning with faculty members, who would be expected to have a much greater role in mentoring and advising their students. Costs associated with supporting and rewarding this expanded role would have to include changes in the incentives that help determine faculty roles and behavior. These, in turn, will require institutions, working with departments and graduate schools, to realign their incentives systems vis-à-vis the relative weights assigned to teaching or mentoring and doing research. Research institutions as a whole will need to adjust the way they weigh their roles in teaching and research, and those funding agencies that traditionally have weighed research productivity most heavily in evaluating projects to fund, even if they have substantial responsibilities within them for graduate student education, will have to adjust their project selection criteria. None of this will be easy, and many of the committee's recommendations may incur substantial costs, although the estimations for these costs were not provided because each program, department, and institution will face a different set of variables, constraints, and preexisting resources that will make the implementation of the recommendations vary significantly. In fact, the difficulty and costs in achieving the kind of cultural change recommended in this report may be the main reasons that earlier reports on graduate education have not been well implemented.

Additionally, the level of resources available at each institution can vary dramatically campus to campus. Many institutions that serve graduate students face considerable challenges related to funding instability, existing work burden on faculty, and strain on administration and support staff. For the changes called for in this report to flourish in a sustainable way, they might require institutions and departments to reflect on the existing structure of their graduate programs. Although pilot initiatives and optional programs can help develop ideas and test efficacy within a department or an institution, the recommendations point to a cultural change resulting from committed leadership, widespread faculty support, and shifts in the allocation of resources and the incentive structure.

There are some examples where large-scale efforts are under way, directed at the kinds of system changes recommended here, and they are cause for encouragement that change is possible. A variety of academic institutions have already mounted experimental programs and made substantial changes that will help move graduate education at the local level in the directions outlined in this report.

At the national level, the United Kingdom provides an example of policies aspiring to drive cultural and behavioral changes. A new statement of expectations (UK Research and Innovation, 2018) from all seven of the UK Research councils and some other funders is attempting to stimulate major changes in the way graduate education is conceived and carried out in that country. While the diffuse nature of U.S. higher education makes it a challenge to identify a single leader with the capacity to mandate change, the federal funding agencies have the greatest potential to affect change. Another example of a policy action directed at stimulating significant change in graduate student training in the biomedical sciences is the recent release by the U.S. National Institute of General Medical Sciences at the National Institutes of Health of a new set of requirements and selection criteria for institutional graduate training grants (Gammie, Gibbs, and Singh, 2018).[2] Again, the effectiveness of these efforts at system-level change, in both cases driven by government agency initiatives, will only be known after they have been in place for several years.

In summary, despite recognized shortcomings, the U.S. system of graduate STEM education has significant strengths and has contributed immensely to the nation's prosperity over the past eight decades. However, even with that, it would be wise to acknowledge and understand the current and future challenges facing this system and take steps now to ensure that it remains vital, adaptable, and relevant for many generations to come. To neglect graduate education, or to ignore threats to its success, puts the economic, social, and cultural well-being of the nation at risk. Such a risk is one the nation can ill afford at a time when other nations are expanding their investment in STEM education.

BACKGROUND OF THE REPORT

To determine how well the current graduate STEM education system is serving the needs of various sectors and stakeholders, and to propose new guiding principles, models, programs, and policies that might be adapted to local needs and contexts, the National Academies convened an ad hoc committee, under the auspices of the Board on Higher Education and Workforce and the Committee on Science, Engineering, Medicine, and Public Policy (COSEMPUP), and liaising with the Government-University-Industry Research Roundtable and the Teacher Advisory Council, to lead a study of STEM graduate-level education in the United States, revisiting and updating a similar COSEMPUP study completed 20

---

[2] See https://loop.nigms.nih.gov/2017/10/new-nigms-institutional-predoctoral-training-grant-funding-opportunity-announcement/ (accessed March 16, 2018).

years ago, *Reshaping the Graduate Education of Scientists and Engineers* (NAS/NAE/IOM, 1995).

The Statement of Task for the Committee on Revitalizing Graduate STEM Education for the 21st Century includes the following specific tasks:

- Conduct a systems analysis of graduate education, with the aim of identifying policies, programs, and practices that could better meet the diverse education and career needs of graduate students in coming years (at both the master's and Ph.D. levels—understanding the commonalities and distinctions between the two levels), and also aimed at identifying deficiencies and gaps in the system that could improve graduate education programs.
- Identify strategies to improve the alignment of graduate education courses, curricula, labs, and fellowship/traineeship experiences for students with the needs of prospective employers—and the reality of the workforce landscape—which include not only colleges and universities but also industry, government at all levels, nonprofit organizations, and others. A key task will be to learn from employers how graduate education can continue to evolve to anticipate future workforce needs.
- Identify possible changes to federal and state programs and funding priorities and structures that would better reflect the research and training needs of graduate students.
- Identify policies and effective practices that provide students and faculty with information about career paths for graduates holding master's and Ph.D. degrees and provide ongoing and high-quality counseling and mentoring for graduate students.
- Identify the implications of the increasingly international nature of graduate education and career pathways, reflecting both the numbers of foreign students who enroll in U.S. graduate schools and the increasing global migration of U.S. STEM graduates.
- Investigate the many new initiatives and models that are influencing graduate education, including massive open online courses, other digital learning programs, increasing numbers of alternative providers of master's and Ph.D. degrees, and opportunities to secure credentials through multiple sources.
- Create a set of national goals for graduate STEM education that can be used by research universities, Congress, federal agencies, state governments, and the private sector to guide graduate-level programs, policies, and investments over the next decade, and ensure that this "blueprint" for graduate education reform is revisited and updated on a periodic basis to reflect changing realities.

Over the course of the resulting 18-month study, the committee held five meetings in Washington, D.C., Raleigh, North Carolina, and San Francisco, California, and convened five focus groups, conducted by Research Triangle International (RTI) in partnership with the National Academies, at Texas A&M Corpus Christi and Kingsville, South Dakota State University, the University of Northern Colorado, Florida Agricultural and Mechanical University, and the 23rd American Indian Science and Engineering Society Conference in Denver, Colorado. The goal of these committee meetings and focus groups was to invite direct input from a range of students, employers, faculty members, and other stakeholders. The committee used the analysis prepared by RTI to better understand perspectives from students and faculty at institutions that might not otherwise be well represented in the research or at other public forums.[3] The committee welcomed feedback from the STEM education community via participation at conferences, discussion sessions, professional society presentations, and webinars through the American Association for the Advancement of Science, American Chemical Society, Association of American Universities, Council of Graduate Schools, Council of Scientific Society Presidents, Duke University, Emerging Researchers National Conference, Federation of American Societies for Experimental Biology, the Graduate Career Consortium, Institute for Teaching and Mentoring, Massachusetts Institute of Technology's Washington, D.C., office, the National Postdoctoral Association, Princeton University, Transforming Postsecondary Education in Mathematics, the University of Michigan, and the University of North Carolina at Chapel Hill. The committee developed a discussion document and associated website to seek input from the broader set of stakeholders involved in U.S. graduate STEM education (Appendix B). To ensure that the concerns of graduate students were at the center of our activities, the committee talked with a number of current and recent graduate students and included as members of our committee early-career members and individuals who are advocates for STEM graduate students. The committee also commissioned a review of the academic literature on how graduate students learn and which conditions could improve retention, persistence, career outcomes, and other indicators of student success. This review was prepared by Margaret Blume-Kohout at Colgate University (Blume-Kohout, 2017). Finally, the committee commissioned a review of the interdisciplinary STEM program frameworks, with a focus on the Institute of Education Sciences Predoctoral Interdisciplinary Research Training Program in the Education Sciences. This paper was prepared by Jennifer Lebrón (Lebrón, 2017). In the review of research, the committee understood the limitations of the evidence. Within the field of education research, a small fraction is conducted on graduate STEM education. Because of the nature of graduate programs, which tend to be smaller than undergraduate programs and more specific to the field of study, there are

---

[3] A summary from RTI is available at http://sites.nationalacademies.org/cs/groups/pgasite/documents/webpage/pga_186164.pdf (accessed May 18, 2018).

challenges in understanding whether a policy, intervention, or program will produce similar results in a different field, institution, or department. Although the papers cited in this report may have limited reach, the committee also referenced a number of previous reports with a focus on graduate STEM education (Hussain, 2017). For all the recommendations in these previous reports, the stakeholders identified will need to design pilot implementation activities and strategies that best meet the needs of the local context.

The summary of the recommendations made in these reports serves as a proxy for the concerns in the field since the NAS/NAE/IOM (1995) report, *Reshaping the Graduate Education of Scientists and Engineers.* This report, the first from the National Academies on the state of graduate STEM education broadly, made an impact on the field by raising awareness and giving stakeholders a set of defined issues to begin discussions. Although there are challenges in connecting specific actions to the 1995 report, graduate education has appeared in other national efforts, from the Carnegie Initiative on the Doctorate[4] to the National Academies' *Rising above the Gathering Storm* (NAS/NAE/IOM, 2007). The latter was used in the development of the 2007 America COMPETES Act (P.L. 110-69), which included provisions for the National Science Foundation regarding Professional Science Master's degree programs and the Integrative Graduate Education and Research Traineeship program.[5]

The committee established several working definitions for the context of this report: STEM stands for science, technology, engineering, and mathematics and includes the social and behavioral sciences. The data in this report refer to the following broad fields: engineering, agricultural sciences; biological sciences; earth, atmospheric, and ocean sciences; computer sciences; mathematics and statistics; chemistry; physics; social and behavioral sciences; and medical and other health sciences (for Ph.D.'s only because these degrees are part of the "doctoral-research/scholarship" category as noted by the National Center for Science and Engineering Statistics). A glossary of terms is included in Appendix A.

In reference to diversity, the committee refers to the following definition: "Diversity in science refers to cultivating talent, and promoting the full inclusion of excellence across the social spectrum. This includes people from backgrounds that are traditionally underrepresented and those from backgrounds that are traditionally well represented" (Gibbs, 2014). Dimensions of diversity to be considered include, but are not limited to, national origin, language, race, color, disability, ethnicity, gender, age, religion, sexual orientation, gender identity, socioeconomic status, veteran status, educational background, and family structures. The concept also encompasses differences among people concerning where they are from and where they have lived and their differences of thought and life experience. When the committee references historically underrepresented

---

[4] See http://gallery.carnegiefoundation.org/cid/ (accessed March 27, 2018).
[5] See https://www.congress.gov/110/plaws/publ69/PLAW-110publ69.pdf (accessed March 27, 2018).

minority groups in STEM (URM), these groups include women, persons with disabilities, and three racial and ethnic groups—blacks, Hispanics, and American Indians or Alaska Natives. Other groups, such as students who identify as Native Hawaiian or Pacific Islander or students who identify as two or more races are acknowledged as underrepresented in STEM; however, because of the way data collection has historically included these groups of students in broader categories (Asian or Other), we are unable to include them in the definition of historically underrepresented groups.

STRUCTURE OF THE REPORT

Recommendations in this report are directed at each of the stakeholders in the U.S. STEM enterprise, including federal and state policy makers and funders, institutions of higher education and their administrators and faculty, leaders in business and industry, and the students that the system is intended to educate. The report acknowledges the multiple roles many of these stakeholders play. For example, federal and state governments and industry serve both as funders of graduate education and as potential employers of master's and doctoral students. The recommendations contained in this report should help the nation's STEM graduate programs meet the needs of their students and the prospective employers of the graduates, as well as the national needs for STEM expertise to address the nation's toughest challenges.

As this report documents, the main obstacles to responding to the needs of both master's and Ph.D. students are largely tied to the academic culture and the current tenure and promotion system that rewards research output over the quality of education, advising, and mentoring. This report serves as a call to action to faculty members, deans, provosts, presidents, and other university administrators to accept responsibility for the role that the policies and culture of academic research institutions play in creating barriers that complicate graduate student exploration of the range of career options in today's rapidly changing science-related work environment.

The committee also offers recommendations directed to state and federal research and education funding agencies because they contribute both directly and indirectly to the academic incentive system through their specific funding policies. Finally, the committee calls upon prospective and current STEM graduate students to be more intentional about recruiting supportive mentors, creating professional development plans, fulfilling the core principles and learning objectives of STEM graduate training, and advocating for and helping to develop additional resources as needed for career exploration sufficient to inform confident career choices by the time of completion of graduate training.

Following this introductory chapter, the remainder of this report, dealing with both master's and doctoral STEM education, lays out the committee's analysis of the current education system and the nation's needs in Chapter 2. Chapters

3, 4, and 5 offer recommendations to ensure that the system remains dynamic by addressing current needs and anticipating future contexts in graduate education. Chapter 6 presents a summary of what an ideal graduate education system would be like if all the recommendations in this report were to be implemented. It also provides a listing of the committee's recommendations organized by stakeholder to make clear what each must do to actualize the revised graduate STEM education system that the committee envisions.

REFERENCES

Blume-Kohout, M. 2017. *On What Basis? Seeking Effective Practices in Graduate STEM Education.* Commissioned paper prepared for the Committee. Available: http://sites.nationalacademies.org/cs/groups/pgasite/documents/ webpage/ pga_186176.pdf (accessed May 7, 2018).

Bush, V. 1945. *Science: The endless frontier.* Washington, DC: U.S. Government Printing Office.

Denecke, D., K. Feaster, and K. Stone. 2017. *Professional development: Shaping effective programs for STEM graduate students.* Washington, DC: Council of Graduate Schools.

Fayer, S., A. Lacey, and A. Watson. 2017. STEM occupations: Past, present, and future. U.S. Department of Labor, Bureau of Labor Statistics. Available: https://www.bls.gov/spotlight/2017/science-technology-engineering-and-mathematics-stem-occupations-past-present-and-future/home.htm (accessed January 22, 2017).

Fuhrmann, C. N., D. G. Halme, P. S. O'Sullivan, and B. Lindstaedt. 2011. Improving graduate education to support a branching career pipeline: Recommendations based on a survey of doctoral students in the basic biomedical sciences. *CBE Life Sciences Education* 10(3):239-249.

Gammie, A., A. Gibbs., and S. Singh. 2018. *Catalyzing the modernization of graduate biomedical training.* Bethesda. MD: National Institute of General Medical Sciences. Available: https://www.nigms.nih.gov/training/instpredoc/documents/ABRCMS.pdf (accessed May 20, 2018).

Gibbs, K., Jr. 2014. Diversity in STEM: What it is and why it matters. *Scientific American.* Voices blog. Available https://blogs.scientificamerican.com/voices/diversity-in-stem-what-it-is-and-why-it-matters/ (accessed March 16, 2018).

Golde, C. M., and T. M. Dore. 2001. *At cross purposes: What the experiences of today's doctoral students reveal about doctoral education.* Philadelphia: Pew Charitable Trusts.

Hussain, Y. 2017. *Key Recommendations from Selected Recent Reports on Graduate Education (1995-2017).* Commissioned paper prepared for the Committee. Available: http://sites.nationalacademies.org/cs/groups/pgasite/ documents/webpage/pga_186162.pdf (accessed May 7, 2018).

Lebrón, J. 2017. *Forming Interdisciplinary Scholars: An Evaluation of the IES Predoctoral Interdisciplinary Training Program.* Commissioned paper prepared for the Committee. Available: http://sites.nationalacademies.org/cs/ groups/pgasite/documents/webpage/pga_186161.pdf (accessed May 7, 2018).

NASEM (National Academies of Sciences, Engineering, and Medicine). 2016. *Developing a national STEM workforce strategy: A workshop summary.* Washington, DC: The National Academies Press.

NAS/NAE/IOM (National Academy of Sciences, National Academy of Engineering, and Institute of Medicine). 1995. *Reshaping the graduate education of scientists and engineers.* Washington, DC: National Academy Press.

NAS/NAE/IOM. 2007. *Rising above the gathering storm: Energizing and employing America for a brighter economic future.* Washington, DC: The National Academies Press.

NAS/NAE/IOM. 2014. *The postdoctoral experience revisited.* Washington, DC: The National Academies Press.

NSB (National Science Board). 2015. *Revisiting the STEM workforce: A companion to Science & Engineering Indicators 2014.* NSB-2015-10. Arlington, VA: National Science Foundation. Available: https://www.nsf.gov/pubs/2015/nsb201510/nsb201510.pdf (accessed January 3, 2018).

NSB. 2016a. Science & Engineering Indicators 2016: Appendix Table 2-24, S&E graduate enrollment, by sex and field: 2000–13. National Science Foundation, National Center for Science and Engineering Statistics. Available: https://nsf.gov/statistics/2016/nsb20161/uploads/1/12/at02-24.pdf (accessed January 3, 2018).

NSB. 2016b. Science & Engineering Indicators 2016: Appendix Table 2-26, S&E graduate enrollment, by citizenship, field, race, and ethnicity: 2000–13. National Science Foundation, National Center for Science and Engineering Statistics. Available: https://nsf.gov/statistics/2016/nsb20161/uploads/1/12/at02-26.pdf (accessed January 3, 2018).

NSF (National Science Foundation). 2018. NSF FY 2018 Budget Request to Congress. Available: https://www.nsf.gov/about/budget/fy2018/pdf/01_fy2018.pdf (accessed March 18, 2018).

St. Clair, R., T. Hutto, C. MacBeth, W. Newstetter, N. A. McCarty, and J. Melkers. 2017. The "new normal": Adapting doctoral trainee career preparation for broad career paths in science. *PloS ONE* 12(5):e0177035.

Thiry, H., S. L. Laursen, and H. G. Loshbaugh. 2015. "How do I get from here to there?" An examination of Ph.D. science students' career preparation and decision making. *International Journal of Doctoral Studies* 10:237-256.

Thomasian, J. 2011. *Building a science, technology, engineering, and math education agenda: An update of state action.* Washington, DC: National Governors Association Center for Best Practice.

UK Research and Innovation. 2018. *Statement of Expectations for Postgraduate Training.* Available: https://www.ukri.org/files/legacy/skills /statementofexpectation-revisedseptember2016v2-pdf/ (accessed March 18, 2018).

Xue, Y., and R. Larson. 2015. STEM crisis or stem surplus? Yes and yes. *Monthly Labor Review.* Available: https://www.bls.gov/opub/mlr/2015/article/stem-crisis-or-stem-surplus-yes-and-yes.htm (accessed January 22, 2018).

2

Trends in Graduate STEM Degrees
Earned in the United States

The committee's vision for science, technology, engineering, and mathematics (STEM) graduate education in the 21st century builds on the strengths of the current system. This system has consistently produced both master's and Ph.D. graduates who leave their graduate universities with a deep understanding of their disciplines' content areas and who have learned the practical skills and sophisticated analytical methods needed to conduct research, and it remains the largest destination for graduate education in the world (OECD, 2017). However, as the committee looks to the future needs of graduate students, the science and engineering enterprises, the U.S. economy, and society at large, there are aspects of the current graduate STEM education system that need to change to better serve all four. This is particularly true when one considers the following:

- The pool of *potential* STEM graduate students is increasingly diverse, and research disciplines and institutions are striving—though many continue to struggle—to be more inclusive and equitable, in terms of both representation and institutional climate. Progress in increasing diversity and improving the success of all students, notably students from groups historically underrepresented in STEM, is needed to produce the talent pool that drives the discovery of knowledge and the application of that knowledge in all sectors of life.
- The nature of STEM research and other kinds of work, driven by developments such as "big data" and artificial intelligence, is changing and becoming evermore technology enabled, multidisciplinary, collaborative, and international.

- Increasing numbers of graduates are likely to have multiple jobs over the course of their careers and work in a range of sectors.
- STEM graduate degrees holders are increasingly in demand in traditionally non-STEM fields, such as policy, law, media and communications, nonprofits, and government (AAAS, 2009; NSB, 2018c).

The subsequent chapters of this report focus on these issues. To provide a basis for those discussions, this chapter focuses on the current state of graduate STEM education and important trends in student characteristics of gender, race and ethnicity, citizenship, and disability status. Unless otherwise specified, numbers will include both master's and doctoral students. Additional information on issues and trends specific to master's or doctoral education, such as career outcomes, appear in Chapters 4 and 5, respectively. Note that the broad umbrella term "STEM" comprises many individual disciplines that can vary substantially, and the majority of the report reflects the Statement of Task and focuses on STEM broadly defined. However, to help establish a better understanding of the graduate education system, this chapter does provide data presented by broad discipline (agricultural sciences; biological sciences; earth, atmospheric, and ocean sciences; computer sciences; mathematics and statistics; chemistry; physics; social and behavioral sciences; and medical and other health sciences). A review of data collection mechanisms and initiatives appears in Chapter 3 as a crosscutting issue.

ENROLLMENT, DEGREES, AND TRENDS IN U.S. GRADUATE STEM EDUCATION

The number of students enrolled in graduate STEM education system has grown steadily, increasing from 303,000 in 1975 (NCSES, 2004) to nearly 668,000 students in 2015 (NSB, 2018c). According to the National Center for Science and Engineering Statistics (NCSES), as stated in Science and Engineering Indicators (SEI) 2018, "Most of the growth in this period [in graduate STEM enrollment] occurred in the 2000s, with stable enrollment between 2008 and 2013 and resumed growth in 2014 and 2015" (NSB, 2018h[1]).

The number of degrees awarded over the 2000-2015 period has also grown substantially. In 2015, approximately 225,500 graduate STEM degrees were awarded, with 181,000 at the master's level (NSB, 2018d) and 44,500 at the doctoral level (NSB, 2018f; see also Figure 2-1 and Table 2-1).

Overall, the total number of degrees awarded in STEM fields increased at every level between 2000 and 2015. The number of master's degrees has shown the largest growth, increasing by nearly 88 percent over the 15-year period. In

---

[1] See https://www.nsf.gov/statistics/2018/nsb20181/report/sections/higher-education-in-science-and-engineering/graduate-education-enrollment-and-degrees-in-the-united-states (accessed March 12, 2018).

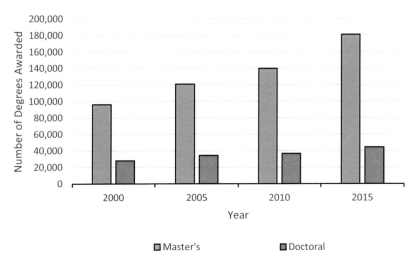

FIGURE 2-1 Graduate degrees awarded in STEM fields, by degree level, 2000-2015 selected years.
SOURCES: NSB, 2018d,f.

comparison, the number of doctoral STEM degrees increased by 60 percent (NSB, 2018b). Regarding proportion of STEM degrees awarded compared to non-STEM degrees, STEM master's degrees accounted for 24.7 percent of all master's degrees awarded in 2015 (NSB, 2018d), while at the doctoral level, STEM degrees accounted for 64.4 percent of all Ph.D.'s awarded in 2015 (NSB, 2018f).

While looking at graduate STEM education as a whole can give a broad perspective of the enterprise, reviewing the data at the discipline level can add nuance to the understanding. According to SEI 2018:

> The highest enrollment growth was recorded in computer sciences, mathematics and statistics, medical sciences, and engineering. Most other S&E[2] fields also had substantial growth. Enrollment in the social sciences grew from 83,000 in 2000 to 111,000 in 2011, then declined to 103,000 by 2015. Enrollment in computer sciences had increased gradually or remained stable through 2012, then accelerated from 52,000 to more than 86,000 in only 3 years. Temporary visa students accounted for most of this growth. Along the same lines, the number of first-time, full-time graduate students in computer sciences, an indicator of developing trends, nearly doubled in the last 3 years. (NSB, 2018h[3])

---

[2] The National Science Foundation uses the term S&E (science and engineering) to denote STEM fields.

[3] See https://www.nsf.gov/statistics/2018/nsb20181/report/sections/higher-education-in-science-and-engineering/graduate-education-enrollment-and-degrees-in-the-united-states (accessed March 12, 2018).

TABLE 2-1 Comparison of Master's and Doctoral Degrees Awarded in STEM Disciplines, in 2000 and 2015

| | Master's | | | |
Field	2000	2015	Numerical Change	Percentage Change
S&E	96,230	180,955	84,725	88.0
Engineering	25,738	49,207	23,469	91.2
Science	70,492	131,748	61,256	86.9
Agricultural sciences	3,858	5,792	1,934	50.1
Biological sciences	6,329	14,370	8,041	127.1
Earth, atmospheric, and ocean sciences	1,345	2,212	867	64.5
Computer sciences	14,986	31,552	16,566	110.5
Mathematics and statistics	3,295	8,269	4,974	151.0
Chemistry	1,909	2,491	582	30.5
Physics	1,244	1,934	690	55.5
Social and behavioral sciences	37,166	64,809	27,643	74.4
Medical and other health sciences	–	–	–	–

[a] The fields for doctoral, which include medical and other health sciences, reflect degrees in the category with doctor's-research/scholarship. These do not include medical or health degrees in the doctor's- professional practice category. The National Center for Science and Engineering does not include the master's degrees in this category in the Science and Engineering Indicators, and they do not appear in this report.
SOURCES: NSB, 2018d, f.

The selection above highlights the magnitude of change that can occur within each discipline. Additional focus on graduate education trends by citizenship appears below in the section on Current State of Graduate STEM Education by Citizenship.

To show the trends in each discipline, Table 2-1 also includes the percentage change within each discipline between 2000 and 2015. While all STEM disciplines listed in Table 2-1 have experienced growth at the master's and Ph.D. levels, the degree to which the fields have increased varies considerably. Following the trends in enrollment, the degrees awarded in computer science at the master's and doctoral levels show some of the highest levels of increase, at 110.5 percent and 151.1 percent, respectively. Other categories that saw a doubling in degrees awarded from 2000 to 2015 include master's degrees in biological sciences (127.1 percent) and mathematics and statistics (151.0 percent) and doctoral degrees in medical and other health sciences (119.1 percent). Engineering experienced relatively high and similar levels of growth in both master's (91.2 percent) and doctoral (93.3 percent) degrees. At the other end of the spectrum, chemistry

Doctoral[a]

2000	2015	Numerical Change	Percentage Change
27,862	44,521	16,659	59.8
5,384	10,406	5,022	93.3
22,478	34,115	11,637	51.8
984	1,381	397	40.3
4,992	7,890	2,898	58.1
579	827	248	42.8
777	1,951	1,174	151.1
1,081	1,802	721	66.7
2,090	2,906	816	39.0
1,208	1,840	632	52.3
8,182	9,950	1,768	21.6
2,439	5,343	2,904	119.1

experienced the lowest overall growth at 30.5 percent for master's and 39.0 percent for doctoral degrees, followed by agricultural sciences at 50.1 percent for master's degrees and 40.3 percent for Ph.D.'s. The social and behavioral sciences saw the lowest level of growth at the doctoral level, with a 21.6 percent increase, although the number of master's degrees increased by 74.4 percent.

DATA AND TRENDS BY GENDER

From 2000 to 2015, annual degree attainment for both genders increased at the master's and doctoral levels (NBS, 2018d,f; Figure 2-2). For women, the number of STEM master's degrees increased from 41,700 in 2000 to 81,700 in 2015, while the number of doctoral degrees rose from 9,300 to 16,300 (Tables 2-2 and 2-3; NSB, 2018d,f). Men earned a larger number of degrees overall, increasing at the master's level from 54,600 in 2000 to 92,000 in 2015 and at the doctoral level from 16,100 to 22,900 (NSB, 2018d,f). For context, at the bachelor's degree level, women earned 201,000 STEM degrees in 2000 and 322,900

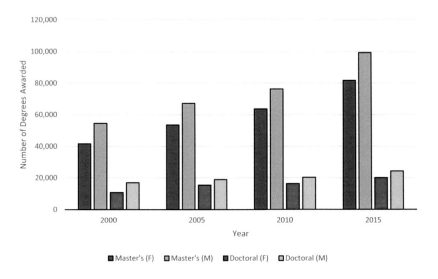

FIGURE 2-2 Graduate degrees awarded in STEM fields, by degree level and gender, 2000-2015, selected years.
SOURCES: NSB, 2018d,f.

TABLE 2-2 Comparison of Master's Degrees Awarded in STEM Disciplines in 2000 and 2015, by Gender

	Master's Degrees Earned by Women			
Field	2000	2015	Numerical Change	Percentage Change
S&E	41,670	81,673	40,003	96.0
Engineering	5,342	12,282	6,940	129.9
Science	36,328	69,391	33,063	91.0
Agricultural sciences	1,819	3,228	1,409	77.5
Biological sciences	3,513	8,326	4,813	137.0
Earth, atmospheric, and ocean sciences	513	955	442	86.2
Computer sciences	5,003	9,607	4,604	92.0
Mathematics and statistics	1,498	3,380	1,882	125.6
Chemistry	823	1,109	286	34.8
Physics	244	436	192	78.7
Social and behavioral sciences	22,767	42,217	19,450	85.4

SOURCES: NBS, 2018d,f.

degrees in 2015, while men earned 197,700 and 327,100 degrees, respectively. At the undergraduate level, the differences in degree attainment by gender have declined. In the 2000 to 2013 period, women earned more degrees than men, while in 2014 and 2015 men earned less than 1 percent more bachelor's degrees than women (NSB, 2018b).

While men earned more STEM graduate degrees, the rate at which women earned graduate STEM degrees has increased more from 2000 to 2015 (Tables 2-2 and 2-3). For master's degrees, women earned 96 percent more degrees in 2015 than in 2000, while men earned 82 percent more. At the doctoral level, women earned 74 percent more degrees in 2015 than 2000, while men earned 43 percent more (NSB, 2018d,f). The increase in degrees earned at the undergraduate level shows a different trend, reflecting that women and men earned bachelor's degrees in STEM at similar levels from 2000 to 2015. From 2000 to 2015, the number of women and men earning bachelor's degrees increased by 61 percent and 66 percent, respectively (NSB, 2018b).

The comparison between women and men in terms of annual degrees awarded varied significantly between disciplines (Tables 2-2 and 2-3). One of the starkest differences in the number of degrees awarded was in engineering versus the sciences. At both levels of graduate education, men earned more degrees in engineering than women, and women earned more degrees in the sciences than men in 2015 (NSB, 2018d,f). In 2000, men also earned more degrees in

Master's Degrees Earned by Men			
2000	2015	Numerical Change	Percentage Change
54,560	99,282	44,722	82.0
20,396	36,925	16,529	81.0
34,164	62,357	28,193	82.5
2,039	2,564	525	25.7
2,816	6,044	3,228	114.6
832	1,257	425	51.1
9,983	21,945	11,962	119.8
1,797	4,889	3,092	172.1
1,086	1,382	296	27.3
1,000	1,498	498	49.8
14,399	22,592	8,193	56.9

TABLE 2-3 Comparison of Doctoral Degrees Awarded in STEM Disciplines in 2000 and 2015, by Gender

Field	Doctoral Degrees Earned by Women			
	2000	2015	Numerical Change	Percentage Change
S&E	10,838	20,150	9,312	85.9
Engineering	835	2,426	1,591	190.5
Science	9,329	16,264	6,935	74.3
Agricultural sciences	321	665	344	107.2
Biological sciences	2,202	4,179	1,977	89.8
Earth, atmospheric, and ocean sciences	166	359	193	116.3
Computer sciences	131	439	308	235.1
Mathematics and statistics	274	503	229	83.6
Chemistry	664	1,206	542	81.6
Physics	158	367	209	132.3
Social and behavioral sciences	4,540	6,046	1,506	33.2
Medical and other health sciences	1,509	3,886	2,377	157.5

SOURCES: NBS, 2018d,f.

engineering than women at both levels; however, in the sciences, women earned more master's degrees than men, though men earned more doctoral degrees. In particular, looking at the largest fields at the doctoral level, women's growth in the biological sciences more than doubled that of men, as they earned 2,000 more degrees in 2015 than in 2000 while men earned 920 more (NSB, 2018d,f).

In terms of growth, as measured by the increase in annual degrees awarded, the trends at the broader STEM level generally apply to growth at the master's and doctoral levels within each STEM discipline (Tables 2-2 and 2-3). Except for master's degrees in computer sciences and mathematics and statistics, the increase in annual degrees awarded to women was greater than the increase for men between 2000 and 2015. As noted previously for engineering, men earned more degrees per year than women did, but women have seen greater annual percentage increases. The number of engineering master's and doctoral degrees that women earned annually increased by 130 and 190 percent, respectively, from 2000 to 2015, while those earned by men increased by 81 percent and 75 percent, respectively. Similarly, women saw greater percentage increases than men in both master's and doctoral degrees awarded between 2000 and 2015—91 percent versus 82 percent for master's degrees and 74 percent versus 31 percent for doctoral degrees. In addition to the growth in the biological sciences, women have earned more degrees than men and had a greater increase in growth in the

Doctoral Degrees Earned by Men			
2000	2015	Numerical Change	Percentage Change
17,024	24,371	7,347	43.2
4,549	7,980	3,431	75.4
12,475	16,391	3,916	31.4
663	716	53	8.0
2,790	3,711	921	33.0
413	468	55	13.3
646	1,512	866	134.1
807	1,299	492	61.0
1,426	1,700	274	19.2
1,050	1,473	423	40.3
3,642	3,904	262	7.2
930	1,457	527	56.7

social and behavioral sciences at both the master's and doctoral levels. Although women have earned fewer degrees in the computer sciences and mathematics and statistics than men, the annual numbers of degrees awarded to women in those fields at both degree levels increased by at least 84 percent between 2000 and 2015 (NBS, 2018d,f).

DATA AND TRENDS BY RACE AND ETHNICITY

The greatest benefit to U.S. society will only come when students from all segments of U.S. society and backgrounds succeed in graduate school through a supportive atmosphere that begins to reverse a long history of underrepresentation and exclusion across many STEM and non-STEM fields alike. NCSES data show that the makeup of the student population in STEM graduate programs does not reflect the diversity of the United States.[4] The demographic composition of the U.S. resident population is shifting, as noted in Figure 2-3, with the percentage of individuals identifying as white falling from nearly 70 percent in the 24 to 65 age group to slightly above 50 percent for those under age 18. In contrast,

---

[4] This report uses the racial and ethnic group categories as defined by the U.S. Office of Management and Budget and adopted by the National Science Foundation (NCSES, 2017b).

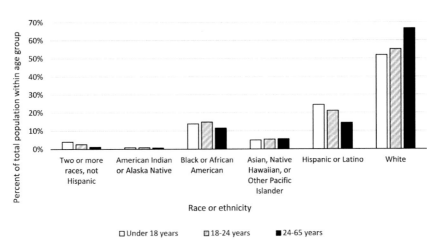

FIGURE 2-3 Proportion of U.S. resident population, by race and or ethnicity, across age groups, in 2014.
NOTE: Hispanic may be of any race. While additional figures in this chapter include the category "Other or unknown race and ethnicity," the data made available in the source material did not include this category. For consistency with the other figures in this report, the category "Asian, Native Hawaiian, or Other Pacific Islander" combines the categories of "Asian" and "Native Hawaiian or Other Pacific Islander." The field used in Figure 2-3 and for subsequent figures reference categories that shifted over time. Two or more races were not collected until 2011.
SOURCE: NCSES, 2017b.

the proportion of individuals identifying as Hispanic or Latino/a, belonging to two or more racial groups (non-Hispanic), or as American Indian or Alaska Native (AIAN) increases steadily as the age of the group declines. For blacks or African Americans, the proportion increases in the 18- to 24-year-old group, and while the proportion decreases for those under age 18, it remains higher than the proportion of the oldest age group. Overall, these shifts in the composition of younger U.S. residents mean that the pool of potential graduate students will change as well.

The way in which federal agencies have collected information on race and ethnicity has also changed between 2000 and 2015:

> Beginning in 2011, some students may be classified as multiracial who in the past may have been reported as American Indian or Alaska Native, Asian and Pacific Islander, black, Hispanic, or white. The number of students with a mul-

tiracial identity accounted for about 500 doctoral degree awards in 2015. (NSB, 2018h[5])

Figures 2-4, 2-5, 2-6, and 2-7 include the two or more races category beginning in 2015. Although the number of degrees awarded to this group in 2015 was not insignificant (3,105 at the master's and 505 at the doctoral level), the NCSES states that the addition of the category did not likely have a major impact on the trends in race and ethnicity regarding how those data had been collected prior to 2011 (NSB, 2018h[6]).

Historically underrepresented racial and ethnic groups who hold master's degrees significantly outnumber those with Ph.D.'s in STEM fields, but witness similar kinds of trends in terms of gender and racial/ethnic representation. NCSES notes that at the master's level, the proportion of STEM degrees earned by students from historically underrepresented racial and ethnic groups increased from 14 percent to 21 percent in 2000 to 2015 (NSB, 2018h[7]), with Hispanic and Latino/a students showing the largest growth at nearly 202 percent. AIAN students, on the other hand, experienced the slowest rate of growth at the master's level overall, at close to 43 percent.

At the doctoral level, the number of degrees earned by all racial and ethnic groups grew between 2000 and 2015. One of the most historically well-represented groups, white students, had the lowest increase in annual degrees earned between 2000 and 2015, at 32 percent. Trends for Asian students, another historically well-represented group, are more challenging to isolate due to the data collection practices mentioned previously; however, given the relatively small number of students in 2015 who identified as Native Hawaiian or Pacific Islander, Figures 2-5 and 2-6 show a general increasing trend for Asian students. Hispanic or Latino/a students, in comparison, had the greatest increase in that time period at 160 percent.

While the view of STEM degrees earned by each racial and ethnic group provides a broad understanding of degrees earned annually, the trends within group at the disciplinary level can identify fields that have experienced increases in representation at the graduate level. In the following analyses by racial or ethnic group, note that in the event of a low base number, the percentage change between 2000 and 2015 in degrees earned per year is more significant.

From 2000 to 2015, AIAN students saw the most growth in agricultural

---

[5] See https://www.nsf.gov/statistics/2018/nsb20181/report/sections/higher-education-in-science-and-engineering/graduate-education-enrollment-and-degrees-in-the-united-states#s-e-doctoral-degrees (accessed March 16, 2018).

[6] See https://www.nsf.gov/statistics/2018/nsb20181/report/sections/higher-education-in-science-and-engineering/graduate-education-enrollment-and-degrees-in-the-united-states#s-e-doctoral-degrees (accessed March 16, 2018).

[7] See https://www.nsf.gov/statistics/2018/nsb20181/report/sections/higher-education-in-science-and engineering/graduate-education-enrollment-and-degrees-in-the-united-states#s-e-master-s-degrees (accessed March 16, 2018).

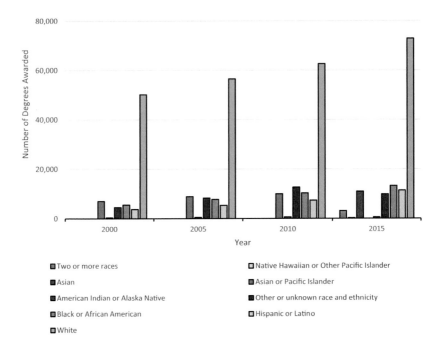

FIGURE 2-4 Master's degrees awarded in STEM fields, by race and ethnicity, 2000-2015, selected years.
NOTES: Asian or Pacific Islander was a category from 2000 to 2010. Starting in 2011, the two categories split into Asian and Native Hawaiian or Other Pacific Islander.
SOURCE: NBS, 2018e.

sciences at the master's level at nearly 74 percent, while the number of AIAN master's students in engineering, chemistry, and earth, atmospheric, and ocean sciences, experienced sharp decreases of 7.8, 20.0, and 33.3 percent, respectively, and no growth in mathematics and statistics (Table 2-4). For STEM doctoral degrees, where the annual number of degrees awarded remains small in relation to the total number of degrees awarded to all racial and ethnic groups and subject to sharper percentage changes, the largest growth for AIAN students was in the agricultural sciences, with a 300 percent increase, but there was no growth in computer sciences and a decrease in the number of AIAN doctoral students in earth, atmospheric, and ocean sciences, mathematics and statistics, and chemistry at 50.0, 50.0, and 28.6 percent, respectively.

For Asian, Pacific Islander, or Native Hawaiian students, because of the

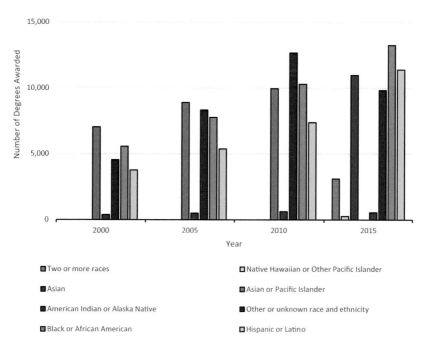

FIGURE 2-5 Detail of master's degrees awarded in STEM fields, for racial and ethnic minorities, 2000-2015, selected years.
NOTES: Asian or Pacific Islander was a category from 2000 to 2010. Starting in 2011, the two categories split into Asian and Native Hawaiian or Other Pacific Islander.
SOURCE: NSB, 2018e.

changes in the data collection process, the trends between the two groups over the 2000 to 2015 time period are more difficult to discern. In Table 2-5, the master's and doctoral degrees awarded for Asian or Pacific Islander appear as a comparison between 2000 and 2010. Starting in 2011, NCSES changed the categories, offering students the opportunity to identify as Asian or as Native Hawaiian or Other Pacific Islander. Going forward, the division will allow researchers to differentiate the trends between Asian students, who have historically been well represented, and Native Hawaiian or Other Pacific Islander students, which have been less well represented in graduate STEM education. To align with the other tables, the degrees awarded in 2015 for these groups are noted. In the 2000 to 2010 period, master's and doctoral degrees awarded to Asian or Pacific Islander students increased in almost every field, except for doctoral degrees in earth, atmospheric, and oceanic studies (which remained flat) and notably, master's degrees, which decreased from 2,068 to 1,470.

For black and African American students, there has been growth in almost

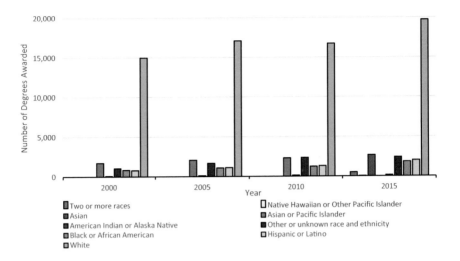

FIGURE 2-6 Doctoral degrees awarded in STEM fields, by race and ethnicity, 2000-2015, selected years.
SOURCE: NSB, 2018g.

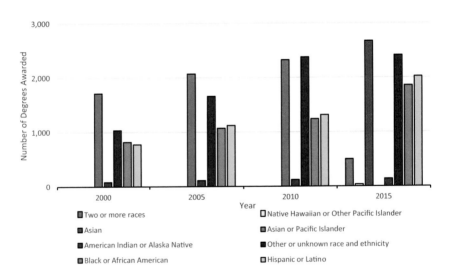

FIGURE 2-7 Detail of doctoral degrees awarded in STEM fields, for racial and ethnic minorities, 2000-2015, selected years.
SOURCE: NSB, 2018g.

every field at both degree levels, aside from physics; however, the small base number renders the percentage change prone to dramatic swings (Table 2-6). For instance, the field that saw the most growth at the master's level was earth, atmospheric, and ocean sciences, with a nearly 550 percent growth from 2000 to 2015, resulting from an increase from 7 to 45 degrees awarded per year. In a more robust field, engineering master's degrees doubled over the 15-year period. Also notable was the 23 percent decrease in master's degrees conferred among this group for physics. For black and African American students, overall growth in STEM doctoral degrees at 126 percent exceeded that of engineering at 81 percent, while the number of computer science doctoral degrees and medical and other health sciences degrees increased by 280 percent and 420 percent, respectively, from 2000 to 2015. Black and African American students earned 5 percent fewer doctoral degrees in physics over this period.

Hispanic and Latino/a students earning engineering master's degrees increased at a slower rate than their rate for STEM master's overall, but still with significant gains at 169 percent change over 15 years (Table 2-7). Strikingly, every discipline at the master's level for this group saw greater than 100 percent change during this time. Hispanic and Latino/a doctoral students earned degrees in engineering and earth, atmospheric, and ocean sciences at nearly twice their rate of STEM overall, nearly 233 and 245 percent change compared to 160 percent. Additionally, medical and health sciences grew by 400 percent. The only discipline with less than 100 percent growth at the doctoral level for Hispanic and Latino/a students was the social and behavioral sciences, at almost 95 percent.

For the relatively small number of students identifying as two or more races, the largest percentage change at the master's level over the 2000-2015 period occurred in earth, atmospheric, and ocean sciences at nearly 270 percent (Table 2-8). At the Ph.D. level, the increase in number of students of two or more races earning Ph.D.'s in engineering exceeded that of STEM overall, 172 percent compared to 148.5 percent.

For students of other or unknown race, the greatest growth at the master's level occurred in the biological sciences, with just over a 200 percent increase, while the smallest increase occurred in chemistry, at just over a 20 percent increase (Table 2-9). At the doctoral level, students of other or unknown race increased the number of medical and other health sciences and agricultural sciences Ph.D.'s they earned by 415 percent and 259 percent, respectively, nearly double that of the 133 percent increase in all STEM Ph.D.'s they earned.

From 2000 to 2015, the number of master's degrees in engineering conferred to white students rose by nearly 40 percent, just shy of growth among that population for STEM master's degrees overall at 45 percent change (Table 2-10). With a 75 percent increase, the biological sciences saw the largest growth in master's degrees awarded to white students. At the doctoral level, the medical and other health sciences experienced the large growth—an almost 105 percent increase—while physics and biological sciences kept pace with overall STEM growth at

TABLE 2-4 Comparison of Master's and Doctoral Degrees Awarded in STEM Disciplines, by American Indian or Alaska Native Students, in 2000 and 2015

Field	Master's Degrees Earned by American Indian or Alaska Native Students			
	2000	2015	Numerical Change	Percentage Change
S&E	383	548	165	43.1
Engineering	64	59	−5	−7.8
Science	319	489	170	53.3
Agricultural sciences	23	40	17	73.9
Biological sciences	26	43	17	65.4
Earth, atmospheric, and ocean sciences	9	6	−3	−33.3
Computer sciences	32	53	21	65.6
Mathematics and statistics	9	9	0	0.0
Chemistry	5	4	−1	−20.0
Physics	3	3	0	0.0
Social and behavioral sciences	211	331	120	56.9
Medical and other health sciences	–	–	–	–

SOURCES: NSB, 2018e,g.
NOTE: Data not available for Master's Degrees awarded in this field.

TABLE 2-5 Comparison of Master's and Doctoral Degrees Awarded in STEM Disciplines, by Asian, Pacific Islander, Native Hawaiian, or Other Pacific Islander Students, in 2000, 2010, and 2015

Field	Master's Degrees			
	Asian or Pacific Islander		Asian	Native Hawaiian or Other Pacific Islander
	2000	2010	2015	2015
S&E	7,032	9,959	10,976	269
Engineering	2,380	3,736	3,469	35
Science	4,652	6,223	7,507	234
Agricultural sciences	94	165	166	12
Biological sciences	595	1,245	1,723	20
Earth, atmospheric, and ocean sciences	22	45	53	2
Computer sciences	2,068	1,470	2,174	38
Mathematics and statistics	180	459	553	4
Chemistry	172	186	183	1
Physics	53	93	73	1
Social and behavioral sciences	1,453	2,548	2,566	156
Medical and other health sciences	–	–	–	–

SOURCES: NSB, 2018e,g.
NOTE: Data not available for Master's Degrees awarded in this field.

Doctoral Degrees Earned by American Indian or Alaska Native Students

2000	2015	Numerical Change	Percentage Change
82	137	55	67.1
5	12	7	140.0
77	125	48	62.3
2	8	6	300.0
8	24	16	200.0
6	3	−3	−50.0
0	4	4	0.0
2	1	−1	−50.0
7	5	−2	−28.6
0	5	5	0.0
43	54	11	25.6
8	20	12	150.0

Doctoral Degrees

Asian or Pacific Islander		Asian	Native Hawaiian or Other Pacific Islander
2000	2010	2015	2015
1,518	2,325	2,669	34
380	517	664	1
1,334	1,808	2,005	33
26	32	35	1
429	650	667	8
15	15	17	1
56	124	112	0
71	84	80	2
124	151	174	3
52	60	73	2
355	415	484	8
196	271	354	8

TABLE 2-6 Comparison of Master's and Doctoral Degrees Awarded in STEM Disciplines, by Black or African American Students, in 2000 and 2015

| Field | Master's Degrees Earned by Black or African American Students | | | |
	2000	2015	Numerical Change	Percentage Change
S&E	5,563	13,239	7,676	138.0
Engineering	658	1,323	665	101.1
Science	4,905	11,916	7,011	142.9
Agricultural sciences	84	189	105	125.0
Biological sciences	223	847	624	279.8
Earth, atmospheric, and ocean sciences	7	45	38	542.9
Computer sciences	650	1,913	1,263	194.3
Mathematics and statistics	98	204	106	108.2
Chemistry	65	97	32	49.2
Physics	44	34	−10	−22.7
Social and behavioral sciences	3,726	8,579	4,853	130.2
Medical and other health sciences	–	–	–	–

SOURCES: NSB, 2018e,g.

TABLE 2-7 Comparison of Master's and Doctoral Degrees Awarded in STEM Disciplines, by Hispanic or Latino/a Students, in 2000 and 2015

| Field | Master's Degrees Earned by Hispanic or Latino/a Students | | | |
	2000	2015	Numerical Change	Percentage Change
S&E	3,762	11,392	7,630	202.8
Engineering	852	2,290	1,438	168.8
Science	2,910	9,102	6,192	212.8
Agricultural sciences	133	314	181	136.1
Biological sciences	268	916	648	241.8
Earth, atmospheric, and ocean sciences	30	104	74	246.7
Computer sciences	308	1,056	748	242.9
Mathematics and statistics	100	298	198	198.0
Chemistry	56	123	67	119.6
Physics	34	100	66	194.1
Social and behavioral sciences	1,975	6,182	4,207	213.0
Medical and other health sciences	-	-	-	-

SOURCES: NSB, 2018e,g.

Doctoral Degrees Earned by Black or African American Students

2000	2015	Numerical Change	Percentage Change
821	1,855	1,034	125.9
91	165	74	81.3
730	1,690	960	131.5
20	31	11	55.0
106	219	113	106.6
3	11	8	266.7
15	57	42	280.0
13	20	7	53.8
45	88	43	95.6
19	18	−1	−5.3
414	757	343	82.9
94	488	394	419.1

Doctoral Degrees Earned by Hispanic or Latino/a Students

2000	2015	Numerical Change	Percentage Change
775	2,019	1,244	160.5
86	286	200	232.6
689	1,733	1,044	151.5
13	47	34	261.5
149	425	276	185.2
9	31	22	244.4
13	42	29	223.1
12	35	23	191.7
45	100	55	122.2
19	44	25	131.6
370	719	349	94.3
56	280	224	400.0

TABLE 2-8 Comparison of Master's and Doctoral Degrees Awarded in STEM Disciplines, by Students Identifying with Two or More Races, in 2000 and 2015

Field	Master's Degrees Earned by Students Identifying Two or More Races			
	2000	2015	Numerical Change	Percentage Change
S&E	1,335	3,105	1,770	132.6
Engineering	296	585	289	97.6
Science	1,039	2,520	1,481	142.5
Agricultural sciences	48	128	80	166.7
Biological sciences	110	332	222	201.8
Earth, atmospheric, and ocean sciences	9	33	24	266.7
Computer sciences	107	345	238	222.4
Mathematics and statistics	34	101	67	197.1
Chemistry	17	50	33	194.1
Physics	9	29	20	222.2
Social and behavioral sciences	698	1,495	797	114.2
Medical and other health sciences	–	–	–	–

SOURCES: NSB, 2018e,g.

TABLE 2-9 Comparison of Master's and Doctoral Degrees Awarded in STEM Disciplines, by Students Identifying Other or Unknown Race and Ethnicity, in 2000 and 2015

Field	Master's Degrees Earned by Students Identifying Other or Unknown Race and Ethnicity			
	2000	2015	Numerical Change	Percentage Change
S&E	4,545	9,833	5,288	116.3
Engineering	940	1,723	783	83.3
Science	3,605	8,110	4,505	125.0
Agricultural sciences	144	290	146	101.4
Biological sciences	284	853	569	200.4
Earth, atmospheric, and ocean sciences	46	109	63	137.0
Computer sciences	663	1,397	734	110.7
Mathematics and statistics	142	278	136	95.8
Chemistry	82	99	17	20.7
Physics	42	101	59	140.5
Social and behavioral sciences	2,190	4,963	2,773	126.6
Medical and other health sciences	–	–	–	–

SOURCES: NSB, 2018e,g.

Doctoral Degrees Earned by Students Identifying Two or More Races

2000	2015	Numerical Change	Percentage Change
202	502	300	148.5
32	87	55	171.9
170	415	245	144.1
5	14	9	180.0
44	110	66	150.0
1	8	7	700.0
3	16	13	433.3
2	8	6	300.0
14	32	18	128.6
9	10	1	11.1
69	145	76	110.1
20	68	48	240.0

Doctoral Degrees Earned by Students Identifying Other or Unknown Race and Ethnicity

2000	2015	Numerical Change	Percentage Change
1,034	2,408	1,374	132.9
146	382	236	161.6
888	2,026	1,138	128.2
22	79	57	259.1
187	381	194	103.7
32	51	19	59.4
29	98	69	237.9
33	78	45	136.4
85	142	57	67.1
57	102	45	78.9
378	782	404	106.9
57	294	237	415.8

TABLE 2-10 Comparison of Master's and Doctoral Degrees Awarded in STEM Disciplines, by White Students, in 2000 and 2015

Field	Master's Degrees Earned by White Students			
	2000	2015	Numerical Change	Percentage Change
S&E	50,130	72,869	22,739	45.4
Engineering	11,020	15,263	4,243	38.5
Science	39,110	57,606	18,496	47.3
Agricultural sciences	2,864	3,860	996	34.8
Biological sciences	4,183	7,309	3,126	74.7
Earth, atmospheric, and ocean sciences	1,036	1,512	476	45.9
Computer sciences	4,641	7,223	2,582	55.6
Mathematics and statistics	1,655	2,730	1,075	65.0
Chemistry	930	1,058	128	13.8
Physics	585	903	318	54.4
Social and behavioral sciences	22,956	32,825	9,869	43.0
Medical and other health sciences	–	–	–	–

SOURCES: NSB, 2018e,g.

38 percent and almost 37 percent, respectively, and the social and behavioral sciences saw a slight decrease of 4 percent.

Reviews of data and trends by gender or by race and ethnicity can highlight important issues; however, the segmentation solely in those major categories can obscure trends at the intersection of gender and race and ethnicity. Identifying trends not only across disciplines, but also within specific groups, provides a much more thorough perspective on the state of representation in STEM higher education as a whole. According to the SEI 2018:

> In 2015, women earned more than half of the master's degrees awarded to their respective racial or ethnic group in the social and behavioral sciences and in non-S&E fields but less than half of those in the natural sciences and engineering. Between 2000 and 2015, the proportion of natural sciences and engineering master's degrees awarded to women rose among American Indians or Alaska Natives, declined among blacks, and remained relatively stable among Hispanics. (NSB, 2018h[8])

---

[8] See https://www.nsf.gov/statistics/2018/nsb20181/report/sections/higher-education-in-science-and-engineering/graduate-education-enrollment-and-degrees-in-the-united-states (accessed March 16, 2018). The natural sciences include agricultural sciences, biological sciences, and earth, atmospheric, and ocean sciences. At the doctoral level, medical sciences and other health sciences are included under natural sciences and consequently under S&E because at this level, these degrees are research degrees.

Doctoral Degrees Earned by White Students

2000	2015	Numerical Change	Percentage Change
14,975	19,714	4,739	31.6
1,948	3,023	1,075	55.2
13,027	16,691	3,664	28.1
470	673	203	43.2
2,845	3,886	1,041	36.6
344	444	100	29.1
289	535	246	85.1
457	676	219	47.9
1,030	1,243	213	20.7
561	774	213	38.0
5,406	5,190	−216	−4.0
1,544	3,155	1,611	104.3

Additionally,

> In 2015, women earned half or more of the doctoral degrees awarded to their respective racial or ethnic groups in the natural sciences, the social and behavioral sciences, and in non-S&E fields. Since 2000, the proportion of women earning doctorates increased in the natural sciences, social and behavioral sciences, and engineering in all racial and ethnic groups except for American Indians or Alaska Natives. (NSB, 2018h[9])

These data do not account for trends over time, but rather present a snapshot of the system in 2015. One finding from these trends is that engineering students at both the master's and doctoral levels and across all racial and ethnic groups are predominantly men (Table 2-11). The natural sciences follow this trend as well, though the difference between the percentage of male and female students is smaller than that within engineering. In the social and behavioral sciences, on the other hand, students at both the master's and doctoral levels are predominantly female. In engineering, for all groups and at both the master's and doctoral levels, men earn more degrees in engineering than women, and the total number of women earning those degrees represent roughly a third or less of the total students across all racial and ethnic groups. In the natural sciences, the numbers

---

[9] See https://www.nsf.gov/statistics/2018/nsb20181/report/sections/higher-education-in-science-and-engineering/graduate-education-enrollment-and-degrees-in-the-united-states (accessed March 16, 2018).

TABLE 2-11 Master's and Doctoral Degrees Awarded to U.S. Citizens and Permanent Residents, by Sex, Race, Ethnicity, and Broad Field Category in 2015

Race or Ethnicity	All	Female	Male	Percentage Female	Percentage Male
Master's Degrees					
American Indian or Alaska Native					
S&E	548	311	237	56.8	43.2
Engineering	59	18	41	30.5	69.5
Natural sciences	158	71	87	44.9	55.1
Social and behavioral sciences	331	222	109	67.1	32.9
Black or African American					
S&E	13,239	8,415	4,824	63.6	36.4
Engineering	1,323	370	953	28.0	72.0
Natural sciences	3,337	1,538	1,799	46.1	53.9
Social and behavioral sciences	8,579	6,507	2,072	75.8	24.2
Hispanic or Latino/a					
S&E	11,392	6,008	5,384	52.7	47.3
Engineering	2,290	555	1,735	24.2	75.8
Natural sciences	2,920	1,238	1,682	42.4	57.6
Social and behavioral sciences	6,182	4,215	1,967	68.2	31.8
White					
S&E	72,869	34,368	38,501	47.2	52.8
Engineering	15,263	3,275	11,988	21.5	78.5
Natural sciences	24,781	10,267	14,514	41.4	58.6
Social and behavioral sciences	32,825	20,826	11,999	63.4	36.6

continued

Asian or Pacific Islander				
S&E	11,245	4,968	6,277	44.2	55.8
Engineering	3,504	1,031	2,473	29.4	70.6
Natural sciences	5,019	2,183	2,836	43.5	56.5
Social and behavioral sciences	2,722	1,754	968	64.4	35.6
Other or unknown race and ethnicity				
S&E	12,938	6,661	6,277	51.5	48.5
Engineering	2,308	536	1,772	23.2	76.8
Natural sciences	4,172	1,750	2,422	41.9	58.1
Social and behavioral sciences	6,458	4,375	2,083	67.7	32.3
Doctoral Degrees				
American Indian or Alaska Native				
S&E	131	78	53	59.5	40.5
Engineering	12	4	8	33.3	66.7
Natural sciences	65	34	31	52.3	47.7
Social and behavioral sciences	54	40	14	74.1	25.9
Black or African American				
S&E	1,593	1,186	618	74.5	38.8
Engineering	165	55	110	33.3	66.7
Natural sciences	671	422	249	62.9	37.1
Social and behavioral sciences	757	549	208	72.5	27.5
Hispanic or Latino				
S&E	1,869	1,005	864	53.8	46.2
Engineering	286	72	214	25.2	74.8
Natural sciences	864	441	423	51.0	49.0

TABLE 2-11 Continued

Race or Ethnicity	All	Female	Male	Percentage Female	Percentage Male
Social and behavioral sciences	719	492	227	68.4	31.6
White					
S&E	18,544	8,828	9,716	47.6	52.4
Engineering	3,023	707	2,316	23.4	76.6
Natural sciences	10,331	4,908	5,423	47.5	52.5
Social and behavioral sciences	5,190	3,213	1,977	61.9	38.1
Asian or Pacific Islander					
S&E	2,495	1,256	1,239	50.3	49.7
Engineering	665	205	460	30.8	69.2
Natural sciences	1,338	713	625	53.3	46.7
Social and behavioral sciences	492	338	154	68.7	31.3
Other or unknown race and ethnicity					
S&E	2,757	1,337	1,420	48.5	51.5
Engineering	469	121	348	25.8	74.2
Natural sciences	1,361	743	771	54.6	56.6
Social and behavioral sciences	927	589	338	63.5	36.5

NOTE: At the doctoral level, medical sciences and other health sciences are not included under natural sciences and consequently under S&E. While previous tables and figures have separated Asian or Pacific Islander in 2015, the source data for this table provided a single category for this tabulation.
SOURCES: Adapted from NSB (2018a) and WebCASPAR.

are slightly more balanced, and in social and behavioral sciences, the situation is reversed, with women in all groups earning at least two-thirds of the degrees at both the master's and doctoral levels. Overall, black and African American students account for the greatest proportional difference within groups between genders among all racial and ethnic groups, most notably in natural sciences and social and behavioral sciences. Interestingly, white women have the lowest share of engineering master's and doctoral degrees compared to other gender splits among the other racial and ethnic groups.

DATA AND TRENDS BY CITIZENSHIP

Another critical component of graduate student demographics is the increasing proportion of international students in the STEM graduate student population. Individuals who do not hold U.S. citizenship or permanent residence and who pursue higher education in the United States do so under a special class of nonimmigrant visa, category F-1 (USCIS, 2018b). This visa allows students to study full-time at an accredited college or university providing the program ultimately confers a degree, diploma, or certificate. Students on F-1 visas are not eligible to work off campus during their degree with certain exemptions such as a STEM Optional Practical Training Extension (OPT) (USCIS, 2018a). These are 24-month extensions available to students who have earned a bachelor's, master's, or doctoral degree from an accredited school. Individuals on F-1 visas also do not have the same access to federal funding sources as American citizens or permanent residents, and are similarly not eligible for government-sponsored aid programs such as the Pell Grant, the Federal Supplemental Education Opportunity Grant, Stafford Loan, Perkins Loan, PLUS Loan, and Federal Work-Study program. This restriction excludes students with an Arrival-Departure Record (I-94) from U.S. Citizen and Immigration Services (USCIS), or who qualify as a "battered immigrant-qualified alien" (U.S. Department of Education, 2010). According to the Brookings Institution, the number of students studying in the United States on F-1 visas has grown dramatically in recent years, and they are disproportionately studying STEM and business.

Over the past 20 years, temporary visa holders earning doctorates have increasingly preferred to stay in the United States immediately following graduation, a measure referred to as the "stay rate." For instance, as of 2014, 45 percent of international students extended their visas in order to work in the United States after graduation, primarily in the same geographic area in which they earned their degrees. The lack of longitudinal data on international student employment limits the granularity of data available on stay rates. However, this influx of global talent has boosted the economy in significant ways, including contributing to an increase of more than $39 billion to our economy in 2016 (IIE, 2017). Stay rates are highest in fields where temporary visa holders are most prevalent: engineering, physical sciences, and life sciences (NCSES, 2017a).

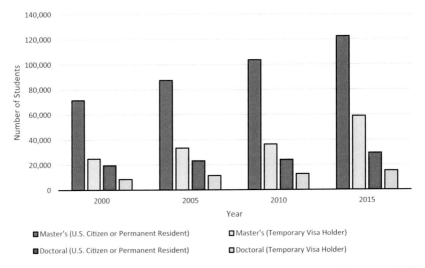

FIGURE 2-8 Graduate degrees awarded in STEM fields, by citizenship status, 2000-2015. SOURCES: NSB, 2018e,g.

For STEM master's degrees, the rate of temporary visa holders continued a general upward trend and increased dramatically from 2014 to 2015, especially remarkable when compared to rates for white and ethnic minorities during that same time (see Figure 2-8 and NSB, 2018i, Fig. 2-15).

At the doctoral level, the rate of visa holders earning STEM Ph.D.'s tapered off from 2014 to 2015, after a gradual rate of growth for several years earlier. For that last year of data collection, the rate of growth for white students and students from underrepresented minorities earning STEM Ph.D.'s outpaced that of visa holders, Asian or Pacific Islanders, and those of unknown or other race or ethnicity (NSB, 2018i, Fig. 2-18).

In terms of the most popular countries of origin for temporary visa holders in the U.S. graduate STEM education system, NCSES reports:

> The top sending locations in 2017 continued to be India and China, accounting for 69 percent of the international S&E graduate students in the United States, followed by Iran, South Korea, Saudi Arabia, and Taiwan (Appendix Table 2-26). Compared to 2016, the number of graduate S&E students from India, Saudi Arabia, Iran, and South Korea declined in 2017 (by 19, 11, 1, and 1 percent respectively) while the number from China and Taiwan increased (by 4 and 5 percent respectively).

> About 8 in 10 graduate students from India, Iran, Bangladesh, and Sri Lanka and more than 6 in 10 of graduate students from China, Pakistan, and Nepal

were enrolled in an S&E field. In the case of Iran, more than half of them were enrolled in engineering; in the case of Bangladesh, 42 percent. In contrast, more than 60 percent of the international students from Canada, South Korea, Brazil and Japan were enrolled in non-S&E fields. (NSB, 2018h[10])

From 2000 to 2015, temporary visa holders earning master's degrees in STEM increased by more than 136 percent, compared to just over 71 percent for American citizens (see Table 2-12). Similarly, temporary visa holders earning doctoral degrees in STEM increased by more than 80 percent over the same period of time despite the tapering between 2014 and 2015 mentioned previously, while the number of American citizens earning doctoral STEM degrees increased by just over 40 percent (see Table 2-13). Temporary visa holders have seen a higher percentage increase in degrees earned in every field at the master's and doctoral levels, except for physics and social and behavioral sciences at the master's level and agricultural sciences at the doctoral level. For overall enrollment, the Council of Graduate Schools (CGS) found for fall 2016 that "International students comprised the largest share of first-time graduate students in mathematics and computer sciences (60 percent), followed closely by engineering (55.7 percent)" (CGS, 2017).

The most recent data from CGS show that there was a decline in temporary visa holder enrollment between 2016 and 2017 in all fields. For STEM, graduate enrollment for first-time international students declined 5 percent in the biological and agricultural sciences; 10 percent in engineering; 2 percent in mathematics and computer sciences; 6 percent in physical and earth sciences; and 1 percent in social and behavioral sciences (Okahana and Zhou, 2017). Graduate deans have faced challenges in interpreting the recent decline in enrollment:

> We do not know whether this is because of fewer applications submitted, fewer applications approved, or a combination of both. An examination of admission yields offers additional insight, as the decline suggests that fewer students are willing to pursue opportunities for graduate education in the United States, even when acceptance into a degree program is offered to them. . . . While the survey [CGS Pressing Issues Survey] cannot pinpoint particular factors that might be shaping such shifts, the uncertainty with prospects of post-graduate school employment under optional practical training and/or H-1B visa programs, as well as opportunities to pursue graduate education in other English-speaking countries, may in part explain some of the declines graduate deans are observing.

Of course, national visa and immigration policies will continue to play a critical role in the continuing participation of international students, who have the potential to contribute to innovation and discovery, in the U.S. scientific enterprise.

---

[10] See https://www.nsf.gov/statistics/2018/nsb20181/report/sections/higher-education-in-science-and-engineering/graduate-education-enrollment-and-degrees-in-the-united-states#graduate-enrollment-by-field (accessed March 16, 2018).

TABLE 2-12 Comparison of Master's Degrees Awarded in STEM Disciplines, by Citizenship Status, in 2000 and 2015

Field	Master's Degrees Earned by Temporary Visa Holders			
	2000	2015	Numerical Change	Percentage Change
S&E	24,815	58,724	33,909	136.6
Engineering	9,824	24,460	14,636	149.0
Science	14,991	34,264	19,273	128.6
Agricultural sciences	516	793	277	53.7
Biological sciences	750	2,327	1,577	210.3
Earth, atmospheric, and ocean sciences	195	348	153	78.5
Computer sciences	6,624	17,353	10,729	162.0
Mathematics and statistics	1,111	4,092	2,981	268.3
Chemistry	599	876	277	46.2
Physics	483	690	207	42.9
Social and behavioral sciences	4,655	7,712	3,057	65.7

SOURCES: NSB, 2018e,g.

TABLE 2-13 Comparison of Doctoral Degrees Awarded in STEM Disciplines, by Citizenship Status, in 2000 and 2015

Field	Doctoral Degrees Earned by Temporary Visa Holders			
	2000	2015	Numerical Change	Percentage Change
S&E	8,461	15,183	6,722	79.4
Engineering	2,728	5,786	3,058	112.1
Science	5,733	9,397	3,664	63.9
Agricultural sciences	431	493	62	14.4
Biological sciences	1,268	2,170	902	71.1
Earth, atmospheric, and ocean sciences	170	261	91	53.5
Computer sciences	375	1,087	712	189.9
Mathematics and statistics	493	902	409	83.0
Chemistry	754	1,119	365	48.4
Physics	500	812	312	62.4
Social and behavioral sciences	1,216	1,811	595	48.9
Medical and other health sciences	484	676	192	39.7

SOURCES: NSB, 2018e,g.

Master's Degrees Earned by U.S. Citizens

2000	2015	Numerical Change	Percentage Change
71,415	122,231	50,816	71.2
15,914	24,747	8,833	55.5
55,501	97,484	41,983	75.6
3,342	4,999	1,657	49.6
5,579	12,043	6,464	115.9
1,150	1,864	714	62.1
8,362	14,199	5,837	69.8
2,184	4,177	1,993	91.3
1,310	1,615	305	23.3
761	1,244	483	63.5
32,511	57,097	24,586	75.6

Doctoral Degrees Earned by U.S. Citizens

2000	2015	Numerical Change	Percentage Change
19,401	29,338	9,937	51.2
2,656	4,620	1,964	73.9
16,745	24,718	7,973	47.6
553	888	335	60.6
3,724	5,720	1,996	53.6
409	566	157	38.4
402	864	462	114.9
588	900	312	53.1
1,336	1,787	451	33.8
708	1,028	320	45.2
6,966	8,139	1,173	16.8
1,955	4,667	2,712	138.7

DATA AND TRENDS BY DISABILITY STATUS

When considering issues of diversity and inclusion in STEM, it is important to consider other traditionally underrepresented groups such as those who have disabilities. The Americans with Disabilities Act defines a disability as "a physical or mental impairment that substantially limits one or more major life activities."[11] In STEM, this population is not insignificant: there were approximately 50,800 graduate students enrolled in STEM fields with a disability in 2012 (NCSES, 2017b[12]).

From SEI 2018:

> In 2014, 7% of S&E doctorate recipients reported having a disability; they were fairly similar to those who did not report a disability in terms of broad field of study. Nearly half of the S&E doctorate recipients who reported one or more disabilities of any type indicated that they had visual disabilities, 40% reported cognitive disabilities, 18% reported hearing disabilities, 10% reported lifting disabilities, and 6% reported walking disabilities. (NSB, 2018h[13])

Notably absent from the indicators are any data concerning similar trends within disciplines or at the master's level, which limits their generalizability in comparison to the data presented earlier in this chapter. Additionally, these numbers may be low as a result of underreporting. Organizations such as the American Association for the Advancement of Science have specific programming directed at making STEM graduate education more accessible to students with disabilities,[14] with the aim of increasing the representation of this population in engineering and the sciences. Future efforts at supporting graduate students with disabilities would be bolstered by more thorough accounting of these individuals among the various STEM disciplines.

REFERENCES

AAAS (American Association for the Advancement of Science). 2009. *Career trends: Careers away from the bench. Advice and options for scientists.* Available: http://www.sciencemag.org/sites/default/files/documents/away_from_the_bench_1.pdf (accessed January 22, 2018).
CGS (Council of Graduate Schools). 2017. Healthy growth in master's enrollment continues at U.S. graduate schools. Available: http://cgsnet.org/healthy-growth-master%E2%80%99s-enrollment-continues-us-graduate-schools (accessed March 18, 2018).

---

[11] See https://adata.org/faq/what-definition-disability-under-ada (accessed March 20, 2018).
[12] See https://www.nsf.gov/statistics/2017/nsf17310/static/data/tab3-7.pdf (accessed March 16, 2018).
[13] See https://www.nsf.gov/statistics/2018/nsb20181/report/sections/higher-education-in-science-and-engineering/graduate-education-enrollment-and-degrees-in-the-united-states (accessed March 16, 2018).
[14] See https://www.aaas.org/program/entrypoint (accessed March 21, 2018).

IIE (Institute of International Education). 2017. Open Doors 2017 Executive Summary. Available: https://www.iie.org/Why-IIE/Announcements/2017-11-13-Open-Doors-2017-Executive-Summary (accessed March 16, 2018).

NCSES (National Center for Science and Engineering Statistics). 2004. *Science and engineering indicators 2004*. Appendix Table 2-13. S&E graduate enrollment, by field and sex: Selected years, 1975–2001. Arlington, VA: National Science Foundation. Available https://wayback.archive-it.org/5902/20150818164912/http://www.nsf.gov/statistics/seind04/append/c2/at02-13.pdf (accessed March 16, 2018).

NCSES. 2017a. *Doctorate recipients from U.S. universities: 2015*. Special Report NSF 17-306. Arlington, VA: National Science Foundation. Available: https://www.nsf.gov/statistics/2017/nsf17306/static/report/nsf17306.pdf (accessed March 26, 2018).

NCSES. 2017b. Technical notes in *Women, minorities, and persons with disabilities in science and engineering: 2017*. Special Report NSF 17-310. Arlington, VA: National Science Foundation. Available: https://www.nsf.gov/statistics/2017/nsf17310/technical-notes.cfm#reporting-categories (accessed December 21, 2017).

NSB (National Science Board). 2018a. Appendix Table 2-20, Degrees awarded to U.S. citizens and permanent residents, by sex, race, ethnicity, broad field category, and degree level: 2000–15. *Science and engineering indicators 2018*. NSB-2018-1. Alexandria, VA: National Science Foundation. Available: https://www.nsf.gov/statistics/2018/nsb20181/assets/561/tables/at02-20.pdf (accessed March 20, 2018).

NSB. 2018b. Appendix Table 2-21, Earned bachelor's degrees, by sex and field: 2000–15. *Science and engineering indicators 2018*. NSB-2018-1. Alexandria, VA: National Science Foundation. Available: https://www.nsf.gov/statistics/2018/nsb20181/assets/561/tables/at02-21.pdf (accessed March 13, 2018).

NSB. 2018c. Appendix Table 2-23, S&E graduate enrollment, by field: 2000–15. *Science and engineering indicators 2018*. NSB-2018-1. Alexandria, VA: National Science Foundation. Available: https://www.nsf.gov/statistics/2018/nsb20181/assets/561/tables/at02-23.pdf (accessed March 26, 2018).

NSB. 2018d. Appendix Table 2-27, Earned master's degrees, by sex and field: 2000–15. *Science and engineering indicators 2018*. NSB-2018-1. Alexandria, VA: National Science Foundation. Available: https://www.nsf.gov/statistics/2018/nsb20181/assets/561/tables/at02-27.pdf (accessed March 13, 2018).

NSB. 2018e. Appendix Table 2-28, Earned master's degrees, by citizenship, field, race, and ethnicity: 2000–15. *Science and engineering indicators 2018*. NSB-2018-1. Alexandria, VA: National Science Foundation. Available: https://www.nsf.gov/statistics/2018/nsb20181/assets/561/tables/at02-28.pdf (accessed March 16, 2018).

NSB. 2018f. Appendix Table 2-29, Earned doctoral degrees, by citizenship, field, and sex: 2000–15. *Science and engineering indicators 2018*. NSB-2018-1. Alexandria, VA: National Science Foundation. Available: https://www.nsf.gov/statistics/2018/nsb20181/assets/561/tables/at02-29.pdf (accessed March 13, 2018).

NSB. 2018g. Appendix Table 2-32, Earned doctoral degrees, by citizenship, field, race, and ethnicity: 2000–15. *Science and engineering indicators 2018*. NSB-2018-1. Alexandria, VA: National Science Foundation. Available: https://www.nsf.gov/statistics/2018/nsb20181/assets/561/tables/at02-32.pdf (accessed March 16, 2018).

NSB. 2018h. Higher education in science and engineering. Chapter 2 in *Science and engineering indicators 2018*. NSB-2018-1. Alexandria, VA: National Science Foundation. Available: https://www.nsf.gov/statistics/2018/nsb20181/report/sections/higher-education-in-science-and-engineering/graduate-education-enrollment-and-degrees-in-the-united-states (accessed March 12, 2018).

NSB. 2018i. *Science and engineering indicators 2018*. NSB-2018-1. Alexandria, VA: National Science Foundation.

OECD (Organisation for Economic Co-operation and Development). 2017. *Education at a glance 2017: OECD Indicators.* Table C4.1: International student mobility and foreign students in tertiary education (2015). Paris: OECD Publishing. Available: http://www.keepeek.com/Digital-Asset-Management/oecd/education/education-at-a-glance-2017_eag-2017-en#page302 (accessed January 22, 2018).

Okahana, H., and E. Zhou. 2017. *Graduate enrollment and degrees: 2006 to 2016.* Council of Graduate Schools. Available: http://cgsnet.org/ckfinder/userfiles/files/Intl_Survey_Report_Fall2017.pdf (accessed March 18, 2018)

USCIS (U.S. Citizenship and Immigration Services). 2018a. Optional practical training extension for STEM students (STEM OPT). Available: https://www.uscis.gov/working-united-states/students-and-exchange-visitors/students-and-employment/stem-opt (accessed March 16, 2018).

USCIS. 2018b. Students and employment. Available: https://www.uscis.gov/working-united-states/students-and-exchange-visitors/students-and-employment (accessed March 16, 2018).

U.S. Department of Education, Office of Federal Student Aid. 2010. Student aid eligibility—Eligibility for Title IV aid for "battered immigrants-qualified aliens" as provided for in the Violence Against Women Act. Available: https://ifap.ed.gov/dpcletters/GEN1007.html (accessed March 16, 2018).

3

Crosscutting Themes in
Graduate STEM Education

Over the course of its research and deliberations, the committee identified several issues that apply to both master's and Ph.D. levels of graduate science, technology, engineering, and mathematics (STEM) education. These crosscutting themes are the subject of this chapter. Issues particular to master's or Ph.D. education are discussed in Chapters 4 and 5, respectively. The crosscutting issues include:

- improving STEM graduate education by adjusting faculty rewards and incentives as they pertain to teaching and mentoring;
- collecting and disseminating data to increase transparency for prospective and current STEM graduate students about institutional degree and career outcomes, among other metrics;
- increasing diversity, equity, and inclusiveness throughout STEM graduate programs to cultivate talent from all backgrounds and promote continued scientific leadership;
- building the ability of the STEM graduate education system to adjust to the dynamic nature of the scientific enterprise and the career options available to its students; and
- optimizing the experiences that graduate students have while in their programs.

One of the main themes of this report is its call for cultural change at the nation's universities that puts students at the center of the graduate school experience. This change in culture, coupled with the set of actions laid out in this and subsequent chapters, would move the graduate education system significantly closer to the ideal set of educational experiences articulated in Chapter 6 and in the Summary of this report. It would also help bridge the partial disconnect between the full range of faculty activities needed to prepare STEM graduate students for the 21st-century work environment writ large—including appropriate advising and mentoring and exposing them to career options outside of academia—and the incentives that drive faculty behavior in terms of tenure, promotion, and merit raises that are based largely on research productivity and results.

ADJUSTING FACULTY REWARDS AND INCENTIVES TO IMPROVE GRADUATE STEM EDUCATION

At most research universities, the incentive and reward system for faculty emphasizes publication rate and amount of grant funding as the main metrics for tenure and promotion. Although the evaluations of the quality of teaching and mentoring activities are collected, these qualities do not receive as much emphasis in the overall evaluation (NAS/NAE/IOM, 1996, 1997). This imbalance is well known throughout academia, and addressing it has been the subject of recommendations in previous reports, on both graduate STEM education and reform in higher education broadly (NRC, 2012).

In addition to the adverse effects that the current incentive structure can have on graduate education, many programs do not employ teaching or mentoring practices based on the emerging evidence base about the most effective pedagogical practices or about the ways adults learn. Research on undergraduate education, for example, has demonstrated that using effective pedagogical practices, such as "active learning," increases student learning and retention (Freeman et al., 2014). Regarding mentoring, the Center for the Improvement of Mentored Experiences in Research at the University of Wisconsin–Madison[1] has developed a wealth of resources for institutions to improve research mentoring relationships. Another potential resource for faculty members is the National Research Mentoring Network,[2] supported by the National Institutes of Health (NIH), which is developing a research base around the science of mentorship. The network has already developed a variety of curricular offerings to promote effective and inclusive mentoring practices.

Although high-quality and student-focused faculty mentoring and advising are essential to the education of STEM graduate students, the academic ecosystem does not reward these behaviors as highly as it does research productivity, publications, and other traditional metrics of success. Faculty members should be given the time, resources, know-how, and incentives to devote attention to mentorship. Early-career faculty in the process of establishing themselves in a

---

[1] See http://cimerproject.org/#/ (accessed January 22, 2018).
[2] See https://nrmnet.net/ (accessed January 22, 2018).

department may require a primer on effective approaches to mentoring, while more senior faculty would benefit from establishing a baseline of existing mentoring and advising skills and from periodic refreshers to explore new skills or techniques in supporting student success.

Education researchers have noted how important it is for institutional leaders to create a set of rewards, incentives, and well-defined criteria (Filetti, 2009; Law et al., 2014; Marcellino, 2011) that encourage advisors and mentors to deliver quality guidance (Drake, 2008; Habley, 2007) and research opportunities (Davis et al., 2015; Schultheis et al., 2011). Although some faculty may strongly resist changing tenure and promotion policies to reward activities outside of research achievements (Brownell and Tanner, 2012), at least a few institutions have overcome faculty objections to reward such activities as they relate to undergraduate students (Purdue University, 2015; University of Arkansas, 2011). Institutional leadership plays a critical role in promoting and sustaining faculty incentive policies that acknowledge the importance of engaging in student-centered activities (Fountain and Newcomer, 2016).

In its advice to new graduate students, the NIH Office of Intramural Training and Education says the best mentors are advisors, coaches, counselors, and supporters all at the same time.[3] They are experienced scientists who guide graduate students, but also challenge them to develop their independence. A good mentor helps students define their research goals and then supports them in their quest to achieve those goals.

Both the paper by Margaret Blume-Kohout that was commissioned for this study and findings in the mentoring literature claim that those students who were most satisfied with their mentors reported that those mentors had several attributes in common (Blume-Kohout, 2017). These mentors challenged and stimulated their students' thinking, were helpful and encouraging, were enthusiastic about the student's research, and contributed to the student's professional development. They were also approachable and generous with their time, gave appropriate amounts of freedom and direction, and provided regular and constructive feedback on both research and academic progress. (Lovitts, 2004; Zhao et al., 2007).

It is uncommon that a student will find a single individual or advisor who has all these attributes. In many instances, students can benefit from having multiple mentors (Higgins, 2000) given that different mentors can provide guidance on different topics. At least one institution, the Watson School of Biological Sciences at Cold Spring Harbor, requires that students have a "research mentor," and separately, an "academic mentor."

One of the key themes that students raised in the focus groups conducted by Research Triangle International (RTI) for this study[4] was how much their gradu-

---

[3] See https://www.training.nih.gov/mentoring_guidelines (accessed January 22, 2018).

[4] See http://sites.nationalacademies.org/cs/groups/pgasite/documents/webpage/pga_186164.pdf (accessed May 16, 2018).

ate school experience depended on their supervising faculty advisor and their relationship with him or her. Participants noted challenges they faced when their educational and career goals differed from those of their advisor. Many of these students did not feel comfortable pursuing courses, workshops, or other professional development opportunities outside the focus of the advisor's research for fear of putting the relationship at risk. The stigma, whether real or perceived, associated with a student's pursuit of a career outside academia also needs to be addressed. Adjusting the incentive system, perhaps by including metrics on student outcomes beyond traditional measures, such as placement of students at research-intensive institutions, is one approach that may be effective in achieving the goals discussed in this section.

Given the importance of effective teaching and mentoring to providing a more effective, student-centered graduate school experience, the committee makes the following two recommendations:

RECOMMENDATION 3.1—Rewarding Effective Teaching and Mentoring: Advancement procedures for faculty, including promotion and tenure policies and practices, should be restructured to strengthen recognition of contributions to graduate mentoring and education.

- Federal and state funding agencies should align their policies and award criteria to ensure that students in the programs they support experience the kind of graduate education outlined in this report and achieve the scientific and professional competencies articulated here, whether they are on training or research grant mechanisms.
- Institutions should increase priority and reward faculty for demonstrating high-quality teaching and inclusive mentoring practices for all graduate students, including the recognition of faculty teaching in master's degree programs, based on the results of restructured evaluations.
- Institutions should include teaching and mentoring performance as important considerations for reappointment, promotion, annual performance review, and tenure decisions. Institutions should also nominate faculty for external awards (such as those from technical societies) that reward teaching excellence.

RECOMMENDATION 3.2—Institutional Support for Teaching and Mentoring: To improve the quality and effectiveness of faculty teaching and mentoring, institutions of higher education should provide training for new faculty and should offer regular refresher courses in teaching and mentoring for established faculty.

- Institutions should require faculty and postdoctoral researchers who have extensive contact with graduate students to learn and demonstrate evidence-based and inclusive teaching and mentoring practices.
- Graduate programs should facilitate mentor relationships between the graduate student and the primary research advisors, as well as opportunities for students to develop additional mentor or advisor relationships, including with professionals in industry, government laboratories, and technical societies.
- Graduate schools should provide extra-departmental mentoring and support programs.
- Graduate students should seek multiple mentors to meet their varied academic and career needs.

INCREASING DATA COLLECTION, RESEARCH, AND TRANSPARENCY ABOUT GRADUATE STEM EDUCATION OUTCOMES

The ability to understand the current state of and emerging trends in the graduate STEM enterprise depends on the quality, breadth, and transparency of data and research about graduate education. For data, a number of organizations collect information ranging from longitudinal datasets to periodic collections held by institutions or professional societies. These data shed light on specific components of the system, such as individual disciplines; however, previous reports on graduate education have called on the primary collectors of data, including federal agencies, institutions, and professional societies, to collect and, more critical, share a broader array of standardized, common metrics on a regular basis. Those recommendations have not generally been implemented or have been implemented unevenly across institutions (Hussain, 2017). As a result, it is difficult, for example, to track how graduate students fare during their programs and after graduation.

The federal government is one of the principal collectors of longitudinal STEM graduate education data. With specific attention to the post-baccalaureate-level population, the National Science Foundation's (NSF's) National Center for Science and Engineering Statistics conducts the following surveys:

- National Survey of College Graduates, a longitudinal biennial survey conducted since the 1970s that provides data on the nation's college graduates, with particular focus on those in the science and engineering workforce;
- Survey of Graduate Students and Postdoctorates in Science and Engineering, an annual census of all U.S. academic institutions;

- Survey of Earned Doctorates, an annual census of all research doctorate recipients;
- Survey of Doctoral Recipients, a sample designed to provide a cross-sectional estimate of the activities of research doctorate recipients; and
- Early Career Doctorates Survey, which gathers in-depth information about individuals who earned their first doctoral degree (Ph.D., M.D., or equivalent) in the past 10 years.

In addition, the National Center for Education Statistics (NCES) conducts a variety of national assessments that include longitudinal data on postsecondary education, including graduate-level metrics across all disciplines. NCES also administers the Baccalaureate and Beyond Longitudinal Study, which examines students' education and work experiences after they complete a bachelor's degree, with a special emphasis on the experiences of new elementary and secondary teachers. The Bureau of Labor Statistics (BLS) also provides career outcome data by levels of educational attainment.

Outside of the federal government, professional societies also play a key role in collecting and sharing data for their constituent audiences. The Council of Graduate Schools (CGS) has provided a report on annual Graduate Enrollments and Degrees, a joint effort with the Graduate Record Examinations (GRE) Board, since 1986 (Okahana and Zhou, 2017). CGS also releases data through a variety of other annual surveys, such as the International Graduate Admissions and Pressing Issues Survey, and through issue-oriented projects, such as the Doctoral Initiative on Minority Attrition and Completion and the recently launched data phase of the Understanding PhD Career Pathways for Improvement Program. Disciplinary professional societies also collect information on graduate education as a part of the information-gathering activities on the state of the field. In December 2017, a coalition of 10 university presidents—the Coalition for Next Generation Life Sciences—announced plans for their institutions to collect and report comprehensive data on graduate student outcomes (Blank et al., 2017).[5]

A lack of publicly available data on graduate student outcomes at the institutional levels makes it difficult for students to make informed choices about their training activities and for universities to prepare graduate students for a full range of careers (Blank et al., 2017). Lacking the information needed to fully understand the path ahead of them can limit students' ability to choose a suitable institution and discipline and be clear about the career options available to them with the degree they decide to pursue (Polka et al., 2015). National data-gathering efforts, such as the NSF surveys described above, provide coverage at a broad STEM or discipline level. However, there are data at the institutional level that should be captured to provide potential students the ability to compare programs and for departments to make data-driven decisions to inform continuous im-

---

[5] See http://nglscoalition.org/ (accessed March 16, 2018).

provement. Many institutions collect these data for internal purposes, though few choose to share their data with the public. The critical data points, which would benefit from regularly scheduled updates, include

- number of applicants and accepted students;
- metrics on current student population by gender, race and ethnicity, and visa status;
- time to candidacy, time to degree, and completion rate, aggregated for all students;
- percentage of students funded with tuition and living expenses, along with percentages of source of funding (assistantships, traineeships, fellowships, faculty members' research grants);
- debt level of undergraduates entering the graduate program and of graduates upon completion for an understanding of how incoming financial aid may affect student outcomes and career decisions;
- positions obtained by alumni of graduate programs at 1, 5, 10, and 15 years after graduation in *all* workforce sectors, and salary and job satisfaction at those time points; and
- student satisfaction with their graduate program and career options and opportunities for employers to provide feedback regarding strengths and gaps in skills and competencies of hired graduates.

In addition to collecting data about students, universities—and particularly financial aid offices—should provide information to all entering students on national salary data by field. Because salary information does not create a complete picture of student satisfaction, institutions should make additional efforts to include other metrics to indicate how graduates relate their education to their career. Financial aid offices should also provide entering graduate students with information on the total cost of their graduate experience, including living expenses, and the various forms of financial support, including student loans, available for graduate students.

There is some promising activity under way to address the current lack of transparency. The Association of American Universities (AAU) in 2017 issued a policy statement (Flaherty, 2017) calling on "all Ph.D. granting universities and their respective Ph.D. granting colleges, schools and departments, to make a commitment to providing prospective and current students with easily accessible information." The AAU stated explicitly that such data should include student demographics, average time to finish a degree, financial support, and career paths and outcomes both inside and outside academia. The presidents of 10 leading research-intensive universities announced that they would collect and make publicly available comprehensive data on graduate student outcomes (Blank et al., 2017), and the University of Michigan Rackham Graduate School has been collecting such data since 2003. The University of Michigan data are now accessible for every graduate department through an interactive dashboard highlighted as the first item on the graduate school's home page.[6] Some federal grant programs, such as the National Institute of General Medical Sciences' T32 Institutional Predoctoral Training grants, also require reporting on career outcomes.[7]

The CGS Understanding PhD Career Pathways for Improvement Program builds on 3 years of work with institutions, survey researchers, professional and disciplinary associations, and labor force economists. This effort will provide more extensive information on the nature of work by collecting information about currently enrolled doctoral students and alumni from 61 participating institutions. Unlike previous efforts that broadly describe occupational functions or provide information only on tenure-track academic positions, the CGS project will capture data on all graduates, including those employed in industry, government, and nonprofits, who no longer produce peer-reviewed publications and were not supported on federal traineeships, research assistantships, or fellowships during graduate school.

The Institute for Research on Innovation and Science (IRIS), based at the University of Michigan, provides a platform for linking university administrative records with U.S. Census data, as well as linking administrative data with other databases, including patents and publications.[8] One recent study using the IRIS system was able to identify where recent science and engineering Ph.D.'s are finding jobs (Zolas et al., 2015). In 2016, the University of Minnesota released IPUMS Higher Ed,[9] a publicly available tool that harmonizes multiple NSF datasets—the National and International Survey of Doctoral Researchers[10] databases and Survey of College Graduates[11] and National Survey of Recent College Graduates[12] databases—from 1990 to 2013. IPUMS Higher Ed provides a user-friendly data extraction system to track career trajectories of Ph.D.'s across different occupations, including in academia, government, industry, and other types of research involvement.

These actions are important steps toward addressing the information gap and increasing transparency about STEM graduate education and career outcomes. As these initiatives and other efforts continue to increase the amount of data available, one challenge that may arise is the ability to compare or to cross-walk metrics from one dataset to the next. In July 2017, NORC at the University of Chicago held a stakeholder workshop on existing efforts to track the career paths and professional outcomes of graduate degree holders. This workshop also

---

[6] See https://tableau.dsc.umich.edu/t/UM-Public/views/ProgramStatisticsPhD2016/ProgramStatistics?embed=y&showShareOptions=true&display_count=no&FOSDParameter=All%20Rackham&:isGuestRedirectFromVizportal=y&:embed=y (accessed March 20, 2018).
[7] See https://www.nigms.nih.gov/Training/InstPredoc/Pages/default.aspx (accessed January 22, 2018).
[8] See http://iris.isr.umich.edu/ (accessed January 22, 2018).
[9] See https://highered.ipums.org/highered/ (accessed January 22, 2018).
[10] See https://www.nsf.gov/statistics/srvydoctoratework/ (accessed January 4, 2018).
[11] See https://www.nsf.gov/statistics/srvygrads/ (accessed January 4, 2018).
[12] See https://www.nsf.gov/statistics/srvyrecentgrads/ (accessed January 4, 2018).

examined ways that programs can use data to inform program effectiveness, as well as how to support coordination and partnerships to improve the network of efforts in this area.[13] At the institutional level, there is an opportunity to define and to collect metrics in a standardized way across departments that could make aggregation feasible with other institutions and scale to a national level.

The availability of data also improves the capacity of the research community to understand the graduate STEM education enterprise and help plan any needed adjustments. While there has been increased attention to the pedagogy and practice in effective STEM undergraduate education, which includes critical components of active learning, blended classrooms, and discipline-based education research, there is a relatively smaller proportion of educational research targeted toward understanding effective models and practices in graduate education.[14] Given the importance to the future of the STEM research enterprise of increasing retention and degree completion rates for historically underrepresented minorities, there is a critical need for research on the programs and models that most effectively support those students (NAE, 2014; NAS/NAE/IOM, 2011).

Currently, most studies of this sort employ a small sample size from a single discipline, making it challenging to determine whether the findings can be generalized to other groups of students or to other disciplines. One notable exception is the NIH Broadening Experiences in Scientific Training (BEST) program.[15] Started in 2013, the BEST program funded 17 sites with the focus on improving career exploration in the biomedical sciences. Each site designed an experimental approach, based on the local context of the institution, as well as an assessment to evaluate the outcomes and impact of the work. The predominant goal of the BEST program has been to identify evidence-based practices that other institutions could adopt or adapt. Toward that end, the program includes a continuous and rigorous evaluation process. Given the significant level of investment from federal agencies in graduate-level STEM training and education programs, the products of those investments have the potential to grow beyond the individual student participants and expand into a set of evidence-based practices for other institutions to adopt or adapt. For example, the University of California, San Francisco, and the University of California, Davis, reported that the programs students participate in to expand career development skills and promote career exploration did not increase median time to degree for the 217 Ph.D. students in the BEST programs at those institutions (Schnoes et al., 2018).

---

[13] See https://www.spencer.org/graduate-degree-holder-career-paths-workshop (accessed January 22, 2018).

[14] See online resource at http://sites.nationalacademies.org/cs/groups/pgasite/documents/webpage/pga_186176.pdf for literature review.

[15] See http://www.nihbest.org/ (accessed March 8, 2018).

RECOMMENDATION 3.3—Comprehensive National and Institutional Data on Students and Graduates: Graduate programs should collect, update, and make freely and easily accessible to current and prospective students information about master's- and Ph.D.-level educational outcomes. In addition, to make appropriate future adjustments in the graduate education system, it is essential that comprehensive datasets about the system, its participants, and its outcomes be collected in a standard format, be fully transparent, and be easily accessible and transferable across multiple computer and statistical analysis platforms.

- Federal and state funding agencies should require institutions that receive support for graduate education to develop policies mandating that these data be collected and made widely available to qualify for traineeships, fellowships, and research assistantships.
- Institutions should develop a uniform, scalable, and sustainable model for data collection that can operate beyond the period of extramural funding. The data collection should follow standard definitions that correspond with national STEM education and workforce surveys to help inform benchmarking or higher education research.
- Departments and programs should review their own data from current students and alumni to inform curricula and professional development offerings, and they should provide these data to current and prospective students.
- Prospective students should use these data to inform graduate program selection, educational goal development, and career exploration.

RECOMMENDATION 3.4—Funding for Research on Graduate STEM Education: The National Science Foundation, other federal and state agencies, and private funders of graduate STEM education should issue calls for proposals to better understand the graduate education system and outcomes of various interventions and policies, including but not limited to the effect of different models of graduate education on knowledge, competencies, mind-sets, and career outcomes.

- Funders should support research on the effect of different funding mechanisms on outcomes for doctoral students, including traineeships, fellowships, teaching and research assistantships; the effects of policies and procedures on degree completion, disaggregated by gender, race and ethnicity, and citizenship; and the effect of expanding eligibility of international students to be supported on federal fellowships and training grants.

ENHANCING DIVERSITY, EQUITY, AND INCLUSION

Diversity in science refers to cultivating talent and promoting the full inclusion of excellence across the social spectrum, including people from backgrounds that are traditionally underrepresented and those from backgrounds that are traditionally well represented (Gibbs, 2014). The STEM graduate education enterprise as a whole must seek to enable students of all backgrounds to succeed by implementing mentoring practices and pedagogies that create an inclusive institutional environment in terms of gender, age, culture, ethnicity, and nationality; that make available opportunities for productive dialogue; and that encourage diverse perspectives that can lead to a deeper understanding of how people from different backgrounds may approach learning and problem solving in different ways (Gibbs, 2014).

Expansion of educational opportunities and engagement of a broader and more diverse cross section of the U.S. population in STEM fields is a national priority (NAS/NAE/IOM, 2011) given the importance of drawing on the unique perspectives that people from different backgrounds and with different experiences bring to addressing the most challenging scientific problems facing society today. Research has shown, in fact, that scientific creativity benefits from having multiple viewpoints shaped by the different life experiences of its group members (Ferrini-Mundy, 2013; Page, 2008; Reagans and Zuckerman, 2001; Roberge and Van Dick, 2010; Saxena, 2014). In addition, the enormous output of the U.S. scientific community depends on a constant supply of scientific talent, and a lack of diversity represents a loss of talent (NAS/NAE/IOM, 2011). Diversity of ideas also comes with diversity of the talent pool. As NIH Director Francis Collins and Lawrence Tabak, NIH's principal deputy director, have stated, a lack of diversity in the STEM student body and workforce leads to "the inescapable conclusion that we are missing critical contributions" (Tabak and Collins, 2011, p. 941). Given that the demographics of the U.S. population have shifted over the past 50 years—most children born today in the United States are not white, and a growing fraction of the workforce is female (U.S. Census Bureau, 2012)—tapping into every available pool of talent is essential for the United States to retain its world leadership in science, engineering, and technology.

Moreover, improving representation in STEM graduate education is critical to future employment needs and to ensuring equity for the growing minority-majority population in the United States. According to the BLS, employment in STEM and STEM-associated occupations is projected to grow faster than the average for all occupations (Vilorio, 2014). BLS estimates that overall STEM employment will grow approximately 13 percent between 2012 and 2022, faster than the 11 percent projected growth for all occupations over the same period. Moreover, BLS predicts that nearly all STEM occupations, which pay on average nearly double the median wage for all workers, will experience growth during that time.

Currently, graduate programs do not attract or develop talent from all sectors of the nation's population; women and certain racial and ethnic groups remain underrepresented in many (but not all) disciplines. As a result, graduate programs need to strengthen the culture of equity and inclusion that prepares all students for successful careers and that equips all students with the career skills needed to overcome the challenges they will face in graduate school and beyond. Comparative research to understand how certain departments, institutions, and disciplines have been successful in increasing both the number and success of underrepresented students in graduate programs could help others who are facing similar challenges.

The past few decades have seen increases in the participation of students from historically underrepresented groups and female students; however, progress toward parity looks different from discipline to discipline. Overall, data from the NSF show that the number of minority students pursuing graduate STEM degrees more than doubled in the two decades from 1989 to 2009, with the number of Hispanic and Latino/a graduate students in STEM programs nearly tripling and the number of black or African American students more than doubling (Einaudi, 2011, p. 4). The inclusion of historically underrepresented minorities, notably at the doctoral level, is intertwined with the challenges in developing the equitable representation around faculty. As noted in the National Academies report, *Expanding Underrepresented Minority Participation*, "Not only does it provide underrepresented minorities [doctoral students] an opportunity to contribute to teaching and research, but it is at this level that increases can have a multiplier effect. . . . As the number of underrepresented minorities in faculty positions increases, the more role models underrepresented minority students have who 'look like them' and the higher rate at which underrepresented minority students enroll and graduate." (NAS/NAE/IOM, 2011, pp. 46-47)

Research has already shown that mentoring that intentionally addresses the challenges faced by underrepresented groups can be highly effective at empowering student success (Carver et al., 2017; Griffin et al., 2010; Lewis et al., 2016; May, 2016; Packard, 2015). The development of scalable and sustainable initiatives comes with significant challenges. Revisiting admissions policies can expand traditional definitions of merit to include characteristics that recognize student potential, particularly to the benefit of students from historically underrepresented groups. For example, the Fisk-Vanderbilt Master's-to-PhD Bridge Program, designed to provide underrepresented minority (URM) students a pathway to doctoral studies, added a question to its selection process to assess the applicants' understanding of their own grit[16] and resilience. Since 2004, the program has demonstrated positive results, with 81 percent of those entering the program having gone on to enter doctoral programs (Posselt, 2016).

The extensive effort associated with various intervention programs, edu-

---

[16] Grit is a predisposition for pursuing long-term, challenging goals with passion and perseverance. From http://fisk-vanderbilt-bridge.org/grit-better-than-gre-for-predicting-grad-student-success/ (accessed January 18, 2018).

cational approaches, and modified federal policies has driven the increase in underrepresented student populations (Covington et al., 2017; Fleming et al., 2013; Maton and Hrabowski, 2004; Rincon and George-Jackson, 2016; Stassun et al., 2011; Tanner, 2013; Valantine et al., 2016). One program is the NSF's undergraduate-focused Louis Stokes Alliances for Minority Participation Program[17] (LSAMP), an alliance-based initiative that helps universities and colleges transform undergraduate STEM education through innovative, evidence-based recruitment and retention strategies and relevant educational experiences in support of racial and ethnic groups historically underrepresented in STEM discipline. The last full evaluation of this program in 2005 found that the vast majority of program graduates sought additional education after their bachelor's degrees, and two-thirds of participants later enrolled in graduate school, working toward a master's, Ph.D., or professional degree (Clewell et al., 2005). At the time of this evaluation, one in four LSAMP graduates had completed a STEM graduate degree. In addition, the majority of LSAMP graduates reported that the program had been helpful as they sought their bachelors' degrees in STEM and had influenced their decisions to attend graduate school. A comparison between LSAMP and a nationally representative sample of URMs and white and Asian students revealed that LSAMP participants pursued post-bachelor's coursework, enrolled in graduate programs, and completed advanced degrees at greater rates than did the national comparison groups.

Similarly, the NSF's Alliances for Graduate Education and the Professoriate[18] (AGEP) program seeks to advance knowledge about models to improve pathways to the professoriate and success for historically underrepresented minority doctoral students, postdoctoral researchers, and faculty in specific STEM disciplines and/or STEM education research fields. AGEP has, in fact, enhanced institutions' efforts to recruit underrepresented minorities into STEM graduate programs. According to a 2011 evaluation of the AGEP program, alliances and institutions funded by the program experienced both successes and challenges in their recruitment efforts (Rodriguez et al., 2011). Reported successes included increased URM enrollments in specific disciplines and a change in campus culture to one that was more supportive and welcoming of diverse students into STEM programs. Challenges included the limited pool of students that universities were drawing from and competition with industry or other institutions.

Evaluations of two programs developed by the National Institute of General Medical Sciences—the Maximizing Access to Research Careers Undergraduate Student Training in Academic Research (MARC U-STAR) Program[19] and the Postbaccalaureate Research Education Program (PREP)[20]—have also shown

---

[17] See https://www.nsf.gov/funding/pgm_summ.jsp?pims_id=13646 (accessed December 21, 2017).

[18] See https://www.nsf.gov/funding/pgm_summ.jsp?pims_id=5474 (accessed December 21, 2017).

[19] See https://www.nigms.nih.gov/Training/MARC/Pages/USTARAwards.aspx (accessed January 22, 2018).

[20] See https://www.nigms.nih.gov/Training/PREP/Pages/default.aspx (accessed January 22, 2018).

gains with respect to entry and completion of doctoral graduate degrees by groups that have been historically underrepresented in the biomedical sciences. Among alumni of the MARC U-STAR Program, which provide trainees with multiyear structured training programs and a summer research experience at a research-intensive institution outside the home institution, approximately 59 percent enrolled in Ph.D. programs and two-thirds completed their degrees (Hall et al., 2016). In addition, 65 percent of PREP scholars, who receive support to work as apprentice scientists in a mentor's laboratory and participate in courses for skills development, matriculated into Ph.D. programs and were found to complete at or above the national average for other students from underrepresented minority groups (Hall et al., 2015). Nonetheless, despite these and other effective programs, such as the NIH Ruth L. Kirschstein National Research Service Award (NRSA) Institutional Research Training Grant (T32), most racial and ethnic groups other than whites and some Asian groups remain underrepresented in the STEM graduate student population compared to the composition of the U.S. population.[21]

Research has demonstrated that GRE scores used in isolation may have only modest predictive power for many measures of graduate school performance and that reliance on standardized tests can lead to disproportionate selection bias against women and scientists from URM backgrounds (Hall et al., 2017; Miller and Stassun, 2014; Moneta-Koehler et al., 2017). That is not to say that institutions should abandon traditional measures, such as undergraduate grade point average or GRE scores, entirely. However, programs should also be aware that the Educational Testing Service itself, the sponsoring body of the GRE, describes the scores as an "inexact measure" and that "a cut-off score (i.e., a minimum score) should never be used as the only criterion for denial of admission or awarding of a fellowship" (Educational Testing Service, 2017). Alternatively, departments can use data on completion rates and other student metrics to evaluate the degree to which the admissions process is inclusive and equitable.

STEM master's degree and Ph.D. programs should continuously expose students to multiple worldviews, promote interdisciplinary activities involving individuals from different backgrounds, welcome international students, and employ diverse approaches to teaching and learning. Toward those ends, graduate schools should design programs that account for the complexity of how cultural diversity and career diversity interface with one another (Godwin et al., 2016; Layton et al., 2016). As the trainee pool becomes more diverse, faculty and administrators should consider how to design pedagogical experiences and training opportunities that are inclusive of cultural and societal differences. Attrition rates can be deeply impacted by bringing students from historically underrepresented backgrounds into environments that are not inclusively designed to maximize the likelihood of their success. In other words, if the trainers and environment in science and engineering are largely the reason various branches of these enterprises historically have not been an inclusive space, increasing the number of trainees from

---

[21] Available at https://ncsesdata.nsf.gov/gradpostdoc/2016/ (accessed May 9, 2018).

historically underrepresented backgrounds but placing them in this same historic environment will keep them in a system that is biased against their success.

Professional development modules should be required for faculty to learn how to advise and mentor students from different backgrounds and to raise awareness and accountability about their role in changing the training and mentoring environment (Carver et al., 2017; Museus and Liverman, 2010; Packard, 2015). Examples of the types of issues that modules could cover include a step-by-step walk-through on implementing a mentoring compact, how faculty have an impact on trainee self-efficacy, and how to provide the same quality of mentorship to each student without bias.

Graduate programs will have to increase programmatic flexibility to be able to tailor training and career preparation for each student while considering the different needs and cultural values of each individual, and how those values affect future career decisions. All programs also should have access to experts in this sort of work who can assist in correctly identifying and determining student needs for mentoring, personal and professional development, career advice, etc. This may require hiring faculty, administrators, or other experts within each school.

RECOMMENDATION 3.5—Ensuring Diverse, Equitable, and Inclusive Environments: The graduate STEM education enterprise should enable students of all backgrounds, including but not limited to racial and ethnic background, gender, stage of life, culture, socioeconomic status, disability, sexual orientation, gender identity, and nationality, to succeed by implementing practices that create an equitable and inclusive institutional environment.

- Faculty and administrators involved in graduate education should develop, adopt, and regularly evaluate a suite of strategies to accelerate increasing diversity and improving equity and inclusion, including comprehensive recruitment, holistic review in admissions, and interventions to prevent attrition in the late stages of progress toward a degree.
- Faculty should cultivate their individual professional development skills to advance their abilities to improve educational culture and environments on behalf of students.
- Institutions, national laboratories, professional societies, and research organizations should develop comprehensive strategies that use evidence-based models and programs and include measures to evaluate outcomes to ensure a diverse, equitable, and inclusive environment.
- Institutions should develop comprehensive strategies for recruiting and retaining faculty and mentors from demographic groups historically underrepresented in academia.
- Federal and state agencies, universities, professional societies, and non-governmental organizations that rate institutions should embed diversity and inclusion metrics in their criteria.

- Federal and state funding agencies and private funders that support graduate education and training should adjust their award policies and funding criteria to include policies that incentivize diversity, equity, and inclusion and include accountability measures through reporting mechanisms.

RESPONDING TO THE DYNAMIC NATURE OF 21ST-CENTURY STEM

As noted in the Summary and Chapter 1, the research enterprise itself—the way research is done in the United States and abroad—is constantly evolving. This evolution is largely the result of technological advances that have enabled new methods of inquiry, analysis, and collaboration, and advances in knowledge that are enabling the research enterprise to tackle bigger problems that can best—or only—be addressed through a combination of disciplinary approaches and technologies (Disis and Slattery, 2010; NRC and IOM, 2003; Van Noorden, 2015). From basic science through applied research and development, the opportunities made available through the impressive advances of recent decades in instrumentation and across all of science, as well as in the ability and focused efforts to turn scientific advances into technological ones, and vice versa, have yielded robust opportunities (NRC and IOM, 2003). The era of big data and cloud computing, team science that crosses disciplinary boundaries, online publishing, artificial intelligence, nanotechnology, gene editing, and other developments are expanding the ways science is done and the ways researchers think about conducting their studies. STEM graduate education must actively embrace and integrate these new areas and approaches to scientific research to continue educating and training the STEM workforce of the future.

Many fields of science were historically rather solitary activities that, over time, evolved into a "typical" form where a single principal investigator pursued research projects along with a small cadre of graduate students and perhaps a few postdoctoral fellows. That structure, however, is not well adapted to address more complex multidimensional and multidisciplinary problems that require multiple levels of analysis at the same time. As a result, team science is becoming a more "typical" model of research—two analyses of research papers and patents issued over five decades found that teams increasingly dominate the production of knowledge (Plume and van Weijen, 2014; Wuchty et al., 2007)—and thus graduate students trained across STEM disciplines and with collaborators should become comfortable working in teams and with collaborators who may approach research problems differently (NRC, 2015).

Although working in teams has long been a tradition in some fields, such as high-energy physics and many engineering disciplines, many other disciplines have yet to focus on developing these skills in their next generation of researchers. Additionally, industry has long valued employees with the capability to work in teams and collaborate across departments, locations, or with partners. Industry leaders who spoke with the committee stressed that they increasingly require individuals who can lead, navigate, and work in teams with others from diverse backgrounds with regard to gender, race, culture, country of origin, and academic discipline (Hart Research Associates, 2015). Moreover, while specialization is as important as ever, scientists and engineers now also need a broader general literacy to enable them to know enough outside of their specialties to appreciate how another strategy, approach, or technology can contribute to solving the problem on which they are working (NRC, 2009, 2014).

Multiple reports have described a current and future world in which societal pressures present scientific and technological challenges that require multi- and transdisciplinary approaches to problem solving. Again, the graduate STEM education enterprise will need to adapt to prepare students to contribute meaningfully to the solutions to those challenges. For example, a 2009 National Research Council report articulates a future world "where there is abundant, healthful food for everyone; where the environment is resilient and flourishing; where there is sustainable, clean energy; and where good health is the norm" (NRC, 2009, p. 9). This report describes these goals as daunting, interconnected challenges that cannot be achieved independently of the others at a time when population growth threatens to outstrip food and energy production, and environmental degradation due to agricultural practices, climate change, and unsustainable manufacturing practices is accelerating (NRC, 2009).

Similarly, a report from the American Academy of Arts and Sciences (2013) argues that these "formidable, urgent, and interconnected societal challenges" present levels of complexity that will require teams of researchers to utilize approaches from the physical sciences, engineering, information sciences, environmental sciences, and social sciences together with an evermore sophisticated understanding of the underlying biology. These reports and others describe in detail how convergent thinking by integrative and collaborative research teams could effectively address these challenges if provided with new educational and training paradigms at the graduate level.

Looking at yet another trend in STEM activity, the 21st-century STEM enterprise is experiencing an explosion of what is called "big data," a term used to describe the emergence of very large datasets that aggregate information from many studies and/or many individuals. This presents a critical, emerging need for analytical training and tools that can enable researchers to integrate and manage those datasets to transform information into knowledge. Some 90 percent of the data in the world today was created in the past 2 years (Hale, 2017), and estimates place the growth of data at 40 percent a year, which if correct would mean the digital universe will comprise 44 zettabytes, or 44 trillion gigabytes, of data by 2020 (NASEM, 2017b; Turner, 2014) (Figure 3-1).

Big data and team science considerations aside, as the rate of scientific and technical advances increases, these advances affect people's everyday lives more than ever. However, they also lead to real concerns about privacy, data

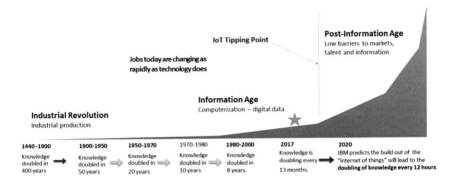

FIGURE 3-1 Knowledge-doubling curve; "Internet of Things" or IoT Tipping Point refers to the anticipated acceleration of knowledge associated with widespread growth of the IoT.
SOURCE: Presentation by Michael Richey, Boeing, at Committee Meeting, September 14, 2017, slide 3.

quality, and technology-driven social and workforce changes. Consequently, it is more important than ever that scientists and engineers consider the societal impacts of science and technology and what they can do to steward responsible discovery and innovation (NASEM, 2017a; NRC, 2011). Today, all STEM graduate students supported by NSF and NIH training grants must take courses on the responsible conduct of research—the "microethics" of authorship rules, research misconduct, and publishing norms, among others—but few graduate programs teach or discuss the "macroethics" of scientific and technological impacts on society (Herkert, 2004). Too few graduate students have opportunities to grapple with the big questions at the intersection of science, technology, and ethics that frequently appear in the news, such as climate change or gene editing (Interacademy Partnership, 2016). Advances in the conduct of STEM research call for graduates who have had the opportunity to learn both foundational and state-of-the-art methods and research skills that reflect the ways in which STEM fields carry out their work, and to develop an understanding of the societal and ethical issues that accompany advances in science and technology. The adoption of evidence-based teaching practices and the regular evaluation and assessment of curricula can help administrators and faculty measure the degree to which the program fulfills these objectives.

One consistent message that speakers from outside of academia made to the committee was that new employees with graduate degrees are well trained regarding their ability to do research. The curricula of graduate education center on building disciplinary knowledge, but there are other professional skills that students can develop during their education based on individual goals, such as appropriate teaching techniques for future faculty or management approaches for positions in industry, government, or nonprofits. One study, conducted in 2017 by the consulting firm PwC for the Business-Higher Education Forum, found that employer demand for students with data science and analytical skills, in addition to their other training, is triple that of the supply of such students (PwC and Business-Higher Education Forum, 2017). The speakers from outside of academia also noted the need for graduates who have broad literacy across STEM fields and the humanities to enable the convergent, interdisciplinary, and team-based research that is needed to solve increasingly complex research problems.

Given the complex nature of interdisciplinary problems, institutions face challenges establishing and sustaining programs across disciplines. In a paper commissioned by the committee, Jennifer Lebrón notes: "There are numerous organizational barriers that interdisciplinary research within institutions including tenure processes which value disciplinary contributions, faculty reward structures which are tied to departments, and financial systems of institutions that discourage faculty from crossing disciplines for collaborative research or teaching" (Lebrón, 2017). The paper goes on to review lessons learned from awards made by the Institute of Education Sciences (IES) Predoctoral Interdisciplinary Research Training Program that was designed "to train a new generation of education researchers to carry out methodologically rigorous research that is relevant and accessible to education practitioners and policymakers." Since IES established the program in 2004, there have been three iterations of multiyear funding to 20 institutions. These institutions developed training programs crossing several disciplines (e.g., economics, education, psychology, public policy, and statistics) and supported 600 doctoral students who have graduated within a traditional academic discipline and earned an Education Sciences Certificate.

Current and previous participants noted that the structure of the IES program, which includes interdisciplinary lectures, provided them with exposure to new subject matter and helped them gain understanding of different disciplines. Internships, which could be hosted at a variety of institutions (e.g., policy organizations, K-12 classrooms, or other independent research centers), allowed students to understand the value of research in practice and to explore career pathways, including the professional skills needed to apply and interview for positions outside of academia. Upon completion of the program, however, alumni integrated their roles as interdisciplinary scholars to mixed effect. For example, alumni who sought positions in policy and research reported that they were able to apply their interdisciplinary training by conceptualizing problems across disciplines and through their ability to adapt discipline-specific language.

From discussions with IES program directors, it remains unclear the degree to which the awards have shifted any of the underlying structures of their institutions, which can limit the ability for faculty to sustain an interdisciplinary program. The resulting challenges can range from logistical, such as scheduling and course offerings; to social and identity-based (language used and expectations set by different departments and disciplines); to financial (sustained funding for the program at the conclusion for the award). Additionally, the program directors raised concerns about the ability to recruit students from historically underrepresented groups into the program and hoped that they could work with the institution to create more inclusive admission policies, thus enlarging the pool of students eligible to apply for the fellowship.

The IES program highlights the nature of the challenges that face the future of higher education. Traditional departmental structure of the university has historically provided researchers and students the ability to develop deep disciplinary knowledge within a structured network. Going forward, the U.S. graduate education system needs to also reflect well the changing nature of scientific work, such as the increasing emphasis on team and multidisciplinary[22] science, as well as the changing needs of an increasingly diverse student body with goals and aspirations that differ from those of many who currently compose the professoriate.

RECOMMENDATION 3.6—A Dynamic Graduate STEM Education System: The STEM education system should develop the capabilities to adjust dynamically to continuing changes in the nature of science and engineering activity and of STEM careers. This includes mechanisms to detect and anticipate such changes, experiment with innovative approaches, implement appropriate educational methods, and support institutional mechanisms on a larger scale.

- Faculty and graduate departments and programs should periodically review and modify curricula, dissertation requirements, and capstone projects to ensure timeliness and alignment with the ways relevant work is conducted, and to provide students with opportunities to work in teams that promote multidisciplinary learning.
- Professional societies and nonprofit organizations should convene and lead discussions with graduate programs, employers, and other stakeholders and disseminate innovative approaches.
- Federal and state funding agencies, professional societies, and private foundations that support or conduct education research should support studies on how different STEM disciplines can integrate the changing scientific enterprise into graduate education programs and curricula.
- Graduate students should learn how to apply their expertise in a variety of professional contexts and seek guidance from faculty, research mentors, and advisors on strategies to gain work-related experience while enrolled in graduate school.

---

[22] Multidisciplinarity juxtaposes two or more disciplines focused on a question, problem, topic, or theme. Interdisciplinarity integrates information, data, methods, tools, concepts, and/or theories from two or more disciplines focused on a complex question, problem, topic, or theme (NRC, 2014).

OPTIMIZING THE GRADUATE STUDENT EXPERIENCE

Physical, mental, and emotional well-being are critical for students to develop and perform at their highest level (Graduate Assembly, 2014). For many students, graduate school is a positive experience. However, there is an expanding body of research suggesting that today's students overall are more stressed in ways that are qualitatively different from those of previous generations of graduate students (Levecque et al., 2017; Pain, 2016, 2017; Tsai and Muindi, 2016), and it is likely that this stress impairs their ability to learn and optimally contribute to their chosen discipline. In addition, the number of graduate students reporting mental health disorders has been rising over the past several years (Garcia-Williams et al., 2014; Kemsley, 2017; Levecque et al., 2017).

According to input from current and recent graduate students, one frequent source of student stress and anxiety stems from the longstanding "power differential" that exists between students and advisors that can reduce a student's ability to comfortably advocate for him- or herself. Investigators have noted that students' and advisors' goals can conflict and that students can be at a considerable disadvantage when conflicts arise, largely because students have no formal power (Chesler and Franklin, 1968; Chesler and Lohman, 1971; Miles, 1967). There have, however, been some recent advances in responding to the negative impacts of power imbalances at universities, including in some graduate programs. For example, several U.S. and Canadian universities have recognized and addressed the power imbalances directly by providing classes about mastering relationships with power imbalances, outlets for voicing concerns, counseling services, and third-party mentors to graduate students (Kim et al., 1998).

Another factor that appears to affect the graduate school experience negatively is stagnant or declining federal research budgets and how they might affect career aspirations. Many authors have commented on the growing hypercompetitive nature of the research environment today (Alberts et al., 2014; Cyranoski et al., 2011; Kimble et al., 2015). In most fields of research, access to funding is limited, variable, and uncertain, creating an important source of stress for graduate students both in its own right and through observing the kinds of stress that their faculty advisors also may be experiencing.

Graduate education can be isolating, too. This is particularly true for students from groups traditionally underrepresented in STEM if they are also underrepresented in their graduate programs and for international students who are dealing with a new culture and language. This isolation can contribute to outsized prevalence of mental health issues in Ph.D. students compared to the highly educated population in general (Graduate Assembly, 2014; Pain, 2016, 2017; Patel, 2016; Tsai and Muindi, 2016). High-pressure environments, cloudy career prospects, an imbalance of work and life, and leadership style of one's advisor also contribute to health problems or unhealthy mental status of graduate students.

Another issue related to campus climate is the ways in which institutions address sexual harassment. Reports from graduate students of sexual harassment by faculty or other graduate students have increased, and there have been increasing numbers of high-profile sexual harassment cases in STEM in recent years. Related to the power differential discussed above, when students feel powerless, they are less likely to seek help in the case of harassment. In 2016, the National Academies of Sciences, Engineering, and Medicine Committee on Women in Science, Engineering, and Medicine began a 2-year consensus study on the influence of sexual harassment in academia on the career advancement of women in the scientific, technical, and medical workforce. The scope of the project includes a review of the research on the extent to which women in the fields of science, engineering, and medicine are victimized by sexual harassment in academic settings; an examination of existing information on the extent to which sexual harassment in academia negatively impacts the recruitment, retention, and advancement of women's careers; and the identification and analysis of policies, strategies, and practices that have been the most successful in preventing and addressing sexual harassment in these settings.[23]

There are steps that universities and students can take to ameliorate student stress and anxiety. Better policies at the graduate program level that help both students and faculty address issues such as the need for parental leave, financial support, unconscious bias training, and harassment training could improve the graduate student experience and increase retention of students from all backgrounds. So, too, would consistent and transparent training environments that enable students to clearly understand exactly what their graduate program entails and the requirements for success.

Students, with the help of their institutions, could form and join supportive communities with their peers across a university's graduate education program. Doing so would enable students to both broaden their perspectives about other disciplines and career options and develop networks that can serve them well throughout graduate school and in their future careers. Graduate programs could help with these student-driven efforts by encouraging students to engage in activities and experiences outside of the laboratory with fellow graduate students from within and outside of their departments. Research has shown that such group-based activities can reduce student isolation and improve student success (Fenning, 2004; Wisker et al., 2007).

RECOMMENDATION 3.7—Stronger Support for Graduate Student Mental Health Services: Institutions should provide resources to help students manage the stresses and pressures of graduate education and maximize their success. Institutions of higher education should work with their faculty to recognize and

---

[23] See http://sites.nationalacademies.org/shstudy/index.htm (this URL reflects the most current website for the National Academies report on the *Sexual Harassment of Women: Climate, Culture, and Consequences in Academic Sciences, Engineering, and Medicine* updated after the public release on June 12, 2018).

ameliorate behaviors that exacerbate existing power differentials and create unnecessary stress for graduate students. Toward that end:

- Institutions should administer periodic climate surveys of graduate students at the departmental level to assess their well-being in the aggregate and make adjustments when problems are identified.
- Institutions should take extra steps to provide and advertise accessible mental health services, such as those already available to veterans and most undergraduate students, at no cost to graduate students.
- Institutions should develop clear policies and reporting procedures for instances of sexual harassment and bullying.
- Graduate programs should fully incorporate awareness of mental health issues into the training experience for both students and faculty and should assess services to ensure that they are meeting the needs of graduate students.
- Faculty should be regularly informed on how to support and engage with students requiring or seeking mental health services.
- Graduate programs should encourage students to engage as a group in activities and experiences outside of traditional academic settings as a means of increasing feelings of inclusion and normalizing feelings associated with negative phenomena, such as imposter syndrome, that can reduce productivity and success in the training experience and extend time to degree.
- Graduate programs should allow students to have an active and collaborative voice to proactively engage in practices that support holistic research training and diverse career outcomes and that allow students to provide feedback on their experiences.

REFERENCES

Alberts, B., M. W. Kirschner, S. Tilghman, and H. Varmus. 2014. Rescuing U.S. biomedical research from its systemic flaws. *Proceedings of the National Academy of Sciences of the United States of America* 111(16):5773-5777.

American Academy of Arts and Sciences. 2013. *Arise 2: Unleashing America's research and innovation enterprise*. Cambridge, MA: American Academy of Arts and Sciences.

Blank, R., R. J. Daniels, G. Gilliland, A. Gutmann, S. Hawgood, F. A. Hrabowski, M. E. Pollack, V. Price, L. R. Reif, and M. S. Schlissel. 2017. A new data effort to inform career choices in biomedicine. *Science* 358(6369):1388-1389.

Blume-Kohout, M. 2017. *On what basis? Seeking effective practices in graduate STEM education*. Available: http://sites.nationalacademies.org/cs/groups/pgasite/documents/webpage/pga_186176.pdf (accessed May 7, 2018).

Brownell, S. E., and K. D. Tanner. 2012. Barriers to faculty pedagogical change: Lack of training, time, incentives, and ... tensions with professional identity? *CBE—Life Sciences Education* 11(4):339-346.

Carver, S., J. Van Sickle, J. Holcomb, C. Quinn, D. Jackson, A. Resnick, S. Duffy, N. Sridhar, and A. Marquard. 2017. Operation STEM: Increasing success and improving retention among first-generation and underrepresented minority students in STEM. *Journal of STEM Education* 18(3):30-39.

Chesler, M. A., and J. Franklin. 1968. Interracial and intergenerational conflict in secondary schools. Paper presented at Annual Meeting of the American Sociological Association, Boston, MA.

Chesler, M. A., and J. E. Lohman. 1971. Changing schools through student advocacy. In *Organization development in schools*, edited by R. Schmuck and M. Miles. Palo Alto, CA: National Press Books, pp. 185-212.

Clewell, B. C., C. C. de Cohen, L. Tsui, L. Forcier, E. Gao, N. Young, N. Deterding, and C. West. 2005. *Final report on the evaluation of the National Science Foundation Louis Stokes Alliances for Minority Participation program*. Washington, DC: Urban Institute.

Covington, M., T. Chavis, and A. Perry. 2017. A scholar-practitioner perspective to promoting minority success in STEM. *Journal for Multicultural Education* 11(2):149-159.

Cyranoski, D., N. Gilbert, H. Ledford, A. Nayar, and M. Yahia. 2011. Education: The PhD factory. *Nature* 472(7343):276-279.

Davis, S. N., D. Mahatmya, P. W. Garner, and R. M. Jones. 2015. Mentoring undergraduate scholars: A pathway to interdisciplinary research? *Mentoring & Tutoring: Partnership in Learning* 23(5):427-440.

Disis, M. L., and J. T. Slattery. 2010. The road we must take: Multidisciplinary team science. *Science Translational Medicine* 2(22):22cm9.

Drake, J. K. 2008. Recognition and reward for academic advising in theory and practice. In *Academic advising: A comprehensive handbook*. 2nd ed., edited by V. N. Gordon, W. R. Habley, and T. J. Grites. San Francisco: Jossey-Bass, pp. 396-412.

Educational Testing Service. 2017. *GRE guide to the use of scores, 2017-2018*. Princeton, NJ: Educational Testing Service.

Einaudi, P. 2011. *Two decades of increasing diversity more than doubled the number of minority graduate students in science and engineering*. InfoBrief. NSF 11-319. Arlington, VA: National Science Foundation.

Fenning, K. 2004. Cohort based learning: Application to learning organizations and student academic success. *College Quarterly* 7(1). Available: http://collegequarterly.ca/2004-vol07-num01-winter/fenning.html (accessed March 16, 2018).

Ferrini-Mundy, J., 2013. Driven by diversity. *Science* 340(6130):278.

Filetti, J. S. 2009. Assessing service in faculty reviews: Mentoring faculty and developing transparency. *Mentoring & Tutoring: Partnership in Learning* 17(4):343-352.

Flaherty, C. 2017. AAU sets expectation for data transparency on Ph.D. program outcomes. *Inside Higher Ed*. Available: https://www.insidehighered.com/quicktakes/2017/09/20/aau-sets-expectation-data-transparency-phd-program-outcomes (accessed January 22, 2018).

Fleming, M., M. S. House, M. V. Shewakramani, L. Yu, J. Garbutt, R. McGee, K. Kroenke, M. Z. Abedin, and D. M. Rubio. 2013. The mentoring competency assessment: Validation of a new instrument to evaluate skills of research mentors. *Academic Medicine* 88(7):1002.

Fountain, J., and K. E. Newcomer. 2016. Developing and sustaining effective faculty mentoring programs. *Journal of Public Affairs Education* 22(4):483-506.

Freeman, S., S. L. Eddy, M. McDonough, M. K. Smith, N. Okoroafor, H. Jordt, and M. P. Wenderoth. 2014. Active learning increases student performance in science, engineering, and mathematics. *Proceedings of the National Academy of Sciences of the United States of America* 111(23):8410-8415.

Garcia-Williams, A. G., L. Moffitt, and N. J. Kaslow. 2014. Mental health and suicidal behavior among graduate students. *Academic Psychiatry* 38(5):554-560.

Gibbs, K., Jr. 2014. Diversity in STEM: What it is and why it matters. *Scientific American*. Voices blog. Available https://blogs.scientificamerican.com/voices/diversity-in-stem-what-it-is-and-why-it-matters/ (accessed March 16, 2018).

Godwin, A., G. Potvin, Z. Hazari, and R. Lock. 2016. Identity, critical agency, and engineering: An affective model for predicting engineering as a career choice. *Journal of Engineering Education* 105(2):312-340.

Graduate Assembly. 2014. *Graduate student happiness & well-being.* Berkeley: University of California.

Griffin, K. A., D. Pérez, A. P. E. Holmes, and C. E. P. Mayo. 2010. Investing in the future: The importance of faculty mentoring in the development of students of color in STEM. *New Directions for Institutional Research* 2010(148):95-103.

Habley, W. R. 2007. Putting students first in the campus community: Pathway five. In *Fostering student success in the campus community*, edited by G. L. Kramer. San Francisco: Jossey-Bass, pp. 407-431.

Hale, T. 2017. How much data does the world generate every minute? *IFLScience.* Available: http://www.iflscience.com/technology/how-much-data-does-the-world-generate-every-minute/ (accessed January 22, 2018).

Hall, A., J. Mann, and M. Bender. 2015. *Analysis of scholar outcomes for the NIGMS Postbaccalaureate Research Education program.* Available: https://www.nigms.nih.gov/News/reports/Documents/PREP-outcomes-report.pdf (accessed March 17, 2018).

Hall, A. K., A. Miklos, A. Oh, and S. D. Gaillard. 2016. *Educational outcomes from the Maximizing Access to Research Careers Undergraduate Student Training in Academic Research (MARC U-STAR) program.* Available: https://www.nigms.nih.gov/News/reports/Documents/MARC-paper031416.pdf (accessed March 17, 2018).

Hall, J. D., A. B. O'Connell, and J. G. Cook. 2017. Predictors of student productivity in biomedical graduate school applications. *PloS ONE* 12(1):e0169121. Available: http://journals.plos.org/plosone/article?id=10.1371/journal.pone.0169121 (accessed March 17, 2018).

Hart Research Associates. 2015. *Falling short? College learning and career success.* Prepared for the Association of American Colleges and Universities. Available: https://www.aacu.org/sites/default/files/files/LEAP/2015employerstudentsurvey.pdf (accessed March 17, 2018).

Herkert, J. 2004. Microethics, macroethics, and professional engineering societies. In *Emerging technologies and ethical issues in engineering: Papers from a workshop.* Washington, DC: The National Academies Press, pp. 107-114.

Higgins, M. C. 2000. The more, the merrier? Multiple developmental relationships and work satisfaction. *Journal of Management Development* 19(4):277-296.

Hussain, Y. 2017. *Key Recommendations from Selected Recent Reports on Graduate Education (1995-2017).* Commissioned paper prepared for the Committee. Available: http://sites.national academies.org/cs/groups/pgasite/ documents/webpage/pga_186162.pdf (accessed May 7, 2018).

Interacademy Partnership. 2016. *Doing global science: A guide to responsible conduct in the global research enterprise.* Princeton, NJ: Princeton University Press.

Kemsley, J. 2017. Grappling with graduate student mental health and suicide. *Chemical & Engineering News* 95(32):28-33.

Kim, S. H., R. H. Smith, and N. L. Brigham. 1998. Effects of power imbalance and the presence of third parties on reactions to harm: Upward and downward revenge. *Personality and Social Psychology Bulletin* 24(4):353-361.

Kimble, J., W. M. Bement, Q. Chang, B. L. Cox, N. R. Drinkwater, R. L. Gourse, A. A. Hoskins, A. Huttenlocher, P. K. Kreeger, P. F. Lambert, M. R. Mailick, S. Miyamoto, R. L. Moss, K. M. O'Connor-Giles, A. Roopra, K. Saha, and H. S. Seidel. 2015. Strategies from UW-Madison for rescuing biomedical research in the US. *Elife* 4:e09305.

Law, A. V., M. M. Bottenberg, A. H. Brozick, J. D. Currie, M. V. DiVall, S. T. Haines, C. Jolowsky, C. P. Koh-Knox, G. A. Leonard, S. J. Phelps, D. Rao, A. Webster, and E. Yablonski. 2014. A checklist for the development of faculty mentorship programs. *American Journal of Pharmaceutical Education* 78(5):98.

Layton, R. L., P. D. Brandt, A. M. Freeman, J. R. Harrell, J. D. Hall, and M. Sinche. 2016. Diversity exiting the academy: Influential factors for the career choice of well-represented and underrepresented minority scientists. *CBE—Life Sciences Education* 15(3), doi:10.1187/cbe.16-01-0066.

Lebrón, J. 2017. *Forming Interdisciplinary Scholars: An Evaluation of the IES Predoctoral Interdisciplinary Training Program*. Commissioned paper prepared for the Committee. Available: http://sites.nationalacademies.org/cs/.

Levecque, K., F. Anseel, A. De Beuckelaer, J. Van der Heyden, and L. Gisle. 2017. Work organization and mental health problems in PhD students. *Research Policy* 46(4):868-879.

Lewis, V., C. A. Martina, M. P. McDermott, P. M. Trief, S. R. Goodman, G. D. Morse, J. G. LaGuardia, D. Sharp, and R. M. Ryan. 2016. A randomized controlled trial of mentoring interventions for underrepresented minorities. *Academic Medicine* 91(7):994-1001.

Lovitts, B. E. 2004. Research on the structure and process of graduate education: Retaining students. In *Paths to the professorship: Strategies for enriching the preparation of future faculty*, edited by D. H. Wulff and A. E. Austin. San Francisco: Josey-Bass, pp. 115-136.

Marcellino, P. A. 2011. Fostering sustainability: A case study of a pilot mentoring program at a private university. *Mentoring & Tutoring: Partnership in Learning* 19(4):441-464.

Maton, K. I., and F. A. Hrabowski III. 2004. Increasing the number of African American PhDs in the sciences and engineering: A strengths-based approach. *American Psychologist* 59(6):547-556.

May, W.-C. J. 2016. Characteristics of U.S. students that pursued a STEM major and factors that predicted their persistence in degree completion. *Universal Journal of Educational Research* 4(6):1495-1500.

Miles, M. B. 1967. Some properties of schools as social systems. In *Change in school systems*, edited by G. Watson. Washington, DC: Cooperative Project for Educational Development, National Training Laboratories.

Miller, C., and K. Stassun. 2014. A test that fails. *Nature* 510:303-304.

Moneta-Koehler, L., A. M. Brown, K. A. Petrie, B. J. Evans, and R. Chalkley. 2017. The limitations of the GRE in predicting success in biomedical graduate school. *PloS ONE* 12(1):e0166742.

Museus, S. D., and D. Liverman. 2010. High-performing institutions and their implications for studying underrepresented minority students in STEM. *New Directions for Institutional Research* 2010(148):17-27.

NAE (National Academy of Engineering). 2014. *Advancing diversity in the US industrial science and engineering workforce: Summary of a workshop*. Washington, DC: The National Academies Press.

NAS/NAE/IOM (National Academy of Sciences, National Academy of Engineering, and Institute of Medicine). 1996. *Careers in science and engineering: A student planning guide to grad school and beyond*. Washington, DC: National Academy Press.

NAS/NAE/IOM. 1997. *Adviser, teacher, role model, friend: On being a mentor to students in science and engineering*. Washington, DC: National Academy Press.

NAS/NAE/IOM. 2011. *Expanding underrepresented minority participation: America's science and technology talent at the crossroads*. Washington, DC: The National Academies Press.

NASEM (National Academies of Sciences, Engineering, and Medicine). 2017a. *Fostering integrity in research*. Washington, DC: The National Academies Press.

NASEM. 2017b. *Refining the concept of scientific inference when working with big data: Proceedings of a workshop*. Washington, DC: The National Academies Press.

NRC (National Research Council). 2009. *A new biology for the 21st century*. Washington, DC: The National Academies Press.

NRC. 2011. *Challenges and opportunities for education about dual use issues in the life sciences*. Washington, DC: The National Academies Press.

NRC. 2012. *Research universities and the future of America: Ten breakthrough actions vital to our nation's prosperity and security*. Washington, DC: The National Academies Press.

NRC. 2014. *Convergence: Facilitating transdisciplinary integration of life sciences, physical sciences, engineering, and beyond*. Washington, DC: The National Academies Press.

NRC. 2015. *Enhancing the effectiveness of team science.* Washington, DC: The National Academies Press.

NRC and IOM (National Research Council and Institute of Medicine). 2003. *Enhancing the vitality of the National Institutes of Health: Organizational change to meet new challenges.* Washington, DC: The National Academies Press.

Packard, B. W.-L. 2015. *Successful STEM mentoring initiatives for underrepresented students: A research-based guide for faculty and administrators.* Sterling, VA: Stylus.

Page, S. E. 2008. *The difference: How the power of diversity creates better groups, firms, schools, and societies* Princeton, NJ: Princeton University Press.

Pain, E. 2016. Trainees and mental health: Let's talk. In *Science Careers.* Washington, DC: American Association for the Advancement of Science.

Pain, E. 2017. Ph.D. students face significant mental health challenges. *Science Careers Blog.* Washington, DC: American Association for the Advancement of Science.

Patel, V. 2016. Grad schools try to ease "culture problem" of anxiety and isolation. *Chronicle of Higher Education* 15-17.

Plume, A., and D. van Weijen. 2014. Publish or perish? The rise of the fractional author. *Research Trends* 38(3):16-18.

Polka, J. K., K. A. Krukenberg, and G. S. McDowell. 2015. A call for transparency in tracking student and postdoc career outcomes. *Molecular Biology of the Cell* 26(8):1413-1415.

Posselt, J. R. 2016. *Inside graduate admissions merit, diversity, and faculty gatekeeping.* Cambridge, MA: Harvard University Press.

Purdue University. 2015. Trustees approve new guidelines for promotion and tenure to highlight mentoring. News Release. Available: http://www.purdue.edu/newsroom/releases/2015/Q4/trustees-change-purdue-polytechnic-department-name-to-reflect-enhancements.html (accessed January 22, 2018).

PwC and Business-Higher Education Forum. 2017. *Investing in America's data science and analytics talent: The case for action.* Available: https://www.pwc.com/us/en/publications/assets/investing-in-america-s-dsa-talent-bhef-and-pwc.pdf (accessed March 17, 2018).

Reagans, R., and E. W. Zuckerman. 2001. Networks, diversity, and productivity: The social capital of corporate R&D teams. *Organization Science* 12(4):502-517.

Rincon, B. E., and C. E. George-Jackson. 2016. STEM intervention programs: Funding practices and challenges. *Studies in Higher Education* 41(3):429-444.

Roberge, M. É., and R. Van Dick. 2010. Recognizing the benefits of diversity: When and how does diversity increase group performance? *Human Resource Management Review* 20(4):295-308.

Rodriguez, C., R. Kirshstein, C. Tanenbaum, C. Storey, T. Chan, L. Turk-Bikakci, S. Francois, R. Miller, M. Cillier, and A. Alsbrooks. 2011. *National evaluation of the alliances for graduate education and the professoriate.* Washington, DC: American Institutes for Research.

Saxena, A. 2014. Workforce diversity: A key to improve productivity. *Procedia Economics and Finance* 11(Suppl. C):76-85.

Schnoes, A. N., A. Caliendo, J. Morand, T. Dillinger, M. Naffziger-Hirsch, B. Moses, J. C. Gibeling, K. R. Yamamoto, B. Lindstaedt, R. McGee, and T. C. O'Brien. 2018. Internship experiences contribute to confident career decision making for doctoral students in the life sciences. *CBE—Life Science Education* 17(1). Available: https://doi.org/10.1187/cbe.17-08-0164 (accessed May 9, 2018).

Schultheis, A. S., T. M. Farrell, and E. L. Paul. 2011. Promoting undergraduate research through revising tenure and promotion policy. *CURQuarterly* 31(4):25-31.

Stassun, K. G., S. Sturm, K. Holley-Bockelmann, A. Burger, D. J. Ernst, and D. Webb. 2011. The Fisk-Vanderbilt Master's-to-Ph.D. Bridge Program: Recognizing, enlisting, and cultivating unrealized or unrecognized potential in underrepresented minority students. *American Journal of Physics* 79(4):374-379.

Tabak, L. A., and F. S. Collins. 2011. Weaving a richer tapestry in biomedical science. *Science* 333(6045):940-941.

Tanner, K. D. 2013. Structure matters: Twenty-one teaching strategies to promote student engagement and cultivate classroom equity. *CBE—Life Sciences Education* 12(3):322-331.

Tsai, J. W., and F. Muindi. 2016. Towards sustaining a culture of mental health and wellness for trainees in the biosciences. *Nature Biotechnology* 34(3):353-355.

University of Arkansas at Little Rock. 2011. Faculty roles and rewards, I: Tenure track. Policy 403.20. Available: http://ualr.edu/policy/home/facstaff/faculty-roles-and-rewards-i/ (accessed January 22, 2018).

U.S. Census Bureau. 2012. Most children younger than age 1 are minorities. Census Bureau Reports (news release). Washington, DC: U.S. Census Bureau.

Valantine, H. A., P. K. Lund, and A. E. Gammie. 2016. From the NIH: A systems approach to increasing the diversity of the biomedical research workforce. *CBE—Life Sciences Education* 15(3):fe4; doi:10.1187/cbe.16-03-0138.

Van Noorden, R. 2015. Interdisciplinary research by the numbers. *Nature News* 525(7569):306-307.

Vilorio, D. 2014. STEM 101: Intro to tomorrow's jobs. *Occupational Outlook Quarterly* (Spring). Available: https://www.bls.gov/careeroutlook/2014/spring/art01.pdf (accessed March 20, 2018).

Wisker, G., G. Robinson, and M. Shacham. 2007. Postgraduate research success: Communities of practice involving cohorts, guardian supervisors and online communities. *Innovations in Education and Teaching International* 44(3):301-320.

Wuchty, S., B. F. Jones, and B. Uzzi. 2007. The increasing dominance of teams in production of knowledge. *Science* 316(5827):1036-1039.

Zhao, C.-M., C. M. Golde, and A. C. McCormick. 2007. More than a signature: How advisor choice and advisor behavior affect doctoral student satisfaction. *Journal of Further and Higher Education* 31(3):263-281.

Zolas, N., N. Goldschlag, R. Jarmin, P. Stephan, J. O. Smith, R. F. Rosen, B. M. Allen, B. A. Weinberg, and J. I. Lane. 2015. Wrapping it up in a person: Examining employment and earnings outcomes for Ph.D. recipients. *Science* 350(6266):1367-1371.

4

The Master's Degree

Master's degree programs in many science, technology, engineering, and mathematics (STEM) fields have a reputation of successfully meeting market and workforce demands, at least in part because of their flexible nature, and because the master's degree opens multiple educational and career pathways for students. As of 2015, there were 3.7 million people in the U.S. labor market whose most advanced degree was a master's in a STEM field (NSB, 2018c). For these reasons, an increasing number of U.S. universities are offering programs designed specifically for students seeking a master's degree. Although the incentives for creating master's programs can be varied and multifaceted, the adaptability of the master's degree is suggested by the high rate of development of new inter- or multidisciplinary programs involving multiple academic departments (CGS, 2005). While career prospects for holders of a master's degree vary by field, a master's program can help students develop research skills, expand on content knowledge, gain technical expertise in a program geared to industry, and for some students, provide an opportunity to explore the discipline in a deeper way either to become a more attractive candidate for a doctoral program or to test interest in a particular field.

Chapter 2 provides detail on the overall landscape of master's level enrollment and degrees awarded by gender, race and ethnicity, citizenship status, and additional breakdowns by broad field of study; however, additional focus on careers appears in this chapter for master's students and in Chapter 5 for Ph.D. students. According to an analysis of Census Bureau data, more gainfully employed STEM professionals have master's degrees than Ph.D.'s, with the one exception being among life and physical scientists (AFL-CIO, 2016). In addition, the Bureau of Labor Statistics (BLS, 2013) projects that occupations requiring STEM master's degrees will be the fastest growing segment in many STEM fields, including those in mathematics and in computer, life, physical, and social sciences.

CORE EDUCATIONAL ELEMENTS OF MASTER'S DEGREES

There are many types of master's programs (NRC, 2008), just as there are many reasons that students pursue the master's degree. Generally, STEM master's degree programs take one of three forms. The more traditional-style STEM master's degree program focuses on building subject matter expertise and includes a research project leading to a thesis or another type of capstone project. Within this type of degree program, there are professions such as engineering and psychology that recognize the master's as a terminal degree, while in others, such as biology and physics, students enroll less frequently with the intent of seeking only a master's degree. Some students may enroll in a Ph.D. program and, during the course of their studies, decide the Ph.D. degree does not fit their career plans, because they do not get the mentoring or other forms of support they need to succeed at that level, or because the master's degree allows them to secure well-paying jobs without having to complete a Ph.D. (CGS, 2010). For others, the decision may not be mutual because institutions have the authority to ask Ph.D. students who do not perform adequately to leave the program early; if they have completed enough requirements of the program, they may receive a master's degree.

Additionally, there are master's degree programs in which students may enroll with the intention of seeking a master's, and then have the option to enroll in a Ph.D. program during the course of their study. Looking at time to completion, 41 percent of students completed their master's degrees within 2 years, 60 percent within 3 years, and 66 percent within 4 years (CGS, 2013).

Another type of STEM master's degree is the 2-year Professional Science master's (PSM). This degree program, developed in the late 1990s with input from industry leaders and funding from the Alfred P. Sloan Foundation, is designed specifically to fill the need for scientists who have been trained to work primarily outside of academia. The PSM degree combines rigorous, discipline-based coursework in science and mathematics with training in management, law, and other business areas. This degree is typically self-financed by the student.

Thanks in part to funding from the Alfred P. Sloan Foundation to establish the program in 1997—the foundation's funding ended in 2010[1]—as well as more recent funding from the National Science Foundation, there are now 355 PSM programs offered by 165 U.S. institutions.[2] The Council of Graduate Schools (CGS) has developed a guide for schools intending to develop a PSM program, and there is a national PSM office, formerly run by CGS and now operated by the Keck Graduate Institute. According to 2014 data, the fields with the most PSM

---

[1] See https://sloan.org/programs/completed-programs/professional-science-masters-degree#history (accessed February 26, 2018).

[2] See https://www.professionalsciencemasters.org/program-locator (accessed January 23, 2018).

programs are environmental and climate sciences (47), biotechnology (41), other biological sciences (36), and computer and information sciences (28) (Komura, 2015). Approximately 80 percent of these programs are delivered at in-person settings, while the remaining 20 percent are delivered online or as a combination of in-person and online instruction. In 2014, slightly over half of the enrollees were male, 15.3 percent were from underrepresented groups, and 21.8 percent were temporary residents. Using the Carnegie Classifications for Higher Education,[3] PSM host institutions vary by research focus and size: 56 master's colleges and universities (larger programs); 43 research universities, very high research activity; 30 research universities, high research activity; 13 doctoral research universities; nine other; six master's colleges and universities (smaller programs); and five master's colleges and universities (medium-size programs).[4]

When CGS asked recent graduates to identify the benefits from having earned a PSM degree, 80.8 percent said it was to acquire specific skills and knowledge, 46.6 percent said it was to increase opportunities for promotions, and 26.5 percent said it was to meet requirements of a current or prospective employer (Allum, 2013). Recent program graduates ranked their satisfaction highly, with 87 percent selecting "very satisfied" or "generally satisfied" for the quality of the scientific and/or mathematics training and the internships and "real world" practical experiences they gained through their programs. Other aspects of the program that recent graduates rated with high satisfaction included the distinctive nature of the program (83 percent); quality of the nonscientific professional training they acquired (82 percent); networking opportunities (78 percent); and post-graduation employment prospects (72 percent) (Allum, 2013).

Many master's programs are characterized by flexibility and adaptability to the changing nature of scientific and technical disciplines and to workforce demands, and many attempt to integrate the physical, biological, and social sciences, and in some cases the humanities and arts. The variation in master's degree programs gives them a comparative advantage over Ph.D. programs in that a given program can tailor the number of credit hours, types of experiences, depth of research, and the development of technical skills and transferrable competencies to quickly meet changing student and employer needs. While master's degree programs can also serve as test beds for innovation in graduate education, the efficacy of the programs requires additional evaluation, assessment, and research. With a shorter time to degree than the Ph.D., and because many students fund their own master's degree program, institutions may establish and adapt master's programs to respond to workforce demands, sometimes in partnership with industry, and to anticipate emerging interdisciplinary fields.

Despite the variation, the committee believes that there should be common criteria for what constitutes a master's degree, no matter the STEM field, as

---

[3] See http://carnegieclassifications.iu.edu/definitions.php (accessed March 26, 2018).

[4] See https://www.professionalsciencemasters.org/reports-statistics/carnegie-classifications (accessed March 26, 2018).

part of providing an ideal graduate STEM education to all students as described in Chapter 6 in full. To find a vision for core educational elements of master's degrees, the committee reviewed CGS's Alignment Framework for the Master's Degree.[5] This alignment framework was the product of a year-long dialogue that included 150 graduate school deans (Augustine, 2017). Of the three defining characteristics of master's degree programs, the section on competencies in the CGS framework describes four elements that should be common among master's degree programs:

1. **Disciplinary and interdisciplinary knowledge:** Master's students should develop core disciplinary knowledge and the ability to work between disciplines.
2. **Professional competencies:** Master's students should develop abilities defined by a given profession (e.g., licensing, other credentials).
3. **Foundational and transferrable skills:** Master's students should develop skills that transcend disciplines and are applicable in any context, such as communications, leadership, and working in teams. These dimensions are especially critical as the lines that traditionally define scientific and engineering disciplines become blurred—and more scientific research and application are characterized by the convergence of disciplines.
4. **Research:** Master's students should develop the ability to apply the scientific method, understand the application of statistical analysis, gain experience in conducting research and other field studies, learn about and understand the importance of research responsibility and integrity, and engage in work-based learning and research in a systematic manner.

RECOMMENDATION 4.1—Core Competencies for Master's Education: Every STEM master's student should achieve the core scientific and professional competencies and learning objectives described above:

- Institutions should verify that every graduate program they offer provides for the master's core competencies outlined in this report and that students demonstrate that they have achieved them before receiving their degrees.
- Graduate departments should publicly post how their programs reflect the core competencies for master's students, including the milestones and metrics they use in evaluation and assessment.
- Federal and state funding agencies should adapt funding criteria for institutions to ensure that all master's students they support—regardless of mechanism of support—are in programs that ensure that they develop,

---

[5] See http://cgsnet.org/alignment-framework-master%E2%80%99s-degree (accessed March 26, 2018).

measure, and report student progress toward acquiring the scientific and professional competencies outlined in this report.

- Graduate students should create an individual development plan that includes the core competencies, as outlined in this report for master's degrees, as a key feature of their own learning and career goals and that utilizes the resources provided by their university and relevant professional societies.

- Students should provide feedback to graduate faculty and deans about how they could help students better develop these competencies.

CAREER OUTCOMES OF STEM MASTER'S DEGREE HOLDERS

As noted above, one of the challenges in understanding how the master's degree fits into the overall STEM career picture arises from the lack of current research and data on the STEM master's degrees. The most recent data on employment of U.S. scientists and engineers with master's degrees were collected in 2013 (NSB, 2016b[6]). These data show that master's degree holders play a vital role in the STEM workforce. Of the 2.6 million employed scientists and engineers with master's degrees as their highest degree, 53 percent work in industry, 12.6 percent work for state and federal governments, 11.7 percent have jobs at 2-year and precollege institutions, and 9.4 percent work at 4-year universities and colleges. Of the 2.9 million STEM master's degree holders in the workforce, the largest fields are social and behavioral sciences at 918,000; engineering at 788,000; and computer science and mathematics at 719,000 (Table 4-1). In terms of the distribution of STEM master's degree holders across broad sectors of employment, the majority were working in business or industry (65.6 percent), followed by education (21.2 percent), and then government (13.2 percent).

In contrast to the job market for STEM Ph.D.'s, where there are concerns about increasingly limited opportunities for tenure-track academic positions, the entry-level job market for those holding master's degrees is projected to grow nearly twice as fast as the entry-level job market overall, in large part because of technology-driven changes in the U.S. economy. According to the BLS, jobs requiring a master's degree for entry are projected to grow the fastest—18.4 percent from 2012 to 2022, compared to 10.8 percent growth in overall employment (BLS, 2013). For example, the BLS projects that employment in occupations requiring master's degrees in computer science or mathematics will grow by 26.3 percent from 2012 to 2022, compared to an 18.0 percent increase for bachelor's degree and 15.3 percent for jobs requiring a Ph.D. Similarly, in the life, physical, and social sciences, the BLS projects the demand for an entry-level master's degree will grow by 13.6 percent and for Ph.D.'s by 12.6 percent. A 2016 analysis

---

[6] See https://www.nsf.gov/statistics/2016/nsb20161/#/report/chapter-3/s-e-workers-in-the-economy (accessed January 23, 2018).

TABLE 4-1 Percentage Distribution of STEM Master's Degree Holders in Broad Employment Sectors, by Field, 2015

Field	Total Number	Education (%)	
		4-Year Institutions	2-Year and Precollege Institutions
S&E	2,934,000	10.6	10.6
Computer science and mathematics	719,000	7.6	7.9
Biological, agricultural, and environmental life sciences	345,000	24.9	11.3
Physical and related sciences	163,000	17.2	12.3
Social and related sciences	918,000	10.2	20.5
Engineering	788,000	6.0	0.9

SOURCE: Adapted from NSB, 2018b.

conducted by *Fortune* magazine and the career site PayScale found that 13 of the top 15 graduate degrees for getting jobs are in STEM fields (Dishman, 2016).

Workforce issues for master's STEM degree holders also vary by citizenship status. International students' degrees were heavily concentrated in computer sciences, economics, and engineering, where they received more than 4 out of 10 of all master's degrees awarded in 2013. Within engineering, students on temporary visas earned more than half of the master's degrees in electrical and chemical engineering (NSB, 2016b). For students interested in pursuing jobs in the tech sector, the job market for domestic talent allows most students to pursue jobs with a bachelor's degree; however, for international students, the master's degree provides them with prospects for employment and residency in the United States (Wingfield, 2017). Given the heavy mix of international students enrolled in STEM master's degree programs, the policies, political landscape, and economic environment in the United States can significantly affect the relationship between master's education and workforce opportunities for international students.

A 2014 study found that employers increasingly view the master's degree as a professional credential in its own right, dispelling the notion prevalent in some disciplines that master's degrees are granted only to students unable to complete a doctoral program (Gallagher, 2014). Employers reported that they viewed the master's degree as a screening tool and as a discrete demonstration of technical skills and competency. The study also showed that employers are increasingly viewing the master's degree as a key qualification for future leadership roles.

The amount a master's degree can enhance one's careers prospects varies by field. For some STEM occupations, there is an associated "wage premium" that varies by specialty (Table 4-2). For example, within engineering, civil engineers,

Business or industry (%)			Government (%)	
For-profit Businesses	Self-Employed, Unincorporated Businesses	Nonprofit Businesses	Federal Government	State or Local Government
53.6	4.0	8.0	6.3	6.9
66.8	2.4	6.0	4.3	4.9
36.8	2.9	8.1	8.1	7.8
52.8	3.7	4.3	5.5	3.7
31.2	6.3	15.4	6.4	10.2
75.1	3.0	2.3	7.4	5.3

mechanical engineers, and architectural and engineering managers had median wages that were between 9 and 13 percent more for workers who had a master's degree compared with those of workers who had a bachelor's degree. In contrast, petroleum, mining, and geological engineers had a median wage that was about 7 percent less for workers with a master's degree than a bachelor's degree, and chemical engineers had a median wage that was about the same for workers who had either education level.

The most recent employment data from CGS (Allum, 2013), which documented initial hiring outcomes for 2012-2013 PSM graduates, found that almost 95 percent of the 2012-2013 graduates were employed in full-time positions, and 67.8 percent reported earning $50,000 or more in annual salary. Data from the National Center for Science and Engineering Statistics show that the median salary for all STEM master's degree holders also exceeded $50,000 in the first 4 years after graduate school (Figure 4-1).

In light of the flexibility of the STEM master's degree, both in terms of the degree structure and career pathways available to graduates, the committee makes the following recommendation.

RECOMMENDATION 4.2—Career Exploration for Master's Students: Master's students should be provided opportunities for career exploration during the course of their studies.

- Faculty, who serve as undergraduate advisors, should discuss with their students whether and how a master's degree will advance the students' long-term educational and career goals.

TABLE 4-2 Selected STEM Occupations in Which Workers with a Master's Degree Earned a Premium Over Workers with a Bachelor's Degree, 2013

Occupation	Employment with Bachelor's Degree	Percentage of Workforce with Bachelor's Degree	Employment with Master's Degree
Mathematicians, statisticians, and other miscellaneous mathematical science occupations	12,613	32	15,340
Environmental scientists and geoscientists	30,737	47	25,079
Network and computer systems administrators	76,462	39	21,479
Web developers	63,354	54	18,520
Biological scientists	26,993	43	21,414
Chemists and materials scientists	35,304	49	15,473
Information security analysts	23,569	45	8,658

[a] The wage premium represents the wage increase for workers with a master's degree over that for workers with a bachelor's degree in the occupation.
SOURCE: Torpey and Terrell, 2015. Adapted from U.S. Census Bureau, American Community Survey.

- Institutions should integrate professional development opportunities, including relevant course offerings and internships, into curriculum design.
- Master's students should seek information about potential career paths, talk to employers and mentors in areas of interest, and choose a master's program optimal for gaining the knowledge and competencies needed to pursue their career interests.
- Industry, nonprofit, government, and other employers should provide guidance and financial support for relevant course offerings at institutions and provide internships and other forms of professional experiences to students and recent graduates.
- Professional societies should collaborate with other sectors to create programs that help master's students make the transition into a variety of careers.

FLEXIBLE AND INNOVATIVE PROGRAMS: CERTIFICATES AND MICROCREDENTIALS

Beyond the growth of traditional master's degrees and PSMs, institutions have increased offerings in certificate or "microcredential" programs to allow

Percentage of Workforce with Master's Degree	Median Annual Wage for Bachelor's Degree	Median Annual Wage for Master's Degree	Wage Premium Amount[a]	Wage Premium Percent
38	$60,000	$80,000	$20,000	33
38	62,000	80,000	18,000	29
11	70,000	88,000	18,000	26
16	61,000	75,000	14,000	23
34	50,000	60,000	10,000	20
22	60,000	71,000	11,000	18
17	85,000	100,000	15,000	18

students to gain skills with a focus on career advancement. A graduate certificate program is a prescribed set of regular graduate-level academic courses, and these credits may fulfill degree requirements. Graduate certificate programs are a means for currently enrolled master's and doctoral students, as well as post-baccalaureate students, to augment or supplement their degree, to explore new career options, and to develop expertise in a content area or skill. For employers, a certificate can signal a prospective employee's competency in a desired specialization. Online graduate certificate programs provide students the flexibility to manage a full-time job or to navigate other personal demands.

The CGS *Graduate Enrollment and Degrees: 2006-2016* (Okahana and Zhou, 2017) recorded 42,886 graduate certificates awarded in 2015-2016 across all fields, an 11.8 percent increase from 2014 to 2015. The predominant fields were education at 30.9 percent, business at 14.7 percent, and health sciences at 14.4 percent. These fields, which tend to have more women than other STEM disciplines, may contribute to the gender difference in graduate certificates awarded, with 63.1 percent going to women and 36.9 going to men. STEM fields comprise relatively smaller fractions of the total graduate certificates earned; however, some of the fields showed robust growth between 2006 and 2016, such as 38.6

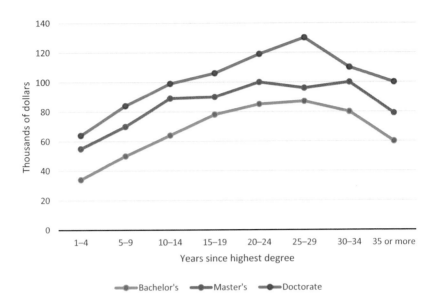

FIGURE 4-1 Median salaries for STEM highest degree holders, by level of and years since highest degree, 2015.
SOURCE: Adapted from NSB, 2018c, Fig. 3-20.

percent growth in engineering and 26.1 percent growth in the biological and agricultural sciences, compared to the 11.8 percent average across all fields.

In 2016, edX,[7] an online learning provider founded by Harvard University and MIT, launched 19 MicroMasters programs at 14 institutions, including MIT, the University of Pennsylvania, Georgia Tech, and the University of Michigan. The MicroMasters programs included a corporate advisory board to help develop the programs with industry employers in mind. These programs allow students the flexibility to advance through the program while maintaining their day jobs, and students can transfer their MicroMasters into academic credit if accepted by the master's degree program at associated institutions. While the MicroMasters programs address a broad range of disciplines, several of the programs focus on developing skills needed in emerging issues in STEM such as data science, artificial intelligence, bioinformatics, and cloud computing.

To date, only one of the edX MicroMasters programs has been completed, the Supply Chain Management program from MIT. For this program, of the 200,000 people enrolled, nearly 19,000 or 9.5 percent were awarded certificates; learners can take the course for free and do not need to pursue the certification.

---

[7] See https://www.edx.org/ (accessed March 17, 2018).

Boston University released information regarding its course in Digital Trans-formation Strategy: 12,153 total enrollments, 587 completed (4.6 percent), and 284 (2.3 percent) completed and verified with a certificate (Smith, 2017). The total enrollment figure might be an outlier attributed to first-run novelty, because the second round of the course enrolled 4,463 students, and low completion rates for online courses remain a concern. In a report released by HarvardX and MITx on their open online courses, these institutions report that 5.5 percent of partici-pants earned certificates from 2012 to 2016; however, the report contends that given that the dearth of data on student intention and motivation for enrolling in the program, certification completion rates may not provide a useful metric for evaluation (Chuang and Ho, 2016). The limited understanding about graduate certificate programs represents an issue for additional research and inquiry.

In addition to online microcredential programs, such as the ones mentioned above, some institutions also offer students the opportunity to earn full master's degrees either through fully online programs or through blended learning, which includes face-to-face and online components. One high-profile example of a recently launched online master's program is the computer science program of-fered by Georgia Tech. Announced in 2013 in partnership with Udacity and with funding from AT&T, the 3-year program features a lower cost to students at less than $7,000 ($134 per credit in comparison to $472 for in-state students and $1,139 for out-of-state students) (Young, 2013). As of fall 2017, the program had enrolled approximately 5,900 students and graduated nearly 600 students; however, there is a notable difference in enrollment between genders with 85.6 percent male and 14.4 percent female (Georgia Tech, 2017). Although it is an imperfect comparison, for reference, in 2013 male students earned 73 percent of all master's computer science degrees (NSB, 2016a). The program states that 15 percent of the students are from historically underrepresented groups compared to 11.5 percent of master's computer science degrees earned by students who identified as black or African American, Hispanic, or American Indian or Alaska Native in 2013 (Georgia Tech, 2017; NSB, 2018a).[8] Citing a positive response, Georgia Tech announced in 2017 that it was offering a fully online master's degree in analytics, again featuring low cost and broader access as key features of the program: "[In 2017] Georgia Tech expects to receive more than 1,000 ap-plications for the residential program [in analytics], which can only fit about 70 students. That means the institute must turn away about 800 qualified applicants" (Straumsheim, 2017). The hope is that some of those 700-plus students will enroll in the online master's program.

According to the website OnlineU, at least 80 accredited institutions offer online master's programs, ranging from chemistry and engineering to clinical

---

[8] These three groups were selected to align with the groups featured in the underrepresented groups in science and engineering according to the *Women, Minorities, and Persons with Disabilities in Sci-ence and Engineering* report (NCSES, 2017).

psychology and physics.[9] While this is not a comprehensive census of available online STEM master's programs, it demonstrates the significant institutional and public interest in distance learning options for these credentials. Despite the range of options, from microcredential to full degree and fully online or blended, there are little data or published research on these programs. The limited amount of research in this area means that the ability to draw broader conclusions from these examples is constrained. As online platforms for education delivery at the degree or microcredential level continue to expand, research on student motivation and intention, enrollment, persistence, and completion could help inform future program design.

As this report discusses in Chapter 3, there is a lack of data collected on the outcomes of STEM graduate programs, and this is certainly true in the case of master's degrees. Indeed, there is a general dearth of data and research on factors such as motivation for seeking a master's degree, the characteristics of programs and institutions that help or hinder completion, and why enrollment among underrepresented minorities continues to lag, though less so than with doctoral programs. In a rapidly evolving environment, it is always important to monitor outcomes and quality of programs and educational and career outcomes of students. Universities and the students they serve would be well served if they monitored these programs, used the resulting information to build a culture that better appreciates master's students, and made the data available to current and prospective students. (See Chapter 3, Recommendation 3.2, for additional information on data transparency.)

CGS reported on the results of a pilot study of STEM master's programs that aimed to identify factors contributing to the successful completion of the degree (CGS, 2013). Students surveyed as part of this study cited the desire to support professional aspirations by increasing knowledge and skills as the most common reason for enrolling in a master's degree program. Other less frequently cited reasons included a desire to increase opportunities for promotion, advancement, or higher pay, and to learn about a new area of interest. This study found that two-thirds of students who enrolled in STEM master's degree programs had completed their degrees within 4 years. Some 10 percent of students left their programs within 6 months, and nearly a quarter had dropped out after 2 years (CGS, 2013). The study found that the two most crucial factors contributing to the successful completion of a master's program were motivation and nonfinancial family support, while conflicts with existing work responsibilities was the main reason students were unable to complete their master's degree programs.

The foregoing discussion emphasizes both that there is a growing demand for STEM master's degree programs from students and employers, and that a growing number of institutions are offering them to meet that demand. It is essential that highly competent faculty are engaged in teaching in those programs.

---

[9] See https://www.onlineu.org/college-list?pid=&lvl=8 (accessed March 26, 2018).

For those reasons, covered in detail in Chapter 3, the committee made Recommendation 3.1, Rewarding Effective Teaching and Mentoring, which included specific provisions for supporting and rewarding faculty contributions to master's students and education.[10]

REFERENCES

AFL-CIO. 2016. The STEM Workforce: An Occupational Overview. Available: http://dpeaflcio.org/programs-publications/issue-fact-sheets/the-stem-workforce-an-occupational-overview/ (accessed May 10, 2018).

Allum, J. R. 2013. *Outcomes for PSM alumni: 2012/13*. Washington, DC: Council of Graduate Schools.

Augustine, R. 2017. The alignment framework for the master's degree. *GradEdge* 6(1). Available: http://cgsnet.org/january-2017-gradedge (accessed May 9, 2018).

BLS (U.S. Bureau of Labor Statistics). 2013. Occupational employment projections to 2022. *Monthly Labor Review*. Available: https://www.bls.gov/opub/mlr/2013/article/occupational-employment-projections-to-2022.htm (accessed March 26, 2018).

Chuang, I., and A. Ho. 2016. HarvardX and MITx: Four years of open online courses—fall 2012-summer 2016. Available at SSRN: https://dx.doi.org/10.2139/ssrn.2889436.

CGS (Council of Graduate Schools). 2005. *Master's education: A guide for faculty and administrators, a policy statement*. Washington, DC: CGS.

CGS. 2010. *Ph.D. Completion project: Policies and practices to promote student success*. Washington, DC: CGS.

CGS. 2013. *Completion and attrition in STEM master's programs*. Washington, DC: CGS.

Dishman, L. 2016. Best and worst graduate degrees for jobs in 2016. *Fortune*, March 21. Available: http://fortune.com/2016/03/21/best-worst-graduate-degrees-jobs-2016/ (accessed March 17, 2018).

Gallagher, S. R. 2014. *Major employers' hiring practices and the evolving function of the professional master's degree*. M.S. thesis, Northeastern University, Boston, MA. Available: http://hdl.handle.net/2047/d20004969.

Georgia Tech. 2017. Online master of science in computer science: 2017 program updates. Available: https://www.omscs.gatech.edu/sites/default/files/images/omscsreport2017.pdf.

Komura, K. 2015. *Enrollment and degrees in professional science master's (PSM) programs, Part I, 2014*. Claremont, CA: Keck Graduate Institute.

---

[10] CHAPTER 3 RECOMMENDATION 3.1—REWARDING EFFECTIVE TEACHING AND MENTORING: Advancement procedures for faculty, including promotion and tenure policies and practices, should be restructured to strengthen recognition of contributions to graduate mentoring and education.

- Federal and state funding agencies should align their policies and award criteria to ensure that students in the programs they support experience the kind of graduate education outlined in this report and achieve the scientific and professional competencies articulated here, whether they are on training or research grant mechanisms.
- Institutions should require faculty and postdoctoral researchers who have extensive contact with graduate students to learn and demonstrate evidence-based and inclusive teaching and mentoring practices.
- Institutions should include teaching and mentoring performance as important considerations for reappointment, promotion, and tenure decisions. Institutions should also nominate faculty for external awards (such as those from technical societies) that reward teaching excellence.

NCSES (National Center for Science and Engineering Statistics). 2017. *Women, minorities, and persons with disabilities in science and engineering: 2017*. Special Report NSF 17-310. Arlington, VA: National Science Foundation.

NRC (National Research Council). 2008. *Science professionals: Master's education for a competitive world*. Washington, DC: The National Academies Press.

NSB (National Science Board). 2016a. Appendix Table 2-28, Earned master's degrees, by sex and field: 2000-13. *Science and engineering indicators 2016*. NSB-2018-1. Alexandria, VA: National Science Foundation. Available: https://nsf.gov/statistics/2016/nsb20161/uploads/1/12/at02-28.pdf (accessed January 23, 2018).

NSB. 2016b. *Science and engineering indicators 2016*. Arlington, VA: National Science Foundation.

NSB. 2018a. Appendix Table 2-28, Earned master's degrees, by citizenship, field, race, and ethnicity: 2000–15. *Science and engineering indicators 2018*. NSB-2018-1. Alexandria, VA: National Science Foundation. Available: https://www.nsf.gov/statistics/2018/nsb20181/assets/561/tables/at02-28.pdf (accessed March 16, 2018).

NSB. 2018b. Appendix Table 3-5: Employment sector of S&E highest degree holders, by level and field of highest degree: 2015. *Science and engineering indicators 2018*. NSB-2018-1. Alexandria, VA: National Science Foundation. Available: https://nsf.gov/statistics/2018/nsb20181/assets/901/tables/at03-05.pdf (accessed March 22, 2018).

NSB. 2018c. *Science and engineering indicators 2018*. NSB-2018-1. Alexandria, VA: National Science Foundation.

Okahana, H., and E. Zhou. 2017. *Graduate enrollment and degrees: 2006 to 2016*. Council of Graduate Schools. Available: http://cgsnet.org/ckfinder/userfiles/files/Intl_Survey_Report_Fall2017.pdf (accessed March 17, 2018).

Smith, J. 2017. BU's first MicroMasters programs off to a great start. Available: https://digital.bu.edu/bus-first-micromasters-programs-off-to-a-great-start/ (accessed March 26, 2018).

Straumsheim, C. 2017. Georgia Tech's model expands. *Inside Higher Ed*, January 12. Available: https://www.insidehighered.com/news/2017/01/12/georgia-tech-launches-second-low-cost-online-masters-degree-program (accessed March 17, 2018).

Torpey, E., and D. Terrell. 2015. Should I get a master's degree? *Career Outlook*. Available: https://www.bls.gov/careeroutlook/2015/article/should-i-get-a-masters-degree.htm#STEM (accessed January 23, 2018).

Wingfield, N. 2017. The disappearing American grad student. *The New York Times*, November 3. Available: https://www.nytimes.com/2017/11/03/education/edlife/american-graduate-student-stem.html (accessed March 17, 2018).

Young, J. R. 2013. Georgia Tech to offer a MOOC-like online master's degree, at low cost. *Chronicle of Higher Education*, May 14. Available: https://www.chronicle.com/article/Ga-Tech-to-Offer-a-MOOC-Like/139245 (accessed March 17, 2018).

5

The Doctoral Degree

The Ph.D. is the highest degree in science, technology, engineering, and mathematics (STEM) fields, resulting from 4 to 7 or more years of intensive coursework and mentored research leading to a dissertation and scholarly publications. While no two Ph.D. experiences are identical, the Ph.D. programs typical of many STEM disciplines include 1 to 2 years of discipline-specific coursework; perhaps 1 or more years serving as a teaching assistant; the search for a dissertation advisor, which may or may not involve a formal system of rotating through several laboratories; comprehensive subject matter examinations; formulation and defense of a dissertation project; 3 to 7 years of mentored research supported by a combination of research assistantships and fellowships; writing the dissertation; and a final defense of the dissertation (O'Leary, 2016). This process is supervised almost exclusively by a primary research advisor or dissertation committee that generally sets guidelines for graduation, oversees the student's development as a researcher, and socializes the student into his or her subfield.

This chapter articulates issues and concerns about STEM Ph.D. education in the United States and frames some potential solutions, beginning with the committee's view of the core competencies that compose an ideal STEM Ph.D. education calibrated for the 21st century. Although the recommendations in this chapter call for other kinds of changes in the graduate education experience, they maintain the integrity of the Ph.D. and promote the possibilities for all students, independently of which institutions they attend, to have the opportunity to develop the core competencies. The discussion in this chapter also addresses issues related to career preparation and exploration for STEM Ph.D.'s and the structure of doctoral education, including the dissertation, curriculum, and coursework. The final section in the chapter serves as a companion to Chapter 3 and includes more information specific to doctoral students on mentoring and advising, mechanisms for funding graduate students, and diversity, equity, and inclusion.

CORE EDUCATIONAL ELEMENTS OF THE PH.D. DEGREE

While STEM Ph.D. education needs to respond to the changing needs and interests of graduate students, evolving methods of scientific research, and workforce needs, it is essential to maintain the core educational elements that define a Ph.D. degree for each specific discipline. The education and training that students receive during their Ph.D. education should provide them with the ability to conduct original scientific research. The core education elements would establish the STEM Ph.D. educational mission, with alignment across the key components of the degree program: core disciplinary coursework, original research, and other intensive experiences in the classroom and laboratory or during fieldwork, workshops, conferences, and internships. That mission establishes a Ph.D. education as one that would stimulate curiosity; develop the intellectual capacity to recognize, formulate, and communicate complex problems; create an iterative approach toward solutions, drawing from discipline-appropriate quantitative, theoretical, or mixed-methods tools; make original discoveries that advance understanding; and communicate the impact of the research beyond their discipline.

Supported by input and ideas received in response to its Call for Community Input (see Appendix B), the committee suggests that the following are the core elements that should characterize all Ph.D. education. Acquiring the skills that these core elements provide will serve as fundamentals underpinning future success in whatever career paths students choose:

1. **Develop Scientific and Technological Literacy and Conduct Original Research**
    a. Develop deep specialized expertise in at least one STEM discipline.
    b. Acquire sufficient transdisciplinary[1] literacy to suggest multiple conceptual and methodological approaches to a complex problem.
    c. Identify an important problem and articulate an original research question.
    d. Design a research strategy, including relevant quantitative, analytical, or theoretical approaches, to explore components of the problem and begin to address the question.
    e. Evaluate outcomes of each experiment or study component and select which outcomes to pursue and how to do so through an iterative process.

---

[1] Transdisciplinarity transcends disciplinary approaches through more comprehensive frameworks, including the synthetic paradigms of general systems theory and sustainability (NRC, 2014). See Appendix A for full definitions.

f. Adopt rigorous standards of investigation and acquire mastery of the quantitative, analytical, technical, and technological skills required to conduct successful research in the field of study.

g. Learn and apply professional norms and practices of the scientific or engineering enterprise, the ethical responsibilities of scientists and engineers within the profession and in relationship to the rest of society, as well as ethical standards that will lead to principled character and conduct.

2. **Develop Leadership, Communication, and Professional Competencies**

a. Develop the ability to work in collaborative and team settings involving colleagues with expertise in other disciplines and from diverse cultural and disciplinary backgrounds.

b. Acquire the capacity to communicate, both orally and in written form, the significance and impact of a study or a body of work to all STEM professionals, other sectors that may utilize the results, and the public at large.

c. Develop professional competencies, such as interpersonal communication, budgeting, project management, or pedagogical skills that are needed to plan and implement research projects.

RECOMMENDATION 5.1—Core Competencies for Ph.D. Education: Every STEM Ph.D. student should achieve the core scientific and professional Ph.D. competencies detailed in this report.

- Universities should verify that every graduate program that they offer provides for these competencies and that students demonstrate that they have achieved them before receiving their doctoral degrees.
- Universities should scrutinize their curricula and program requirements for features that lie outside of these core competencies and learning objectives and that may be adding time to degree without providing enough additional value to students, such as a first-author publication requirement, and eliminate those features or requirements.
- Graduate departments should publicly post how their programs reflect the core competencies for doctoral students, including the milestones and metrics the departments and individual faculty use in evaluation and assessment.
- Federal and state funding agencies should adapt funding criteria for institutions to ensure that all doctoral students they support—regardless of mechanism of support—are in programs that ensure that they develop, measure, and report these scientific and professional competencies.
- Students should create an independent development plan that includes these competencies as a core feature of their own learning and career

goals and that utilizes the resources provided by their university and relevant professional societies.

- Students should provide feedback to the graduate faculty and deans about how they could help students better develop these competencies.

CAREER EXPLORATION AND PREPARATION

For those individuals wanting a tenure track academic job or a position directing a research group in industry, a Ph.D. is a prerequisite and, in many fields, may be followed by one or more postdoctoral positions. Although historically most students enrolled in STEM Ph.D. programs came with the expectation of pursuing a tenure track faculty position, data from the National Science Foundation's (NSF) National Center for Science and Engineering Statistics (NCSES) show fulfillment of that expectation has declined. In 2015, only 17.7 percent of STEM Ph.D.'s across all STEM fields had secured tenure track positions within 5 years of graduating, down from 25.9 percent as recently as 2008 and 27.0 percent in 1993 (NSB, 2018, Table 3-16[2]). The shift in tenure status appears across all age groups as well. In a comparison of tenure status of STEM doctorate holders between 1995 and 2015, the percentage of individuals with tenured positions declined in every age category except the 35-39 group, while those in tenure track positions declined to a lesser degree (Table 5-1). The greatest differences occur in the numbers of STEM doctorate holders in the 50- to 54- and 55- to 59-year-old age groups with an "other" status, which includes individuals at institutions where no tenure is offered or there is no tenure for the position held. This trend parallels the decline in the percentage of doctorate holders with tenured status in the 50-54 and 50-59 age categories with tenure status.

While the U.S. Bureau of Labor Statistics (BLS) projects that the job market for postsecondary educators will grow by some 17.4 percent from 2010 to 2020, most of these positions are expected to be part-time or adjunct, rather than tenure track, appointments (BLS, 2013). NSF data show the shifts in proportions of STEM-trained Ph.D.'s working in academia from 1973 to 2015, noting the decrease in full-time faculty and the increase in other full-time positions, which includes research associates, adjunct appointments, instructors (from 1997 to 2015), lecturers, and administrative positions (Figure 5-1).

The job market in academia was better in some fields than in others. Moreover, the different disciplines have long had different traditions and histories of their students pursuing academic careers versus those in other industries. A BLS analysis (Xue and Larson, 2015) found that although the overall number of STEM Ph.D.'s has been climbing steadily, the number of tenure track positions has remained nearly constant in most fields. The biomedical sciences and

---

[2] See https://www.nsf.gov/statistics/2018/nsb20181/assets/901/tables/tt03-16.xlsx (accessed February 27, 2018).

TABLE 5-1 Tenure Status of STEM Doctorate Holders Employed in Academia, by Age: 1995 and 2015

Age	1995 (%)			2015 (%)		
	Tenured	Tenure Track	Others	Tenured	Tenure Track	Others
Total all ages	52.6	16.7	30.7	46.6	14.7	38.7
Younger than 30[a]	s	25.0	75.0	s	26.9	76.9
30–34	5.2	36.7	58.5	3.2	35.8	61.0
35–39	24.9	35.2	39.8	18.9	35.3	45.9
40–44	47.2	20.5	32.3	43.3	19.3	37.5
45–49	63.1	10.3	26.5	54.4	10.0	35.6
50–54	75.8	5.4	18.5	59.3	4.9	35.9
55–59	80.1	2.0	17.5	64.0	3.9	32.0
60–64	85.8	1.4	12.8	68.1	2.6	29.3
65–75[a]	75.9	s	22.8	68.2	1.4	30.4

NOTES: Academic employment is limited to U.S. doctorate holders employed at 2- or 4-year colleges or universities, medical schools, and university research institutes. Percentages may not add to 100% because of rounding. Others include science and engineering doctorate holders at institutions where no tenure is offered or there is no tenure for the position held.

[a]s = suppressed for reasons of confidentiality and/or reliability.

SOURCE: NSB, 2018, Table 5-12, available at https://nsf.gov/statistics/2018/nsb20181/assets/968/tables/tt05-12.pdf (accessed March 24, 2018).

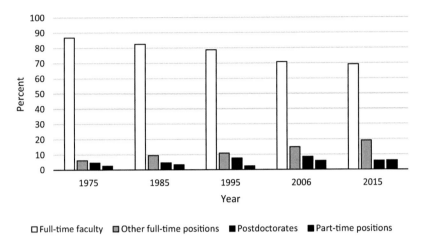

FIGURE 5-1 STEM doctorate holders employed in academia, by percentage of degree holders per position type: 1975–2015.
NOTE: The year 2006 is intentional. No data were available for 2005.
SOURCE: NSB, 2018, adapted from Figure 5-9.

computer science are two exceptions, having seen increases over time resulting from increased investment in biomedical positions following the doubling of the National Institues of Health budget and the increased enrollment in computer science. Despite the stable number of faculty positions overall, each faculty member turns out more Ph.D.'s over the course of a career than the replacement number (Xue and Larson, 2015). The authors of that analysis concluded that there was an oversupply of Ph.D.'s desiring academic careers relative to the paucity of tenure track faculty positions (Bowen and Rudenstein, 1992; Golde and Dore, 2001).

NCSES data also show that of the 992,000 STEM Ph.D.'s in the United States in 2015, 48.3 percent had jobs in business or industry, 43.2 percent had jobs in education, and 8.5 percent were in government (Table 5-2).[3] In contrast to the overall trends, only 24 percent of engineering Ph.D.'s held positions in education while 69.9 percent were employed in business or industry, with 63.9 percent employed by for-profit businesses. Looking within employment subcategories, those with degrees in the social and related sciences show the highest percentage in the category of self-employed, unincorporated businesses (11.5 percent), nonprofit businesses (10.1 percent), and 2-year and precollege institutions (6.8 percent).

Several studies have documented that students' career goals often change dur-

---

[3] Detailed information about Ph.D. programs and student demographics is provided in Chapter 2 and will not be repeated here.

TABLE 5-2 Employment Sector of STEM Doctoral Degree Holders, by Field of Highest Degree, 2015

Field	Total Number	Education (%)		Business or industry (%)			Government (%)	
		4-Year Institutions	2-Year and Precollege Institutions	For-Profit Businesses	Self-Employed, Unincorporated Businesses	Nonprofit Businesses	Federal Government	State or Local Government
All STEM Fields	992,000	39.6	3.6	36.2	5.2	6.9	6.5	2.0
Computer sciences and mathematics	87,000	43.7	2.3	43.7	1.1	1.1	6.9	s*
Biological, agricultural, and environmental life sciences	272,000	45.2	2.9	29.4	2.9	8.5	7.7	2.9
Physical and related sciences	171,000	40.9	3.5	38.6	2.3	5.8	8.2	0.6
Social and related sciences	278,000	42.8	6.8	20.9	11.5	10.1	5.0	2.9
Engineering	183,000	23.5	0.5	63.9	3.3	2.7	4.9	1.1

NOTES: All science and engineering highest degree holders include professional degree holders not reported separately. The 2-year and precollege institutions include 2-year colleges and community colleges or technical institutes. The 4-year institutions include 4-year colleges or universities, medical schools, and university-affiliated research institutes. The education sector includes public and private institutions. Detail may not add to total because of rounding. Numbers are rounded to the nearest 1,000. Percentages are based on rounded numbers.

s* = suppressed for reasons of confidentiality and/or reliability.

SOURCE: NSB, 2018, Table 3-5.

ing their doctoral studies (Fuhrmann et al., 2011; Gibbs et al., 2014; Sauermann and Roach, 2012). While the general assumption has been that this attitudinal change among STEM graduate students has resulted from the realization that academic positions are in short supply or that funding for academic research is becoming more difficult to obtain (Alberts et al., 2014; Cyranoski et al., 2011; Schillebeeckx et al., 2013), a 2017 study found that this decline has more to do with students' changing perceptions of what an academic research career entails vis-à-vis their own abilities and interests as researchers (Roach and Sauermann, 2017). Whatever the impetus, the majority of STEM Ph.D.'s now pursue careers outside of academic research. Since most STEM Ph.D. students no longer enter academic research positions, there is an imperative that the STEM research and education community act on the recommendations of this and many previous reports on the future of graduate education, which date back at least as far as the 1995 National Academies report *Reshaping the Graduate Education of Scientists and Engineers* (NAS/NAE/IOM, 1995).

Numerous reports in the literature have emphasized a lack of preparation for today's workforce, both within and outside of academia, particularly regarding communication skills, the ability to work effectively in teams, business acumen, and leadership competencies (AAU, 1998; Golde and Dore, 2001; Nerad et al., 2006; Nyquist, 2002; Taylor, 2006; Wendler et al., 2012). Moreover, students who submitted entries to NSF's Innovation in Graduate Education Challenge,[4] which was initiated to capture the graduate student voice and solicit student ideas about how to improve graduate education, identified a lack of exposure to transferable professional skills as one of the main problems they wanted to see addressed. Transferable professional skills included science communication, entrepreneurism, leadership, management, outreach, and the ability to work as part of an interdisciplinary team. Students also cited the desire to get more information about and exposure to nonacademic careers.

Even when universities offer opportunities for graduate students to broaden their exposure to such skills or alternative careers, those offerings may not be well publicized and may be of varying effectiveness. In addition, such offerings may be underutilized by students because they are not aware of them, out of concern that their advisors may not support participation, or because their schedules do not allow for it (Denecke et al., 2017). Another underlying reason why these opportunities may be underutilized is that students are not encouraged to develop competencies beyond their own research field, even though leadership, collaboration, project management, and other skills would also help them to be more effective and efficient researchers.

Students may not know how to explore opportunities to broaden their exposure to professional skills because of the mismatch between when students seek

---

[4] See https://www.nsf.gov/news/special_reports/gradchallenge/about.html (accessed January 23, 2018).

career information and when it is provided to them (Gibbs and Griffin, 2013). In addition, students may not have support from their primary research advisor to explore what have historically been career paths outside of academia (Janke and Colbeck, 2008; Laursen et al., 2012). Depending on the field of study, the stigma associated with nonacademic careers can be an issue that many students say needs to be addressed (Gibbs et al., 2015; Pinheiro et al., 2017). Faculty often do not have the expertise to provide students with guidance regarding nonacademic careers, because they have not had first-hand experience in those positions and do not readily receive training in broader career advising. As described in Chapter 6, providing the ideal graduate education involves changing the culture of academia to encourage faculty, administrators, career counselors, and other staff who support graduate education by providing them the time, training, and other resources needed to refer and support students within their career goals.

A central issue relating to career preparation facing STEM Ph.D. programs is how to most appropriately provide students with exposure to these additional skills. Some may worry that these additional experiences will dilute discipline-specific coursework or the core elements of the Ph.D., adding extra burden to already stressed students and administrative budgets or increasing the time to degree. Although more research is needed to determine how professional development activities impact graduate student outcomes, existing evidence suggests that participation in thoughtfully designed professional development experiences do not detract from core elements of the Ph.D. There are graduate programs that have successfully incorporated opportunity-broadening experiences, such as those at 17 institutions funded by the National Institutes of Health's Broadening Experiences in Scientific Training (BEST) program.[5] This program, which started in 2013 and will not fund any new grants, is designed specifically to develop innovative approaches to facilitate career exploration by Ph.D. students and postdoctoral fellows that might be considered, adopted, or adapted by other institutions.

Virtually every stakeholder group from which the committee received input mentioned the need for increased transparency about the metrics for Ph.D. programs, including data on student demographics, time to degree, student life, financial support, and career paths and outcomes within and outside of academia. Much of this concern has to do with providing students with an honest appraisal of the career opportunities awaiting them, particularly regarding careers in academia as discussed above. As mentioned in Chapter 2, institutions have not historically provided sufficient data about how alumni have used their graduate education experiences and accomplishments in the workforce for students to understand the career pathways available to them.

---

[5] See http://www.nihbest.org/about-best/17-research-sites/ (accessed January 23, 2018).

RECOMMENDATION 5.2—Career Exploration and Preparation for Ph.D. Students: Students should be provided an understanding of and opportunities to explore the variety of career opportunities and pathways afforded by STEM Ph.D. degrees.

- Faculty who serve as undergraduate and master's advisors should discuss with their students whether and how a Ph.D. degree will advance the students' long-term educational and career goals.
- Institutions should integrate professional development opportunities, including relevant course offerings and internships, into doctoral curriculum design.
- Institutions, through their career counselors and career centers, should assist students in gaining an understanding of and opportunities to explore career options afforded by STEM Ph.D. degrees.
- Students should seek information about potential career paths, talk to employers and mentors in areas of interest, and choose a doctoral program optimal for gaining the knowledge and competencies needed to pursue their career interests.
- Every student and his or her faculty advisor should prepare an individual development plan.
- Industry, nonprofit, government, and other employers should provide guidance and financial support for relevant course offerings at institutions and provide internships and other forms of professional experiences to students and recent graduates.
- Federal and state agencies and private foundations that support graduate education should require STEM graduate programs to include career exploration curricular offerings and require STEM doctoral students to create and to update annually individual development plans in consultation with faculty advisors to map educational goals, career exploration, and professional development.
- Professional societies should collaborate with leaders in various sectors to create programs that help Ph.D. recipients transition into a variety of careers.

DOCTORAL CURRICULUM, COURSEWORK, AND THE DISSERTATION

One challenge raised frequently by graduate students is finding the balance between the completion of required coursework and degree requirements with other growth opportunities (Lovitts, 2004). In particular, students report that high expectations of faculty about acquisition of deeply technical, disciplinary-specific information limits their growth in other dimensions (Gardner, 2009). In a 2004 study, students felt that they were discouraged from seeking courses in other disciplines or nonacademic professional skills through coursework or internships (Fagan and Suedkamp Wells, 2004). More recently, in the case of chemistry, many U.S. graduate programs have begun to incorporate courses that impart highly valued, nonacademic professional skills, such as professional communication, leadership, and management skills, into their core curricula (Loshbaugh et al., 2011).

In the committee's judgment, one essential element of any Ph.D. program is student access to a variety of research groups to allow them to grow their network of colleagues, to experience different types of research methods and working styles, and to determine whether their department or program is large enough, and to give them a chance to "shop around" for a research topic and advisor(s) most suited to their intellectual interests. In large departments in laboratory-based fields, this could mean rotations through several laboratories lasting from several weeks to a semester. For non-laboratory-based disciplines, departments would develop similar approaches to serve the same purpose of exposing students to a range of options for advisors and mentors.

A common refrain related to the dilemma posed by finding a way to include additional skills and opportunities not directly related to the core Ph.D. research project is the fear of increased time to degree. The 1995 National Academies' report noted that one concern linked to increased time to degree is that the potential financial and opportunity costs would deter prospective applicants (NAS/ NAE/IOM, 1995). The release of that report coincided with the highest recorded median time to degree for STEM Ph.D.'s at 7.7 years for all fields, having increased from 7.2 years in 1985. By 2015, time to degree has steadily declined to an average of 6.8 years across all STEM fields. At the disciplinary level, the median times to degree in 2015 were lower than in 1985, except for computer sciences, which increased from 7.4 to 7.6 years, and engineering, which retained the median of 6.7 years (NSB, 2018, Table 2-30). Other notable decreases from 1985 to 2015 include the social sciences (9.1 to 8.3 years), medical and other health sciences (9.7 to 9 years), and earth, atmospheric, and oceanic sciences (7.4 to 6.9 years) (NSB, 2018).

A program that can serve as an illustrative example of balancing primary degree requirements with additional activities is the former NSF GK-12 program. In this program, graduate students spent 10 to 15 hours on K-12 education activities, and the participants had publication rates and time to degree similar to those of students in typical Ph.D. programs (Gamse et al., 2010). The results from this program suggest that it is possible to build transferrable skills in the context of the graduate program in a way that can enhance research and education outcomes without significantly increasing time to degree. Such opportunities could give students the chance to develop time management skills. For example, students can be more intentional about their dissertation project planning, project management, and collaboration to achieve better outcomes. They could also take on roles that support the scientific enterprise while improving their transferrable skills, such as creating a website to describe their lab's work for public audiences or managing data for multiple projects.

Another central Ph.D. requirement is the dissertation, seen as the primary achievement and a record of the student's contribution to the field, as described in the 1995 National Research Council report:

> The dissertation, as a demonstration of ability to carry out independent research, is the central exercise of the PhD program. When completed, it is expected to describe in detail the student's research and results, the relevance of that research to previous work, and the importance of the results in extending understanding of that topic. (NRC, 1995, p. 49)

Despite changes in many fields to include collaboration as a key part of academic research and the long-standing tradition of teamwork in industry, the written dissertation typically continues to remain the work of a single author. Some programs do allow for research done in teams to be included; however, the end product remains the creation of one student. The opportunity for team or group dissertations may appeal to students, better reflect the nature of work in contemporary science and engineering, and allow students to navigate issues of authorship, research ethics, and scholarly communication practices that they will encounter as STEM professionals (Hakkarainen et al., 2016). Organizations such as the Council of Graduate Schools have initiated projects looking at the future of the dissertation in the face of the changing nature of science and engineering,[6] and the results should be monitored closely.

Beyond producing the dissertation itself, the guidance given for writing in many Ph.D. programs is limited to preparing students to write in a technical manner. However, many of the students who participated in the committee's focus groups expressed a desire to learn to communicate results to a broader audience. This could be demonstrated in a chapter in the dissertation that reflects the value of the findings to society or provides students the opportunity to write to the broader public. Since 2010, the University of Wisconsin–Madison's Wisconsin Initiative for Science Literacy, for example, hosts a dissertation award for chemistry Ph.D. candidates to include a chapter aimed at nonspecialists, such as family members, friends, civic groups, newspaper reporters, and program officers at appropriate funding agencies, state legislators, and members of the U.S. Congress.[7] Other institutions have requirements that dissertations include a lay summary or abstract. While the traditional dissertation format may remain appropriate for many students, programs may consider pilot projects and flexibility within the dissertation to tailor the dissertation more to the educational and career goals of the student and measure the outcomes of such options on students' perceptions

---

[6] See http://cgsnet.org/future-doctoral-dissertation (accessed January 23, 2018).

[7] See http://scifun.chem.wisc.edu/news/thesis_awards.htm (accessed January 23, 2018).

about graduate programs or whether such opportunities have broadened their perspectives about potential career pathways.

RECOMMENDATION 5.3—Structure of Doctoral Research Activities: Curricula and research projects, team projects, and dissertations should be designed to reflect the state of the art in the ways STEM research and education are conducted.

- Universities, professional societies, and higher education associations should take the lead in establishing criteria and updating characteristics of the doctoral research project and dissertation preparation and format.
- Students should seek opportunities to work in cross-disciplinary and cross-sector teams during their graduate education and via extracurricular activities and be incentivized by their departments and faculty advisors to do so.
- Graduate programs and faculty should encourage and facilitate the development of student teams within and across disciplines.

ADDITIONAL FACTORS REQUIRING EVOLUTION OF THE SYSTEM

The evolving 21st century context in which STEM education is imbedded, as discussed earlier in this report, calls for some significant changes in the graduate education system itself. While many of the issues featured below were introduced in Chapter 3, the sections below include detail on how the trends have a specific effect for Ph.D. programs.

Mentoring and Advising

In addition to the detailed review of issues related to mentoring and advising in graduate-level education under the section Adjusting Faculty Rewards and Incentives to Improve STEM Graduate Education in Chapter 3, the importance of the relationship between student and research mentor warrants additional detail here. In addition to a moderate amount of formal coursework, Ph.D. education is typically structured like an apprenticeship, where students work for one primary research advisor who plays a vital role in passing on deep knowledge and sophisticated methodology, imparting the norms of the field, and advising and authorizing the students' graduate activities and experiences.

Mentoring and advising are two different sets of activities and require distinct kinds of expertise and approaches (Paglis et al., 2006; see also Green, 2015; Misra and Lundquist, 2016). In general, the role of a Ph.D. research advisor is to focus more on the academic progress of a student, serve as an information resource regarding courses and university policies, help students develop core capacities as an independent researcher, and help students gain broad scientific literacy. A mentor's role combines academic guidance with career advice, role modeling, and varying amounts of emotional support to help students succeed through graduate school. Students are most successful when their primary research advisor also provides some mentoring. However, recognizing that every faculty member has particular strengths and each student has different goals, most students need multiple advisors and mentors to help them acquire interdisciplinary perspectives, develop broad professional competencies, explore career pathways, navigate graduate school, and support their well-being.

Another issue that needs to be addressed is the power dynamics of the advisor-student relationship, where both the student and the advisor recognize that the advisor is dominant in the relationship, and that in many cases the student becomes a true apprentice working for the benefit of the advisor more than the student. Students are often the literal producers of research products in the form of data and publications, and many have reported that they can feel exploited by their advisors. Although the advisor-student relationship can work adequately, the imbalance in power can also be problematic when the advisor is perceived to have the power to determine the student's future. Addressing this relationship and making it more equal makes the graduate experience more student centered (Graduate Assembly, 2014; Levecque et al., 2017) while still recognizing the needs of the research enterprise and students' advisor's need to secure funding, publish, and gain tenure or promotion. Having different individuals serving as advisor and mentor can help address that power dynamic by dividing responsibilities. In some disciplines and at some universities, the members of a student's dissertation committee play important advising and mentoring roles, which can also ameliorate the power dynamics of the single advisor-student relationship.

A student's relationship with his or her primary advisor is the factor most directly correlated with retention, timely completion, sense of inclusion, career aspirations, and overall satisfaction with her or his graduate experience (O'Meara et al., 2013). Studies have reported that the best faculty advisors improved academic success, research productivity, career commitment, and self-efficacy, commonly defined as one's belief in one's own ability to succeed (Mollica and Nemeth, 2014; Paglis et al., 2006). Recommendation 3.2 on Institutional Support for Quality Teaching and Mentoring includes specific actions related to improving mentoring and advising for doctoral students.[8]

---

[8] RECOMMENDATION 3.2—Institutional Support for Teaching and Mentoring: To improve the quality and effectiveness of faculty teaching and mentoring, institutions of higher education should provide training for new faculty and should offer regular refresher courses in teaching and mentoring for established faculty.

- Institutions should require faculty and postdoctoral researchers who have extensive contact with graduate students to learn and demonstrate evidence-based and inclusive teaching and mentoring practices.
- Graduate programs should facilitate mentor relationships between the graduate student and the primary research advisors, as well as opportunities for students to develop additional mentor

Funding Mechanisms

In addition to the broader issues related to data collection on graduate education and increasing funding for research on outcomes of graduate education in *Increasing Data Collection, Research, and Transparency in Graduate STEM Education* in Chapter 3, the issues facing doctoral students have additional nuance described below.

Approximately 90 percent of Ph.D. recipients in STEM fields fund their graduate education primarily through their advisor's research grants or other institutional sources (Zeiser and Kirschstein, 2014). While there is much discussion about the form of this financial support and the balance in prevalence and use of research and/or teaching assistantships versus traineeships or fellowships, overall there is little definitive information available on how student experiences and outcomes differ based on mechanisms for funding their education, how mechanisms affect students at different points in their education, whether different mechanisms have differential effects on subsets of the student population, and the requirements of funders.

For the approximately 40,000 graduate students supported by the NSF, funds are distributed as follows: 6 to 8 percent traineeships, 10 to 15 percent fellowships, and 80 percent research assistantships (NSF, 2014). NIH reports that out of nearly 109,000 graduate students in the biomedical, behavioral, social, and clinical sciences, approximately 7 percent are supported on traineeships, nearly 14 percent are on fellowships, 29 percent are on research assistantships, and 19 percent are on teaching assistantships, with the remainder supported by other means.[9] In the case of research assistantships, a student's support is tied to his or her mentor's grants and includes obligations to "assist" the principal investigator in addition to receiving training (Bersola et al., 2014; Blume-Kohout and Clack, 2013). Fellowships, on the other hand, allow for increased intellectual freedom and autonomy, which could allow greater participation in professional development outside of the discipline but may also be associated with lower levels of interaction with an advisor (Miller and Feldman, 2015).

Teaching experience can be invaluable to Ph.D. students (Connolly et al., 2015), particularly for those who wish to pursue faculty positions and those who seek to work at primarily teaching institutions. One perceived disadvantage of being supported on a teaching assistantship has been the belief that students who receive them have a longer time to degree compared to students supported on fellowships or research assistantships (Ehrenberg and Mavros, 1995). While the

---

or advisor relationships, including with professionals in industry, government laboratories, and technical societies.

- Graduate schools should provide extra-departmental mentoring and support programs.
- Graduate students should seek multiple mentors to meet their varied academic and career needs.

[9] See https://report.nih.gov/NIHDatabook/Charts/Default.aspx?showm=Y&chartId=235&catId=19 (accessed May 11, 2018).

available research reflects distinct studies focusing on specific disciplines, imply-ing that the conclusions drawn from these studies may not be generalizable to all STEM fields, the existing data do appear to refute this narrative.

According to the Longitudinal Study of Future STEM Scholars, nearly all (94.9 percent) doctoral students taught undergraduates, primarily as research mentors and teaching or lab assistants (Connolly et al., 2016, p. 1). This study found that although coursework-based teaching development programs alone did not affect students' time to degree, actual teaching experience did correlate with an increased time to degree. Other studies, however, have found that structured teaching experiences, such as the NSF Graduate STEM Fellowship in K-12 Education[10] and the University of North Carolina at Chapel Hill's BEST program, do not have longer time to degree. Moreover, students who participate in this type of program and/or serve as teaching assistants appear to be better able to generate testable hypotheses and valid research designs compared to those who serve only as research assistants (Feldon et al., 2011; Trautmann and Krasny, 2006). The reality of the graduate experience is that most students are supported on a mix of fellowships, traineeships, research assistantships, and teaching assistantships over the course of their degree programs, making it difficult to tease out the effects of these different support mechanisms.

Recommendation 3.3 on Comprehensive National and Institutional Data on Students and Graduates includes specific suggestions for additional data collec-tion, and Recommendation 3.4 on Funding for Research on Graduate STEM Edu-cation, include details on researching the effect of different funding mechanisms on STEM Ph.D. students educational and career outcomes.[11]

Diversity, Equity, and Inclusion

While the changing demographics of the pool of potential students are de-tailed in Chapter 2 and issues related to cultivating talent and preparing students from all backgrounds in graduate-level education is reviewed in Enhancing

---

[10] The NSF GK-12's last solicitation deadline was in 2010. See http://www.gk12.org/ (accessed on January 23, 2018).

[11] RECOMMENDATION 3.4—Funding for Research on Graduate STEM Education: The National Science Foundation, other federal and state agencies, and private funders of graduate STEM educa-tion should issue calls for proposals to better understand the graduate education system and outcomes of various interventions and policies, including but not limited to the effect of different models of graduate education on knowledge, competencies, mind-sets, and career outcomes.

- Funders should support research on the effect of different funding mechanisms on outcomes for doctoral students, including traineeships, fellowships, teaching and research assistantships; the effects of policies and procedures on degree completion, disaggregated by gender, race and ethnicity, and citizenship; and the effect of expanding eligibility of international students to be supported on federal fellowships and training grants.

Diversity, Equity, and Inclusion in Chapter 3, the section below features nuance and additional detail related to doctoral STEM degree programs.

Although many institutions have made vigorous efforts to recruit and include students from a wide variety of backgrounds, too many programs have continued to struggle with the creation of an *inclusive and equitable* environment that can improve chances for their academic success and degree completion. Indeed, achieving inclusion and equity may require significant additional efforts to promote full integration of scientists from all backgrounds into teaching, research, and leadership positions (Tienda, 2013). At its core, an inclusive environment not only admits students from all backgrounds through equitable admissions practices, but also ensures that the classroom, lab, and campus environments serve all students equally well throughout their education and that all students receive the mentoring and support they need to succeed in their doctoral programs (CGS, 2009).

Students from all backgrounds cannot be expected to thrive in a system that does not create an inclusive and equitable environment. Efforts to increase diversity and equity require, among other steps, making a commitment to recruiting faculty and other mentors and trainees from historically underrepresented groups. Such efforts also require changing the culture of universities so that equity and inclusion are not viewed as an "add-on," but as an integral and deeply embedded component for promoting the scientific success. NSF has funded programs and initiatives focused on addressing these issues and is also funding research to understand the efficacy of interventions. One program, ADVANCE: Increasing the Participation and Advancement of Women in Academic Science and Engineering Careers, seeks to fund projects that address the fact that women are significantly underrepresented as faculty, particularly in upper ranks, and in academic administrative positions, in almost all STEM fields.[12] The program looks at challenges in recruitment, retention, and advancement of women in STEM and focuses funding to projects developing systemic approaches to increase women's representation and advancement in academic careers, promoting gender equity strategies for all members of the academic workforce, and contributing to the field of equity research. NSF has also launched INCLUDES, a national initiative focused on broadening participation for groups historically underrepresented in STEM.[13] The initiative will fund a group of research-based collaboratives, linking individual projects for collective impact and including an emphasis on evaluation to share lessons learned from each project. Of the 69 pilot awards made in FY 2016 and FY 2017, 20 of them enhance support systems for undergraduate and graduate students.

To create and sustain an inclusive and equitable environment, universities should address institutional structures, policies, and behaviors that can contrib-

---

[12] See https://www.nsf.gov/funding/pgm_summ.jsp?pims_id=5383 (accessed March 27, 2018).

[13] See https://www.nsf.gov/news/special_reports/nsfincludes/index.jsp (accessed March 27, 2018).

ute to a hostile culture that correlates with imposter syndrome,[14] lack of cultural capital,[15] and reduced self-efficacy.[16] They also need to organize experiences in which students and faculty are encouraged to leave homogeneous peer groups and challenge themselves to think critically about their assumptions, seek out knowledge and develop informed perspectives—skills that will translate into a more favorable attitude toward collaborating with colleagues from different backgrounds. Given that each discipline, and even subdiscipline, is characterized by a different demographic profile with regard to gender, race and ethnicity, and international origin, programs should seek to use their own data iteratively to address inequities. Creating solutions within a local context at the department and program levels will be relevant for how graduate students approach career decisions and the overall graduate education experience. Best practices exist to guide the development of local solutions (Bhopal, 2017; Field et al., 2007).

Since faculty have the most direct contact with students and deeply impact perceptions and training experiences, they will need to be at the forefront of creating an inclusive and equitable culture, policies, and practices for all students, which means that they will need to learn how to improve their own cultural awareness about mentoring. Finally, programs will need to prioritize this goal for the sake of improved innovation and funding outcomes in research as well. For example, NIH is advancing policies to require mentor training for faculty as a criterion for receiving a National Institute of General Medical Sciences T32 predoctoral institutional training grant.[17] Recommendation 3.5 on Ensuring Diverse, Equitable, and Inclusive Environments includes specific actions related to improving support for students of all backgrounds.[18]

---

[14] Imposter syndrome is a form of intellectual self-doubt occurring among high achievers who are unable to internalize and accept their own success (Weir, 2013).

[15] Cultural capital in the context of graduate education can be conceptualized as the combination of academic qualifications (skills, knowledge, and value within a group) and the intersection with an individual's social background (Gazley et al., 2015).

[16] Self-efficacy refers to an individual's belief in his or her capacity to execute behaviors necessary to produce specific performance attainments (Carey and Forsyth, n.d.).

[17] See https://researchtraining.nih.gov/programs/training-grants/T32 (accessed May 6, 2018).

[18] RECOMMENDATION 3.5—Ensuring Diverse, Equitable, and Inclusive Environments: The graduate STEM education enterprise should enable students of all backgrounds, including but not limited to racial and ethnic background, gender, stage of life, culture, socioeconomic status, disability, sexual orientation, gender identity, and nationality, to succeed by implementing practices that create an equitable and inclusive institutional environment.

- Faculty and administrators involved in graduate education should develop, adopt, and regularly evaluate a suite of strategies to accelerate increasing diversity and improving equity and inclusion, including comprehensive recruitment, holistic review in admissions, and interventions to prevent attrition in the late stages of progress toward a degree.
- Faculty should cultivate their individual professional development skills to advance their abilities to improve educational culture and environments on behalf of students.

REFERENCES

AAU (Association of American Universities). 1998. *AAU Committee on Graduate Education: Report and recommendations*. Washington, DC: AAU. Available: https://www.aau.edu/sites/default/files/AAU%20Files/AAU%20Documents/GradEdRpt.pdf (accessed March 17, 2018).

Alberts, B., M. W. Kirschner, S. Tilghman, and H. Varmus. 2014. Rescuing U.S. biomedical research from its systemic flaws. *Proceedings of the National Academy of Sciences of the United States of America* 111(16):5773-5777.

Bersola, S. H., E. B. Stolzenberg, J. Love, and K. Fosnacht. 2014. Understanding admitted doctoral students' institutional choices: Student experience versus faculty and staff perceptions. *American Journal of Education* 120(4):515-543.

Bhopal, K. 2017. Addressing racial inequalities in higher education: Equity, inclusion and social justice. *Ethnic and Racial Studies* 40(13):2293-2299.

BLS (U.S. Bureau of Labor Statistics). 2013. Occupational employment projections to 2022. *Monthly Labor Review*. Available: https://www.bls.gov/opub/mlr/2013/article/ occupational-employment-projections-to-2022.htm (accessed March 26, 2018).

Blume-Kohout, M. E., and J. W. Clack. 2013. Are graduate students rational? Evidence from the market for biomedical scientists. *PloS ONE* 8(12):e82759.

Bowen, B., and N. Rudenstine. 1992. *In pursuit of the PhD*. Princeton, NJ: Princeton University Press.

Carey, M. P., and A. D. Forsyth. n.d. Self-efficacy. Teaching Tip Sheet, American Psychlogical Association. Available: http://www.apa.org/pi/aids/resources/education/self-efficacy.aspx (accessed on January 23, 2018).

Connolly, M. R., Y. G. Lee, and L. Hill. 2015. *Why STEM doctoral students participate in teaching development programs*. LSFSS Brief Series, No. 7. Madison: Wisconsin Center for Education Research, University of Wisconsin–Madison.

Connolly, M. R., J. N. Savoy, Y. G. Lee, and L. B. Hill. 2016. *Building a better future STEM faculty: How doctoral teaching programs can improve undergraduate education*. Madison: Wisconsin Center for Education Research, University of Wisconsin–Madison.

CGS (Council of Graduate Schools). 2009. *Ph.D. completion and attrition: Findings from exit surveys of PhD completers*. Washington, DC: CGS.

Cyranoski, D., N. Gilbert, H. Ledford, A. Nayar, and M. Yahia. 2011. Education: The PhD factory. *Nature* 472(7343):276-279.

Denecke, D., K. Feaster, and K. Stone. 2017. *Professional development: Shaping effective programs for STEM graduate students*. Washington, DC: Council of Graduate Schools.

Ehrenberg, R. G., and P. G. Mavros. 1995. Do doctoral students' financial support patterns affect their times-to-degree and completion probabilities. *Journal of Human Resources* 30(3):581-609.

Fagan, A. P., and K. M. Suedkamp Wells. 2004. The 2000 National Doctoral Program Survey: An on-line study of students' voices. In *Paths to the professoriate: Strategies for enriching the preparation of future faculty*, edited by D. H. Wulff and A. E. Austin. San Francisco: Josey-Bass, pp. 74-91.

- Institutions, national laboratories, professional societies, and research organizations should develop comprehensive strategies that use evidence-based models and programs and include measures to evaluate outcomes to ensure a diverse, equitable, and inclusive environment.
- Institutions should develop comprehensive strategies for recruiting and retaining faculty and mentors from demographic groups historically underrepresented in academia.
- Federal and state agencies, universities, professional societies, and nongovernmental organizations that rate institutions should embed diversity and inclusion metrics in their criteria.
- Federal and state funding agencies and private funders that support graduate education and training should adjust their award policies and funding criteria to include policies that incentivize diversity, equity, and inclusion and include accountability measures through reporting mechanisms.

Feldon, D. F., J. Peugh, B. E. Timmerman, M. A. Maher, M. Hurst, D. Strickland, J. A. Gilmore, and C. Stiegelmeyer. 2011. Graduate students' teaching experiences improve their methodological research skills. *Science* 333(6045):1037-1039.

Ferrini-Mundy, J. 2013. Science education. Driven by diversity. *Science* 340(6130):278.

Field, S., M. Kuczera, and B. Pont. 2007. *No more failures: Ten steps to equity in education.* Paris: Organisation for Economic Co-operation and Development

Fuhrmann, C. N., D. G. Halme, P. S. O'Sullivan, and B. Lindstaedt. 2011. Improving graduate education to support a branching career pipeline: Recommendations based on a survey of doctoral students in the basic biomedical sciences. *CBE—Life Sciences Education* 10(3):239-249.

Gamse, B., W. C Smith, A. Parsad, J. Dreier, K. Neishi, J. Carney, L. Caswell, E. Breaux, T. McCall, and J. Spader. 2010. *Evaluation of the National Science Foundation's GK-12 program.* Cambridge, MA: Abt Associates, Inc.

Gardner, S. K. 2009. Student and faculty attributions of high and low-completing doctoral programs in the United States. *Higher Education* 58(1):97-112.

Gazley, J. L., R. Remich, M. E. Naffziger-Hirsch, J. Keller, P. B. Campbell, and R. McGee.2014, Beyond preparation: Identity, cultural capital, and readiness for graduate school in the biomedical sciences. *Journal of Research in Science Teaching* 51(8):1021-1048.

Gibbs, K. D., Jr., and K. A. Griffin. 2013. What do I want to be with my PhD? The roles of personal values and structural dynamics in shaping the career interests of recent biomedical science PhD graduates. *CBE—Life Sciences Education* 12(4):711-723.

Gibbs, K. D., Jr., J. McGready, J. C. Bennett, and K. Griffin. 2014. Biomedical science Ph.D. career interest patterns by race/ethnicity and gender. *PloS ONE* 9(12):e114736.

Gibbs, K. D., Jr., J. McGready, and K. Griffin. 2015. Career development among American biomedical postdocs. *CBE—Life Sciences Education* 14(4):ar44.

Golde, C. M., and T. M. Dore. 2001. *At cross purposes: What the experiences of today's doctoral students reveal about doctoral education.* Philadelphia: Pew Charitable Trusts.

Graduate Assembly. 2014. *Graduate student happiness & well-being.* Berkeley: University of California.

Green, M. 2015. Thanks for listening. *Chronicle of Higher Education,* October 19. Available: http://www.chronicle.com/article/Thanks-for-Listening/233825 (accessed October 13, 2017).

Hakkarainen, K., K. Hytönen, J. Makkonen, and E. Lehtinen. 2016. Extending collective practices of doctoral education from natural to educational sciences. *Studies in Higher Education* 41(1):63-78.

Janke, E. M., and C. L. Colbeck. 2008. Lost in translation: Learning professional roles through the situated curriculum. *New Directions for Teaching and Learning* (113):57-68.

Laursen, S. L., H. Thiry, and C. Liston. 2012. The impact of a university-based school science outreach program on graduate student participants' career paths and professional socialization. *Journal of Higher Education Outreach and Engagement* 16(2):47-78.

Levecque, K., F. Anseel, A. De Beuckelaer, J. Van der Heyden, and L. Gisle. 2017. Work organization and mental health problems in PhD students. *Research Policy* 46(4):868-879.

Loshbaugh, J. G., S. L. Laursen, and H. Thiry. 2011. Reactions to changing times: Trends and tensions in U.S. chemistry graduate education. *Journal of Chemical Education* 88:708-715.

Lovitts, B. E. 2004. Research on the structure and process of graduate education: Retaining students. In *Paths to the professorship: Strategies for enriching the preparation of future faculty,* edited by D. H. Wulff and A. E. Austin. San Francisco: Josey-Bass, pp. 115-136.

Miller, J. M., and M. P. Feldman. 2015. Isolated in the lab: Examining dissatisfaction with postdoctoral appointments. *Journal of Higher Education* 86(5):697-724.

Misra, M., and J. Lundquist. 2016. *The sandwiched midcareer faculty mentor. Inside Higher Ed,* March 10. Available: https://www.insidehighered.com/advice/2016/03/10/how-midcareer-faculty-members-can-find-time-mentoring-essay (accessed October 13, 2017).

Mollica, M., and L. Nemeth. 2014. Outcomes and characteristics of faculty/student mentorships in PhD programs. *American Journal of Educational Research* 2(9):703-708.

Museus, S. D., and D. Liverman. 2010. High-performing institutions and their implications for studying underrepresented minority students in STEM. *New Directions for Institutional Research* 2010(148):17-27.

NAS/NAE/IOM (National Academy of Sciences, National Academy of Engineering, and Institute of Medicine). 1995. *Reshaping the graduate education of scientists and engineers.* Washington, DC: The National Academy Press.

Nerad, M., E. Rudd, E. Morrison, and L. Homer. 2006. Confronting common assumptions: Designing future-oriented doctoral education. Paper read at Doctoral Education and the Faculty of the Future, October 8-9, 2006, Ithaca, NY.

NRC (National Research Council). 1995. *Research doctorate programs in the United States: Continuity and change.* Washington DC: National Academy Press.

NRC. 2014. *Convergence: Facilitating transdisciplinary integration of life sciences, physical sciences, engineering, and beyond.* Washington, DC: The National Academies Press.

NSB (National Science Board). 2018. *Science and engineering indicators 2018.* Arlington, VA: National Science Foundation.

NSF (National Science Foundation). 2014. *NSF FY 2015 budget request.* Arlington, VA: National Science Foundation.

Nyquist, J. 2002. The Ph.D.: A tapestry of change for the 21st century. *Change* 34(6):13-20.

O'Leary, D. P. 2016. *Graduate study in the computer and mathematical sciences: A survival manual.* Available: https://www.cs.umd.edu/~oleary/gradstudy/node5.html (accessed October 15, 2017).

O'Meara, K., K. Knudsen, and J. Jones. 2013. The role of emotional competencies in faculty-doctoral student relationships. *Review of Higher Education* 36(3):315-347.

Page, S. E. 2008. *The difference: How the power of diversity creates better groups, firms, schools, and societies.* Princeton, NJ: Princeton University Press.

Paglis, L. L., S. G. Green, and T. N. Bauer. 2006. Does advisor mentoring add value? A longitudinal study of mentoring and doctoral student outcomes. *Research in Higher Education* 47(7):451-476.

Pinheiro, D. L., J. Melkers, and S. Newton. 2017. Take me where I want to go: Institutional prestige, advisor sponsorship, and academic career placement preferences. *PloS ONE* 12(5):e0176977.

Roach, M., and H. Sauermann. 2017. The declining interest in an academic career. *PloS ONE* 12(9):e0184130.

Sauermann, H., and M. Roach. 2012. Science PhD career preferences: Levels, changes, and advisor encouragement. *PloS ONE* 7(5):e36307.

Schillebeeckx, M., B. Maricque, and C. Lewis. 2013. The missing piece to changing the university culture. *Nature Biotechnology* 31(10):938-941.

Taylor, C. 2006. Heeding the voices of graduate students and postdocs. In *Envisioning the future of doctoral education: Preparing stewards of the discipline. Carnegie essays on the doctorate,* edited by C. M. Golde and G. E. Walker. San Francisco: Jossey-Bass, pp. 46-54.

Tienda, M. 2013. Diversity ≠ inclusion: Promoting integration in higher education. *Educational Researcher* 42(9):467-475.

Trautmann, N. M., and M. E. Krasny. 2006. Integrating teaching and research: A new model for graduate education? *Bioscience* 56(2):159-165.

Weir, K. 2013. Feel like a fraud? *gradPSYCH* 11(4):24-27. Available: http://www.apa.org/gradpsych/2013/11/fraud.aspx (accessed January 23, 2018).

Wendler, C., B. Bridgeman, R. Markle, F. Cline, N. Bell, P. McAllisterm, and J. Kent. 2012. *Pathways through graduate school and into careers.* Princeton, NJ: Educational Testing Service.

Xue, Y., and R. Larson. 2015. STEM crisis or stem surplus? Yes and yes. *Monthly Labor Review.* Available: https://www.bls.gov/opub/mlr/2015/article/stem-crisis-or-stem-surplus-yes-and-yes.htm (accessed January 22, 2018).

Zeiser, K. L., and R. Kirschstein. 2014. *Who pays for the doctorate? A tale of two PhDs.* Washington, DC: American Institutes for Research.

6

A Call for Systemic Change

The committee envisions a 21st-century U.S. graduate science, technology, engineering, and mathematics (STEM) education system that builds on the substantial strengths of the current system but better meets the evolving needs of its students, the scientific enterprise, and the nation. That vision is outlined in the next section. Achieving it will require a clear commitment and changes in both policies and practices throughout the system, as well as focused actions by every stakeholder.

Achieving what the committee sees as an ideal, modern graduate STEM education will require substantial cultural change throughout the system. As discussed throughout this report, the system must become more student-centric and must increase the value it places on best practices of mentorship and advising. The value placed on educating students at the master's level must be increased. The mind-set that seems to be most valued for preparing students at the Ph.D. level for academic research careers must be readjusted to recognize that some of the best students will not pursue academic research but will enter careers in other sectors, such as industry or government.

These cultural changes will come about only if there are changes in the incentive system that appears to drive so much of academia. The current system is heavily weighted toward rewarding faculty for research output in the form of publications and the number of future scientists produced. It must be realigned to increase the relative rewards for effective teaching, mentoring, and advising. Unless faculty behavior can be changed—and changing the incentive system is critical in that regard—the system will not change.

The committee recognizes that these cultural changes will inevitably have costs associated with them but did not attempt to estimate what they might be, since that was not within the committee's statement of task. However, despite any costs, the changes advocated in this report must be achieved. Without such a unified commitment to continue the legacy of excellence in the system, the United States may not unlock the full potential of discovery to power its economy, protect its national interests, and lead the world in addressing the grand challenges of the 21st century.

To make clear the part each stakeholder must play to achieve its vision, the committee lists in this chapter the actions recommended in this report for each participant in the system: state and federal government agencies; private foundations and other nongovernmental organizations; institutions of higher education; faculty; employers in industry, government, and other organizations; professional societies; and students themselves, who are to be the focus of the graduate education system of the future.

AN IDEAL GRADUATE STEM EDUCATION

Implementing the recommendations in this report would produce a U.S. graduate STEM education system that enables graduate students of all backgrounds to meet the highest standards of excellence in 21st-century STEM fields, and to use their knowledge and sophistication across the full range of occupations essential to address global societal needs using science- and technology-informed decision making. These recommendations build on the current strengths of the graduate STEM enterprise, urging careful attention to core educational elements and learning objectives—one set for the master's degree and another for the Ph.D.—that are common across all STEM fields. However, many of the recommendations in this report are also intended to stimulate review and revision of incentive and reward policies, teaching and mentoring practices, and curricular offerings. They may also lead to the expansion of career exploration mechanisms and transparency about trainee outcomes that can inform career paths for students.

Importantly, this report also calls for a shift from the current system that focuses primarily on the needs of institutions of higher education and those of the research enterprise itself to one which is *student centered*, placing greater emphasis and focus on graduate students as individuals with diverse needs and challenges. An ideal, student-centered STEM graduate education system would include several attributes that are currently lacking in many academic institutions. In an ideal STEM graduate education system:

- Prospective graduate students would be able to select their graduate program aided by fully transparent, easily accessible data about costs incurred and viable career pathways and successes of previous students, at the level of the institution and its departments.
- Students would acquire broad technical literacy coupled with deep specialization in an area of interest. They would acquire the core competen-

cies outlined in Chapters 3 and 4. As they acquire this knowledge base, students would have multiple opportunities to understand better and to learn to consider ethical issues associated with their work, as well as the broader implications of their work for society.

- Students from all backgrounds would fully participate and achieve their greatest potential during their educational experience through transparent institutional action to enhance diversity and promote inclusive and equitable learning environments.
- Students would encounter a variety of points of view about the nature, scope, and substance of the scientific enterprise and about the relationships among science, engineering, and society, and they would be encouraged to understand and grapple with differences of opinion, experiences, and ideas as part of their graduate education and training.
- Students would have opportunities to communicate the results of their work and to understand the broader impacts of their research. This includes the ability to present their work and have exposure to audiences outside of their department, ranging from peers in other departments to the broader scientific community and nontechnical audiences. Students would also understand and learn to consider ethical and cultural issues surrounding their work, as well as the broader needs of society.
- Students would be encouraged to create their own project-based learning opportunities—ideally as a member of a team—as a means of developing transferable professional skills such as communication, collaboration, management, and entrepreneurship. Experiences where students "learn by doing," rather than simply learn by lecturing and coursework, would be the norm.
- Students would be encouraged and given time, resources, and space to explore diverse career options, perhaps through courses, seminars, internships, and other kinds of real-life experiences. While some institutions have launched such programs, they should become universal, albeit sensitive to the specific contexts of individual institutions. For example, students clearly interested in future faculty positions might have the opportunity to teach undergraduates from a variety of institutions, from community colleges to research-based universities. Those students wishing to compete for research-intensive university positions would be advised about appropriate postdoctoral positions and the track records of those universities and/or specific faculty members in placing such individuals in faculty positions. Students with potential interests in nonacademic careers would be provided with opportunities to attend workshops and seminars about jobs in a wide range of industries, nonprofit organizations, and government, together with opportunities for placements in nonacademic job settings. Internships with corporations, government agencies, or nonprofit employers during summer months or the school year would become

the norm rather than the exception for graduate students seeking careers outside of academia. Institutions would seek corporate and foundation funding to support such learning experiences.

- Graduate programs and departments would develop more efficient channels for students to communicate with the administration and faculty regarding processes and decisions within the department and the graduate school that affect graduate student education. These channels would facilitate communication in both directions, offering students mechanisms to provide feedback and giving administrators and faculty a better understanding of the student perspectives on issues important to them.
- Graduate programs would develop course offerings and other tools to enable student career exploration and to expose students to career options. Faculty advisors would encourage students to explore career options broadly and would not stigmatize those who favor careers outside of academia.
- Institutions would help students identify advisors and mentors who can best support their academic and career development.
- Institutions would provide faculty with training, resources, and time both to improve their own skills as mentors and to provide for quality mentoring and advising to the graduate students they supervise directly, as well as other students in their departments or from across the institution, as appropriate. Training would provide the mentors with strategies for navigating relationships in which goals and identities (cultural or demographic differences, career aspirations) may differ between mentor and mentee, and mentoring would center on the goals set jointly by the student and mentors and provide strategies for navigating relationships in which goals may differ between supervisor and student. The training would consider the various challenges faculty face at various stages of their own careers. For example, early career faculty who are in the process of establishing themselves in a department with a research group or laboratory may require a primer on best practices for becoming a mentor and advisor. Long-tenured faculty might benefit from periodic refreshers to explore new skills or techniques in supporting student success. Institutions would provide opportunities for students to seek and develop multiple separate mentoring and advising relationships, including those that are interdisciplinary and cross departments. Institutions would also reward faculty for their accomplishments as mentors and advisors.

FEDERAL AND STATE GOVERNMENT AGENCIES

Federal and state governments provide a substantial fraction of the funding for the U.S. scientific enterprise and its graduate STEM education system. For that reason, their funding policies have dramatic effects on the behavior of grantees. In fact, diverse stakeholders in a variety of settings made the argument to the committee that government policies in many ways are responsible for the incentives that drive so much institutional and faculty behavior. Thus, for the system changes recommended in this report to come about, funding policies issued by federal and state government agencies must be aligned with the goals articulated here.

- Federal and state funding agencies should require institutions that receive support for graduate education to develop policies that require data collection on a number of metrics, including but not limited to demographics, funding mechanisms, and career outcomes, on current students and alumni at regular intervals for 15 years after graduation. Institutions should make these data available to qualify for traineeships, fellowships, and research assistantships.
- Federal agencies, such as the National Science Foundation, and state agencies that fund graduate STEM education should issue calls for proposals to better understand the graduate education system and outcomes of various interventions and policies, including but not limited to: the effect of different funding mechanisms on outcomes for doctoral students; studies on career outcomes related to master's students; the ways to integrate master's students into the STEM workforce and research and development ecosystem; the effect of expanding eligibility of international students to be supported on federal fellowships and training grants; and the effect of different models of graduate education on knowledge, competencies, mind-sets, and career outcomes.
- Federal and state funding agencies should align their policies and award criteria to ensure that students in the programs they support experience the kind of graduate education outlined in this report and achieve the scientific and professional competencies articulated here, whether they are on training or research grant mechanisms.
- Federal and state agencies should embed diversity and inclusion metrics in their funding criteria. They should also adjust their grant award policies and funding criteria to include policies that incentivize diversity, equity, and inclusion, and they should include accountability measures through reporting mechanisms.
- Federal and state funding agencies that support or conduct education research should support studies on how different STEM disciplines can integrate the changing scientific enterprise into graduate education programs and curricula.
- Federal and state agencies that support graduate education should require STEM doctoral students to create and update annually individual development plans in consultation with faculty advisors to map educational goals, career exploration, and professional development.

PRIVATE FOUNDATIONS AND OTHER NONGOVERNMENTAL ORGANIZATIONS

In addition to the government funding agencies, private funding organizations play a pivotal role in promoting innovation and research in graduate STEM education, from supporting research directly to funding internships and fellowships, curriculum development, and other programs.

- Private funders of graduate STEM education should issue calls for proposals to better understand the graduate education system and outcomes of various interventions and policies, including but not limited to the effect of different funding mechanisms on outcomes for doctoral students; the effect of expanding eligibility of international students to be supported on federal fellowships and training grants; and the effect of different models of graduate education on knowledge, competencies, mind-sets, and career outcomes.
- Nongovernmental organizations that rate institutions should embed diversity and inclusion metrics in their criteria.
- Private funders of graduate education should adjust their grant award policies and funding criteria to include policies that incentivize diversity, equity, and inclusion and include accountability measures through reporting mechanisms.
- Private foundations that support or conduct education research should support studies on how different STEM disciplines can integrate the changing scientific enterprise into graduate education programs and curricula.
- Nongovernmental organizations should convene and lead discussions among stakeholders and disseminate innovative models, practices, and approaches in graduate STEM education.
- Private foundations that support graduate education should require STEM doctoral students to create and to update annually individual development plans in consultation with faculty advisors to map educational goals, career exploration, and professional development.

INSTITUTIONS OF HIGHER EDUCATION

Many colleges and universities have programs and existing commitments that align with the recommendations made in this report, but the continued excellence of the U.S. graduate STEM education system hinges upon the collective movement of all departments, programs, and institutions. The ways in which institutions reward faculty, collect data, and engage with students are central tenets of graduate STEM education. This report acknowledges the work many institutions have already taken to address the actions below. Not until all institutions act in this way, however, will there be a system of graduate education that ensures that all students have the support and educational experiences needed to fully develop their capacities for research, collaboration, and critical thinking and for success in their STEM careers. Going forward, institutions should

- Verify that every graduate program they offer provides for the master's and Ph.D. core competencies outlined in this report and that students demonstrate they have achieved them before receiving their degrees.
- Increase priority for and reward faculty that demonstrate high-quality teaching and inclusive mentoring practices for all graduate students based on the results of restructured evaluations.
- Require faculty and postdoctoral researchers, who have extensive contact with graduate students, to undergo training, provided by those institutions, to learn evidence-based and inclusive teaching and mentoring practices.
- Integrate professional development opportunities, including relevant course offerings and internships, into graduate curriculum design.
- Develop a uniform, scalable, and sustainable model for data collection that can operate beyond the period of extramural funding. The data collection should occur on a regular basis and follow standard definitions that correspond with national STEM education and workforce surveys to help inform benchmarking or higher education research. Key data elements to be collected include master's degree and Ph.D. completion rates, time to degree, and career outcomes and paths of their graduates spanning 15 years, disaggregated to the extent possible by demographics, including gender, race and ethnicity, and visa status.
- Develop comprehensive strategies that use evidence-based models and programs and include measures to evaluate outcomes to ensure a diverse, equitable, and inclusive environment.
- Administer periodic cultural climate surveys of graduate students at the departmental level to assess their well-being in the aggregate and make adjustments when problems are identified.
- Take extra steps to make available and advertise effective mental health services, such as those already available to veterans and most undergraduate students, at no-cost to graduate students.
- Establish criteria and update characteristics of the doctoral research project and dissertation preparation and format, in collaboration with professional societies and higher education associations.
- Develop comprehensive strategies for recruiting and retaining faculty and mentors from demographic groups historically underrepresented in academia.

GRADUATE SCHOOLS, DEPARTMENTS, AND PROGRAMS

The department is the primary organizational unit on campus. It serves as the primary affiliation for most faculty and students, serving as a key connection to a researcher's identity within his or her field of research. Within the broader academic institutions, graduate schools work with the departments to help address governance and policy issues, to support faculty and students with concerns that rise above the level of the department, and to leverage resources to provide services at scale. These two levels of a university represent key drivers of change within an institution. To achieve the kind of STEM graduate education system outlined in this report, graduate programs should

- Facilitate mentor relationship between the graduate student and the primary research advisors and create opportunities for students to develop additional mentor or advisor relationships with faculty both within and outside of their home department.
- Provide extra-departmental mentoring and support programs and encourage doctoral students to involve dissertation committees more extensively in advising and mentoring.
- Scrutinize their curricula and program requirements for features that lie outside of the core competencies and learning objectives and that may be adding time to degree without providing value to Ph.D. students, such as a first-author publication requirement, and eliminate those features or requirements.
- Review and modify curricula, dissertation requirements, and capstone projects to ensure timeliness and alignment with the ways relevant work is conducted on a periodic basis, and to provide students with opportunities to work in teams that promote multidisciplinary learning.
- Collect and make widely available information about master's degree and Ph.D. completion rates, time to degree, and career outcomes and paths of their graduates spanning 15 years, disaggregated to the extent possible by demographics, including gender, race and ethnicity, and visa status.
- Post publicly how their programs reflect the core competencies for master's and doctoral students, including the milestones and metrics they use in evaluation and assessment.
- Engage in discussions with professional societies, nonprofit organizations, employers, and other stakeholders to disseminate innovative approaches and to receive feedback on how to align graduate curricula and other educational experiences with changes in the nature of science and engineering activity and of STEM careers.
- Incorporate full awareness of mental health issues into the training experience for both students and faculty, and assess services to ensure that they are meeting the needs of graduate students.
- Develop, adopt, and regularly evaluate a suite of strategies to accelerate increasing diversity and improving equity and inclusion, including comprehensive recruitment, holistic review in admissions, and interventions to prevent attrition in the late stages of progress toward a degree.

- Encourage students to engage as a group in activities and experiences outside of traditional academic settings as a means of increasing feelings of inclusion and normalizing feelings associated with negative phenomena, such as imposter syndrome, that can reduce productivity and success in the training experience and extend time to degree.
- Allow students to have an active and collaborative voice to advocate for, and proactively engage in, practices that support holistic academic and social development and that allow students to provide feedback on their experiences.

FACULTY MEMBERS

Faculty play a, if not *the*, central role in fostering the next generation of STEM professionals through their roles as educators, mentors, and advisors. They are what one might consider the "front line" of graduate education. The relationships that graduate students develop with faculty members help shape their interests, build their professional networks, and spark their growth as scientists, technologists, engineers, and mathematicians. Most faculty invest considerable time and resources supporting the development of students, and the recommendations that follow provide details on the ways in which all faculty can ensure that the time spent with students benefits all parties to the fullest extent possible. This list includes some substantial changes in the way some faculty regard and interact with graduate students. The committee recognizes that expecting such changes in faculty behavior will not be possible unless there are broader cultural changes in the entire graduate education system, and that these changes will not be expressed at the faculty level unless the academic incentive system is adjusted as discussed in this report. To play their part in the modernization of the graduate STEM education system, faculty should

- Review and modify curricula, dissertation requirements, and capstone projects to ensure timeliness and alignment with the ways relevant work is conducted on a periodic basis, and to provide students with opportunities to work in teams that promote multidisciplinary learning.
- Develop, adopt, and regularly evaluate a suite of strategies to accelerate increasing diversity and improving equity and inclusion, including comprehensive recruitment, holistic review in admissions, and interventions to prevent late-stage attrition.
- Foster understanding of how to support and engage with students requiring or seeking mental health services and take action when appropriate.
- Use evidence-based and inclusive teaching and mentoring practices for graduate students.
- Cultivate their individual professional development skills to advance their

abilities to improve the educational culture and environment on behalf of students.

- For those who serve as primary research mentors, review their mentees' individual development plans on an annual basis to help students map educational goals, career exploration, and professional development to help students acquire the core competencies, as outlined in this report for master's or doctoral students.
- Discuss with students their areas of interest, educational and professional goals, and potential career paths.
- Discuss with their students, undergraduates interested in graduate education or current graduate students, whether and how a master's or Ph.D. degree will advance the students' long-term educational and career goals.

PROFESSIONAL SOCIETIES

Use of the acronym STEM can appear to flatten the distinctions among fields, but each discipline has its own unique culture, opportunities, and challenges. The professional societies have important roles to play in shaping graduate STEM education in their disciplines by developing appropriate implementation strategies and connecting students, institutions, faculty, and employers with existing resources. To support the recommendations made in this report, professional societies should

- Develop comprehensive strategies that use evidence-based models and programs and include measures to evaluate outcomes to ensure a diverse, equitable, and inclusive environment.
- Convene and lead discussions with those who employ STEM master's and Ph.D. holders, along with other stakeholders, to develop and disseminate innovative approaches to STEM graduate training.
- Participate in and support studies on how different STEM disciplines can integrate the changing scientific enterprise into graduate education programs and curricula.
- Engage with institutions, departments, and students to design and to provide resources on professional and career development.
- Collaborate with other sectors to create programs that help graduate students make the transition into a variety of careers.
- Work with universities and higher education associations to establish criteria and update characteristics of the doctoral research project and dissertation preparation and format.

EMPLOYERS IN INDUSTRY, GOVERNMENT, AND OTHER ORGANIZATIONS

With more students graduating with master's and doctoral degrees in STEM fields, industry, government, and nonprofit employers could tap into a growing pool of highly trained applicants. These stakeholders face the same questions as institutions of higher education with regard to building diverse and inclusive environments, addressing national and global challenges, and driving the frontiers of discovery. They also may seek particular skills in STEM graduates. As such, they develop partnerships with universities and students themselves to communicate their needs and support programs that may advance those skills.

- National laboratories and other research organizations should develop comprehensive strategies that use evidence-based models and programs and include measures to evaluate outcomes to ensure a diverse, equitable, and inclusive environment.
- Employers from all sectors, as key stakeholders in graduate STEM education, should engage with graduate programs, employers, and other stakeholders to provide feedback on how to align graduate curricula and other educational experiences with changes in the nature of science and engineering activity and of STEM careers.
- Industry, nonprofit, government, and other employers should provide guidance and financial support for relevant course offerings at institutions and provide internships and other forms of professional experiences to students and recent graduates.

GRADUATE STUDENTS

While many other stakeholders have more power to change the graduate STEM education system, prospective and current students still play a critical role in driving change. They can and should seek out an education experience that best fits their goals and need to take initiative in shaping their own educations. The committee urges students to use the recommendations in this report as a resource and a guide to help determine their educational experience and advocate for improvements. To seek the ideal graduate education, current and prospective graduate students should

- Discuss with their advisors how a master's or a Ph.D. degree will advance their long-term educational and career goals, including how to explore opportunities within a graduate program to gain the knowledge and competencies needed to pursue their career interests.
- Use a range of data, from national datasets on graduate education and workforce trends to department-level data on current students and alumni,

to inform graduate program selection, educational goal development, and career exploration.

- Seek multiple mentors to meet their varied academic and career needs, such as information about potential career paths and employers.
- Learn how to apply their expertise in a variety of professional contexts and seek guidance from faculty, research mentors, and advisors on strategies to gain work-related experience while enrolled in graduate school.
- Engage in group activities and experiences outside of traditional academic settings to increase feelings of inclusion and to normalize feelings associated with negative phenomena, such as imposter syndrome, that can reduce productivity and success in the training experience and extend time to degree.
- Create an individual development plan that includes the core competencies, as outlined in this report for master's or doctoral degrees, as a key feature of their own learning and career goals and that utilizes the resources provided by their university and relevant professional societies. Students should update these plans annually in consultation with faculty advisors to map educational goals, career exploration, and professional development.
- Communicate with graduate faculty and deans to encourage the implementation of practices that support holistic research training and diverse career outcomes and provide feedback on their experiences.
- Seek opportunities to work in cross-disciplinary and cross-sector teams that promote multidisciplinary learning during their graduate education and via extracurricular activities.

Appendixes

A

Glossary

Adviser is frequently referred to in the context of graduate education as a research adviser. While adviser and mentor are sometimes used interchangeably, the National Academies report, *Adviser, Teacher, Role Model, Friend: On Being a Mentor to Students in Science and Engineering,* highlights some key differences between the roles: "A fundamental difference between mentoring and advising is more than advising; mentoring is a personal, as well as, professional relationship. An adviser might or might not be a mentor, depending on the quality of the relationship" (NAS/NAE/IOM, 1997, p. 1).

Convergence is an approach to problem solving that integrates expertise from life sciences with physical, mathematical, and computational sciences, medicine, and engineering to form comprehensive synthetic frameworks that merge areas of knowledge from multiple fields to address specific challenges (NRC, 2014).

Disciplinarity refers to a particular branch of learning or body of knowledge whose defining elements—such as objects and subjects of study, phenomena, assumptions, epistemology, concepts, theories, and methods—distinguish it from other knowledge formations. Biology and chemistry, for example, are separate domains typically segmented into departments in academic institutions (NRC, 2014).

Diversity "in science refers to cultivating talent and promoting the full inclusion of excellence across the social spectrum. This includes people from backgrounds that are traditionally underrepresented and those from backgrounds that are traditionally well represented." In terms of dimensions to consider for diversity, those characteristics include, but are not limited to, national origin, language, race, color, disability, ethnicity, gender, age, religion, sexual orientation, gender identity, socioeconomic status, veteran status, educational background, and family structures (Gibbs, 2014).

Education (see also Training) refers to activities that enhance knowledge and understanding, typically on a broader scale.

Equity is the fair treatment, access, opportunity, and advancement for all people, while at the same time striving to identify and eliminate barriers that have prevented the full participation of some groups. Improving equity involves increasing justice and fairness within the procedures and processes of institutions or systems, as well as in their distribution of resources (Kapila et al., 2016).

Fellowships are defined as awards that are made to U.S. graduate students in National Science Foundation-supported science, technology, engineering, and mathematics disciplines who are pursuing research-based master's and doctoral degrees at accredited U.S. institutions.[1]

Gender equity refers to the different needs, preferences, and interests of women and men. This may mean that different treatment is needed to ensure equality of opportunity. This is often referred to as substantive equality (or equality of results) and requires considering the realities of women's and men's lives (WHO, 2018).

The Graduate Students and Postdoctorates in Science and Engineering survey is an annual census of all U.S. academic institutions granting research-based master's degrees or doctorates in science, engineering, and selected health fields as of fall of the survey year. The survey, sponsored by the National Science Foundation and the National Institutes of Health, collects the total number of graduate students, postdoctoral appointees, and doctorate-level nonfaculty researchers by demographic and other characteristic such as source of financial support.

Historically underrepresented minority groups in STEM (URM) include women, persons with disabilities, and three racial and ethnic groups—blacks, Hispanics, and American Indians or Alaska Natives (NCSES, 2017).

Impostor syndrome is a specific form of intellectual self-doubt. Impostor feelings are generally accompanied by anxiety and, often, depression (Weir, 2013).

---

[1] See https://www.nsfgrfp.org/ (accessed May 8, 2018).

Inclusion is defined as a culture that connects each employee to the organization; encourages collaboration, flexibility, and fairness; and leverages diversity throughout the organization so that all individuals are able to participate and contribute to their full potential (NSF, 2011).

Interdisciplinary research is a mode of research by teams or individuals that integrates information, data, techniques, tools, perspectives, concepts, and/or theories from two or more disciplines or bodies of specialized knowledge to advance fundamental understanding or to solve problems whose solutions are beyond the scope of a single discipline or area of research practice (NAS/NAE/IOM, 2005).

Massive open online course (MOOC) is defined as a course of study made available over the Internet without charge to a very large number of people.[2]

Mentoring is a collaborative learning relationship that proceeds through purposeful stages over time and has the primary goal of helping mentees acquire the essential competencies needed for success in their chosen career (Pfund et al., 2016).

Micro-credentialing is an opportunity for individuals to demonstrate competency in a specialty area, typically through engagement with a MOOC (Sullivan, 2016).

Multidisciplinarity juxtaposes two or more disciplines focused on a question, problem, topic, or theme. Juxtaposition fosters wider information, knowledge, and methods, but disciplines remain separate and the existing structure of knowledge is not questioned. Individuals and even members of a team working on a common problem such as environmental sustainability or a public health initiative would work separately, and their results typically would be issued separately or compiled in encyclopedic alignment rather than synthesized (NRC, 2014).

The National Center for Science and Engineering Statistics (NCSES), formerly the Division of Science Resources Statistics, was established within the National Science Foundation by Section 505 of the America COMPETES Reauthorization Act of 2010. The name signals the central role of NCSES in the collection, interpretation, analysis, and dissemination of objective data on the science and engineering enterprise. As 1 of 13 federal statistical agencies, NCSES designs, supports, and directs periodic national surveys and performs a variety of other data collections and research.[3]

---

[2] See https://en.oxforddictionaries.com/definition/mooc (accessed May 8, 2018).
[3] See https://www.nsf.gov/statistics/about-ncses.cfm#core (accessed May 8, 2018).

Research assistantships are a financial award given to a graduate student where most of the student's responsibilities are devoted primarily to research assistant activities (NSF/NIH, 2016).

The Survey of Doctorate Recipients (SDR) provides demographic, education, and career history information from individuals with a U.S. research doctoral degree in a science, engineering, or health field. The SDR is sponsored by the National Center for Science and Engineering Statistics and by the National Institutes of Health. Conducted since 1973, the SDR is a unique source of information about the educational and occupational achievements and career movement of U.S.-trained doctoral scientists and engineers in the United States and abroad.[4]

The Survey of Earned Doctorates (SED) is an annual census conducted since 1957 of all individuals receiving a research doctorate from an accredited U.S. institution in a given academic year. The SED is sponsored by the National Center for Science and Engineering Statistics within the National Science Foundation and by five other federal agencies: the National Institutes of Health, U.S. Department of Education, U.S. Department of Agriculture, National Endowment for the Humanities, and National Aeronautics and Space Administration. The SED collects information on the doctoral recipient's educational history, demographic characteristics, and postgraduation plans.[5]

Science and Engineering Indicators (Indicators) is the "gold standard" of high-quality quantitative data on U.S. and international science, engineering, and technology. Indicators is factual, unbiased, and is widely used by state and federal policymakers, businesses, universities, and many others to inform their decisions.[6]

STEM stands for science, technology, engineering, and mathematics. For this report, the field of science includes the social and behavioral sciences. The data in this report refer to the following broad fields: engineering, agricultural sciences; biological sciences; earth, atmospheric, and ocean sciences; computer sciences; mathematics and statistics; chemistry; physics; social and behavioral sciences; and medical and other health sciences (for Ph.D.'s only, as these degrees are part of the "doctoral-research/scholarship" category as noted by the National Center for Science and Engineering Statistics).

Teaching assistantships are a financial award given to a graduate student where most of the student's responsibilities are devoted primarily to teaching assistant activities (NSF/NIH, 2016).

---

[4] See https://www.nsf.gov/statistics/srvydoctoratework/ (accessed May 8, 2018).

[5] See https://www.nsf.gov/statistics/srvydoctorates/ (accessed May 8, 2018).

[6] See https://www.nsf.gov/statistics/2018/nsb20181/ (accessed May 8, 2018).

Trainee may refer to both predoctoral and postdoctoral individuals, regardless of their source of support. Trainee also refers more specifically to individuals appointed to a particular training program.[7]

Training (see also Education) focuses on the development of a skill, trait, or set of abilities related to a specified task or specialization.

Transdisciplinarity transcends disciplinary approaches through more comprehensive frameworks, including the synthetic paradigms of general systems theory and sustainability, as well as the shift from a disease model to a new paradigm of health and wellness. In the late 20th century, it also became aligned with problem-oriented research that crosses the boundaries of both academic and public and private spheres. In this second connotation, mutual learning, joint work, and knowledge integration are key to solving "real-world" problems. The construct goes beyond interdisciplinary combinations of existing approaches to foster new worldviews or domains (NRC, 2014).

REFERENCES

Gibbs, K., Jr. 2014. Diversity in STEM: What it is and why it matters. *Scientific American*. Voices blog. Available https://blogs.scientificamerican.com/voices/diversity-in-stem-what-it-is-and-why-it-matters/.

Kapila, M., E. Hines, and M. Searby; ProInspire. 2016. Why diversity, equity, and inclusion matter. Independent Sector. Available: https://independentsector.org/resource/why-diversity-equity-and-inclusion-matter/.

NAS/NAE/IOM (National Academy of Sciences, National Academy of Engineering, and Institute of Medicine). 1997. *Adviser, teacher, role model, friend: On being a mentor to students in science and engineering.* Washington, DC: National Academy Press.

NAS/NAE/IOM. 2005. *Facilitating interdisciplinary research.* Washington, DC: The National Academies Press.

NCSES (National Center for Science and Engineering Statistics). 2017. Introduction in *Women, minorities, and persons with disabilities in science and engineering:* 2017. Special Report NSF 17-310. Arlington, VA: National Science Foundation. Available: https://www.nsf.gov/statistics/2017/nsf17310/technical-notes.cfm#reporting-categories (accessed December 21, 2017).

NRC (National Research Council). 2014. *Convergence: Facilitating transdisciplinary integration of life sciences, physical sciences, engineering, and beyond.* Washington, DC: The National Academies Press.

NSF (National Science Foundation). 2011. *Diversity and inclusion strategic plan 2012–2016.* Arlington, VA: NSF. Available: https://www.nsf.gov/od/odi/reports/StrategicPlan.pdf (accessed May 8, 2018).

NSF/NIH (National Science Foundation and National Institutes of Health). 2016. Worksheet for Survey of Graduate Students and Postdoctorates in Science and Engineering. Available: https://www.nsf.gov/statistics/srvygradpostdoc/surveys/srvygradpostdoc-2016.pdf (accessed May 8, 2018).

---

[7] See https://www.nigms.nih.gov/training/Pages/New-Training-Tables-FAQs.aspx.

Pfund, C., A. Byars-Winston, J. Branchaw, S. Hurtado, and K. Eagan. 2016. Defining attributes and metrics of effective research mentoring relationships. *AIDS and Behavior* 20(2):238-248.

Sullivan, A. 2016. *A case study in micro-credentialing*. Interstate Renewable Energy Council. Available: https://irecusa.org/wp-content/uploads/2016/03/MicroCredential-Case-Study-FINAL-March-2016.pdf (accessed May 8, 2018).

Weir, K. 2013. Feel like a fraud? *gradPSYCH* 11(4):24-27. Available: http://www.apa.org/gradpsych/2013/11/fraud.aspx (accessed January 23, 2018).

WHO (World Health Organization, Knowledge Centre). 2018. Gender, equity and human rights: Glossary of terms and tools. Available: http://www.who.int/gender-equity-rights/knowledge/glossary/en/ (accessed May 8, 2018).

B

Discussion Document and Call
for Community Input

National Academies of Sciences, Engineering, and Medicine
Committee on Revitalizing Graduate STEM Education for the 21st Century

This document was available on the project site for the Committee on Revitalizing Graduate STEM Education for the 21st Century and the call for community input was open to the public from August 10 to September 22, 2017.

The members of the National Academies of Sciences, Engineering, and Medicine's (National Academies) Committee on Revitalizing Graduate STEM Education for the 21st century are soliciting input into ways to structure U.S. graduate education programs to better serve the needs of diverse students, the scientific enterprise, and the Nation.[1] We would appreciate your reactions to some of the input the Committee has received from various stakeholders (e.g., students, faculty, scientific societies, and funding agencies), as well as your own thoughts on these issues.

BACKGROUND

The National Academies created this Committee to respond to the concern that the current system is inadequately educating graduate students in science, technology, engineering, and mathematics (STEM) to prepare them for productive careers in the 21st century. For example, all available evidence suggests that over 60 percent of new Ph.D. students in STEM do not pursue careers in academia.[2] However, the Ph.D. graduate education system has changed relatively little over the past 100 years, with its fundamental format directed at preparing students primarily for research careers in academia. At the master's level, there

---

[1] Visit the project website for Statement of Task, list of Committee members, and project information.

[2] National Center for Science and Engineering Statistics. 2016. *Doctorate recipients from U.S. universities: 2015.* Special Report NSF 17-306. Arlington, VA: National Science Foundation, Table 46. Available: www.nsf.gov/statistics/2017/nsf17306/.

have been more significant changes over the last decade or two, but there is concern that those changes may have been too few or too small in scale. Given the diversity of career paths that students pursue—coupled with changes in demographics of the student populations, and with the rapid evolution in the ways science itself is conducted—we and others believe that there is an urgent need to ensure that the graduate education system is better aligned with the needs of *all* students, as well as the needs of the scientific enterprise, potential employers, and the broader society. The National Academies charged this Committee with considering the questions of how well the current graduate education system is equipping students for current and anticipated future needs and what changes should be made to increase its effectiveness.

The Committee recognizes that many elements of the existing graduate education system are working well and serve many of the needs of an array of higher education institutions, academic departments, faculty members, and other stakeholders. The Committee will strive to ensure that those benefits are not compromised. Nevertheless, evidence from students, recent graduates, and employers suggest that the system has not fully kept pace with broader changes in society, or in the ways science and engineering are practiced.[3] There is both a demand and opportunities to modernize the system to be more inclusive and to better meet the needs and interests of an increasingly diverse student body pursuing a broad spectrum of careers in a world in which labor markets, funding sources, and institutional policies are undergoing rapid change.[4]

A CALL FOR COMMUNITY INPUT

As a starting point for your thoughts, we ask you to consider a set of competencies, described in the following sections, that might serve as core educational elements or goals at both the master's and Ph.D. levels. These core educational elements would be the foundation for framing programmatic and logistic standards and considerations, such as program structure, curriculum, and how to enhance diversity within the scientific enterprise. We would like to know if the community, writ large, agrees with these core educational goals going forward or whether they should be adjusted to better reflect the context and needs of all 21st-century STEM graduate students. We would value your ideas on what might be missing from these lists, and what additional knowledge, experiences, and skills should be expected of all students. We also ask for your input on other questions

---

[3] National Academies of Sciences, Engineering, and Medicine. 2016. *Developing a national STEM workforce strategy: A workshop summary.* Washington, DC: The National Academies Press. doi: 10.17226/21900.

[4] National Science Foundation. 2016. *The National Science Foundation strategic framework for investments in Graduate Education FY 2016-FY 2020.* NSF-16074. Arlington, VA. Available: www. nsf.gov/pubs/2016/nsf16074/nsf16074.pdf.

we are pondering, listed at the end of the document, that represent focus areas for the eventual development of our report and recommendations.

CORE EDUCATIONAL ELEMENTS: MASTER'S DEGREES

Many master's programs are characterized by flexibility and adaptability to the changing nature of scientific disciplines and to workforce demands, and they often attempt to integrate the physical, biological, and social sciences, and even the humanities and arts. With a shorter time to degree than the Ph.D., and because many students fund their own master's degree program, institutions often establish and adapt master's programs to respond to workforce demands (sometimes in partnership with industry), and to anticipate emerging interdisciplinary fields.

To find a vision for core educational elements of master's degrees, the Committee referred to the Council of Graduate School's (CGS's) *Alignment Framework for the Master's Degree*. This alignment framework was the product of a year-long dialogue that included 150 graduate school deans.[5] Of the three defining characteristics of master's degree programs, the section on competencies describes four developmental dimensions that graduate school deans believe should be common among all or most master's degree programs:

1. **Disciplinary and interdisciplinary knowledge:** Master's students should develop core disciplinary knowledge and the ability to work between disciplines.
2. **Professional competencies:** Master's students should develop abilities defined by a given profession (e.g., licensing and other credentials).
3. **Foundational and transferrable skills:** Master's students should develop skills that transcend disciplines and are applicable in any context, such as communications, leadership, and working in teams. These dimensions are especially critical as the lines that traditionally define scientific and engineering disciplines become blurred—and more scientific research and application is characterized by the convergence of disciplines.
4. **Research:** Master's students should develop the ability to apply the scientific method, understand the application of statistical analysis, gain experience in conducting research and other field studies, and engage in work-based learning and research in a systematic manner.

CORE EDUCATIONAL ELEMENTS: PH.D.

There is a consensus among graduate education leaders and faculty on U.S. university campuses that the education that Ph.D. students receive should at a

---

[5] Council of Graduate Schools. 2016. *The alignment framework for the master's degree*. Washington, DC. Available: http://cgsnet.org/january-2017-gradedge.

minimum provide them the ability to conduct original scientific research and to enhance their capacity to acquire new data, information, and knowledge. That is, the core coursework and other intensive experiences in the classroom and laboratory should prepare students to discover new knowledge, understand the implications of the new knowledge for both the scientific discipline and society at large, and communicate the impact of the research to their peers and the broader public. Taken together, the core educational elements would establish the STEM Ph.D. educational mission: stimulate curiosity; develop intellectual capacity to recognize, formulate, and communicate a complex problem; create multidimensional, quantitative approaches toward its solution; discover knowledge that advances understanding; and communicate the impact of the research to peers and the broader public.

Based on the input and ideas received to date, the Committee is considering some core elements of a quality Ph.D. education:

1. **Scientific literacy, communication, and professional skills**
   a. Acquire basic transdisciplinary knowledge sufficient to address a complex problem using multiple conceptual and methodological approaches.
   b. Develop deep specialized expertise in at least one STEM discipline/approach.
   c. Acquire an appreciation of the ethics and norms of the scientific enterprise and its relationship to the rest of society, as well as a strong and ethical character and exemplary professional conduct.
   d. Develop the ability to work in collaborative and team settings involving colleagues from diverse cultural and disciplinary backgrounds.
   e. Develop management, leadership, financial, and entrepreneurial skills critical to success in any 21st-century career.
   f. Build capacity to communicate the significance and impact of a study or a body of work to all STEM professionals, policy makers, and the public at large.

2. **Conduct of original research**
   a. Identify an important problem and articulate an original research question.
   b. Design a set of studies, including relevant quantitative and analytical approaches, to explore components of the problem and begin to address the research question.
   c. Evaluate outcomes of each experiment or study component and select which outcomes to pursue and how.

    d. Adopt rigorous standards of investigation and acquire mastery of the quantitative and analytical skills required to conduct successful research in the field of study.

Are these effective/appropriate core educational elements for the 21st century, or should they be modified to increase the probability of successful careers for all students? The Committee looks forward to your comments and suggestions.

ADDITIONAL QUESTIONS FOR THE COMMUNITY

The committee also seeks your input on several issues that have arisen during our deliberations to date.

- In addition to the core capabilities described above, the committee has been hearing about other offerings that could augment a graduate STEM degree independently of the student's educational and career goals. These might include mentoring, career exploration, personnel management, cross-cultural competency, budgeting, communication, entrepreneurship, and fundamentals of business development. This raises an array of questions on which the committee seeks input:
  - What are the types of offerings that institutions, employers, professional societies, and other stakeholders should provide to help students acquire the skills to equip them for 21st century careers? To what degree will students and employers find value in emerging credentials offered online and by nontraditional models?
  - Should these offerings be required of all students, or should they be optional? When should they be offered? During or after graduate school?
  - How in-depth and of what duration should the additional educational experiences be?
- Many say that attitudinal and behavioral changes regarding career pathways for STEM graduates among virtually all concerned stakeholders (e.g., students, faculty, institutional leadership, and funding agencies) are necessary to ensure that graduate STEM education is effective and relevant going forward. Given that each group operates within a different context and with its own unique set of incentives and rewards, how might those incentives be adjusted to better align the behavior of various groups to achieving the goals of 21st-century graduate education?
- How can the system most effectively increase the diversity of U.S. STEM graduate student and faculty populations?
- How can the system increase completion rates for all students?
- There appears to be great concern about the issue of time to degree. What level of priority should time to degree receive, and how should it be addressed?

- Since the needs for graduate STEM education will continue to evolve and change over time, what kind of monitoring system can be established to ensure continuous improvement in terms of meeting the needs of diverse stakeholders? What metrics would be used to evaluate progress?
- How might students gain sufficient familiarity with the range of careers available for STEM Ph.D. recipients so that they can make more informed decisions as their education progresses? Should the core of graduate education be in some way adjusted to align better with the perceived needs of the range of future employers? Would internships in nonacademic settings or opportunities to formally mentor other students be appropriate? If so, should those internships and mentoring opportunities be offered during or after graduate school?
- The systematic collection and publication of reliable career placement data are sporadic across graduate schools and individual departments, although the Committee is aware that efforts are under way to remedy this situation. How can we best encourage uniform transparency about career outcomes for prospective students and other stakeholders at the level of individual graduate schools and departments? What would be the impact of publication of these data on prospective students and graduate schools?

You may submit your feedback online at http://nas.edu/GradEdInput **by September 22, 2017,** or you may submit general comments via e-mail to STEMGradEd@nas.edu.

The Committee on Revitalizing Graduate STEM Education for the 21st Century has received support from the following sponsors:

- The Burroughs Wellcome Fund,
- The Institute for Education Sciences,
- The National Science Foundation, and
- The Spencer Foundation.

C

Committee Biographies

Alan I. Leshner (*Chair,* **NAM**) is chief executive officer, emeritus, of the American Association for the Advancement of Science (AAAS) and former executive publisher of the *Science* family of journals. Before joining AAAS, Leshner was director of the National Institute on Drug Abuse at the National Institutes of Health. He also served as deputy director and acting director of the National Institute of Mental Health, and in several roles at the National Science Foundation. Before joining the government, Leshner was professor of psychology at Bucknell University. Leshner is an elected fellow of AAAS, the American Academy of Arts & Sciences, the National Academy of Public Administration, and many others. He is a member and served on the governing council of the National Academy of Medicine (formerly the Institute of Medicine) of the National Academies of Sciences, Engineering, and Medicine. He served two terms on the National Science Board, appointed first by President George W. Bush and then reappointed by President Obama. Leshner received Ph.D. and M.S. degrees in physiological psychology from Rutgers University and an A.B. in psychology from Franklin and Marshall College. Leshner has received many honors and awards, including the Walsh McDermott Medal from the National Academy of Medicine and seven honorary doctor of science degrees.

Sherilynn Black is the associate vice provost for Faculty Advancement, a new position designed to work in collaboration with the vice provost for Faculty Advancement at Duke University School of Medicine to create strategic initiatives and implement practices that support faculty development and advancement. She provides leadership in the area of faculty development and success, including mentoring, support for pre-tenure and mid-career faculty, career pathways, and professional development for nontenure system faculty, and resources and initiatives to increase diversity among the faculty ranks and further develop an inclusive climate within academic units. Black previously served as the founding director of the Office of Biomedical Graduate Diversity for the Duke University School of Medicine. She is currently one of the principal investigators of the Duke Initiative for Maximizing Student Development Program referred to as the Duke Biosciences Collaborative for Research Engagement, which provides extensive mentoring and scientific engagement opportunities for talented and diverse undergraduate and graduate students and faculty in the biomedical and behavioral sciences. Black holds several national appointments relating to faculty development and advancement, including serving on advisory boards, developing strategic initiatives, and holding committee appointments with the National Institutes of Health, the Howard Hughes Medical Institute, the Burroughs Wellcome Fund, the American Association of Medical Colleges, the National Academies of Sciences, Engineering, and Medicine, and the Society for Neuroscience. Black earned her B.A. as a Morehead-Cain Scholar at the University of North Carolina at Chapel Hill and earned her Ph.D. at Duke University. She also completed additional studies in the School of Education at the University of North Carolina at Chapel Hill. Black's research focuses on increasing faculty efficacy through developing cultural awareness in mentoring and assessing effective practices in interventions to increase diversity in academia.

Mary Sue Coleman (NAM) is the president of the Association of American Universities (AAU) and president emerita of the University of Michigan, an institution she led for 12 years before retiring in July 2014. She previously was president of the University of Iowa. Coleman co-chaired the Lincoln Project, an initiative of the American Academy of Arts & Sciences to explore strategies to preserve the strength and diversity of public research universities. She also serves on the Board of Trustees of the Society for Science & the Public, a nonprofit organization dedicated to public engagement in scientific research and education. She is a member of the Board of Trustees of the Kavli Foundation, which is dedicated to advancing science and support for scientists, and the Board of Trustees of the Gates Cambridge Scholars, a graduate student fellowship program. She serves on the Board of Trustees of the Mayo Clinic. In 2010, U.S. Commerce Secretary Gary Locke named her co-chair of the National Advisory Council on Innovation and Entrepreneurship. Her leadership positions in higher education have included membership on the National Collegiate Athletic Association Board of Directors and the Knight Commission on Intercollegiate Athletics. She is a past chair of the Association of American Universities, and also served as chair of the Internet2 Board of Trustees. Elected to the National Academy of Medicine, Coleman also is a Fellow of the American Association for the Advancement of Science and of the American Academy of Arts & Sciences. As a biochemist, Coleman built a distinguished research career through her research on the immune system and malignancies. At Michigan, she holds appointments of professor emerita of biological chemistry in the Medical School and professor emerita of chemistry in the College of Literature, Science, and the Arts. For 19 years she was a member of the biochemistry faculty at the University of Kentucky. Her work in the sciences led to administrative appointments at the University of North Carolina at Chapel Hill and the University of New Mexico, where she served as provost and vice president for academic affairs. Coleman earned her B.S. in chemistry from Grinnell College and her Ph.D. in biochemistry from the University of North Carolina at Chapel Hill.

Jaime Curtis-Fisk is a scientist and STEM education advocate for the Dow Chemical Company. Her primary focus area in education outreach was the development of the Dow STEM Ambassadors, the employee engagement program that focuses on unique approaches to connect the passion of STEM professionals to opportunities for impact in their local communities and through partner universities. Along with employee volunteerism, Curtis-Fisk is also very passionate about building the pipeline of future women scientists. She is involved with several initiatives that support the role of women in STEM, including serving on the American Chemical Society's Women Chemist Committee. In addition to leading STEM education outreach, she is also a practicing STEM professional as an innovation project leader in Dow's Manufacturing & Engineering division. Her technical expertise focuses on polymer chemistry and utilizing material science to develop new delivery systems for active ingredients. Curtis-Fisk received her B.S. in chemistry from Grand Valley State University and her Ph.D. in chemistry with certification in college teaching from Michigan State University.

Kenneth (Kenny) Gibbs, Jr. is a program director in the Division of Training, Workforce Development and Diversity (TWD) at the National Institute of General Medical Sciences (NIGMS) where he leads and administers federal programs that train the next generation of scientists and broaden participation in the research workforce. Previously, Gibbs served as a program analyst in the NIGMS Office of Program Planning, Analysis, and Evaluation where he led evaluation and innovation efforts of NIGMS TWD programs, and supported trans-NIH strategic and programmatic evaluative efforts. Prior to joining NIGMS, Gibbs was a Cancer Prevention Fellow at the National Cancer Institute, and an American Association for the Advancement of Science, Science & Technology Policy Fellow at the National Science Foundation in the Directorate for Education and Human Resources. Gibbs completed his Ph.D. in the immunology program at Stanford University and received his B.S. in biochemistry and molecular biology (summa cum laude) from the University of Maryland, Baltimore County, where he was a Meyerhoff, MARC (Maximizing Access to Research Careers), and Howard Hughes Medical Institute scholar. Gibbs serves as member of the editorial board of the journal *CBE—Life Sciences Education*, has previously served on the board of directors for the National Postdoctoral Association, and has written about scientific training and diversity issues for *Science Careers* and *Scientific American*.

Maureen Grasso, an American Society of Heating, Refrigerating and Air-Conditioning Engineers (ASHRAE) Fellow, is a professor in the College of Textiles at North Carolina State University. As dean of the Graduate School at North Carolina State University, she served as the academic leader responsible for policy with fiscal oversight of the graduate student support plan and fellowships. Grasso provided the administration for more than 220 degree programs serving 7,700 students that spanned the university's 10 colleges. A nationally recognized leader in graduate education, Grasso served as dean of the Graduate School at the University of Georgia for 12 years. As the academic leader at the University of Georgia, she developed and implemented policy and was responsible for graduate student stipends and fellowships for more than 6,600 students, 95 doctoral programs, 138 master's programs, and 17 specialty degree programs that spanned 16 colleges. Among her numerous accomplishments, a focus on graduate student diversity resulted in a 54 percent increase in African American graduate students during her tenure at the University of Georgia. Grasso has received numerous awards and recognition for her work, including the Southern Graduate Schools Achievement Award for Outstanding Contributions to Graduate Education in 2009. She served on the board of directors of the Council of Graduate Schools and in key leadership positions for the Conference of Southern Graduate Schools, including as president. She is a member of ASHRAE where she served in many of its leadership positions including as a member of the board of directors and as a trustee of the ASHRAE Foundation.

Sally Mason is president emerita of the University of Iowa (UI). Trained as a cell developmental biologist, she also holds a full professorship in the Department of Biology in the College of Liberal Arts and Sciences. Currently, Mason is overseeing a historic era of campus transformation, including rebuilding in the wake of the historic 2008 flooding, especially the renewal of an arts campus for the 21st century; the construction of a state-of-the-art children's hospital and biomedical discovery research center; and the first new residence hall since 1968. At Iowa, Mason has also spearheaded a sustainable university initiative, making sustainability a central priority of all aspects of the university enterprise. Under Mason's leadership, the UI has successfully met current economic challenges through careful planning, strategic prioritization, and increased efficiency. Other major accomplishments during President Mason's tenure have been a student success initiative that has led to increased enrollment and student retention, as well as an expansion of partnership agreements with Iowa's community colleges in order to offer UI degrees to students throughout the state through onsite and distance learning programs. Mason successfully advocated for a 2-year tuition freeze for resident undergraduate students for the 2013–2015 academic years, the first such tuition freeze in nearly 40 years. The daughter of an immigrant father and the first child in her family to attend college, Mason received her B.A. in zoology from the University of Kentucky in 1972, her M.S. from Purdue University in 1974, and her Ph.D. in cellular, molecular, and developmental biology from the University of Arizona in 1978. She spent two postdoctoral research years at Indiana University before joining the molecular biosciences faculty at the University of Kansas in 1981, where she received awards for outstanding undergraduate advising and teaching and was awarded a prestigious Kemper Teaching Fellowship. After stints as acting chair of the Department of Physiology and Cell Biology and associate dean in the College of Liberal Arts and Sciences, in 1995 she won appointment as the dean of the College of Liberal Arts and Sciences, the largest academic unit on the University of Kansas campus. Mason served as provost of Purdue University from 2001 to 2007, where she was responsible for planning, managing, and reviewing all academic programs at Purdue's West Lafayette campus and four affiliated branch campuses throughout Indiana. Mason is the author of many scientific papers and has obtained a number of research grants from the National Science Foundation, the National Institutes of Health, the Wesley Research Foundation, and the Lilly Endowment. Her research interests have focused on the developmental biology, genetics, and biochemistry of pigment cells and pigments in the skin of vertebrates, and she served as president of the PanAmerican Society for Pigment Cell Research. Since 2006, Mason has been appointed by the President of the United States to three terms on the National Medal of Science President's Committee, including one term as chair. She has also served as chair of the Advisory Committee to the National Science Foundation (NSF) Directorate for Education and Human Resources (EHR) and chair of the American Association for the Advancement of Science (AAAS) review panel of the NSF Science and Technology Centers Program.

Mary Maxon is the associate laboratory director for Biosciences at Lawrence Berkeley National Laboratory, where she oversees Berkeley Laboratory's Biological Systems and Engineering, Environmental Genomics and Systems Biology, and Molecular Biophysics and Integrated Bioimaging divisions and the Department of Energy Joint Genome Institute. Maxon has been integral to the strategic planning efforts and development of the biosciences area for 4 years, most recently as the biosciences principal deputy. She earned her bachelor's degree in biology and chemistry from the State University of New York at Albany, and her graduate degree in molecular cell biology from the University of California, Berkeley. Maxon has worked in the private sector, in both the biotechnology and pharmaceutical industries, as well as the public sector, highlighted by her tenure as the assistant director for biological research at the White House Office of Science and Technology Policy in the Executive Office of the President, where she developed the National Bioeconomy Blueprint. With her diverse and extensive background in industry, scientific foundations, and both state and federal government, Maxon is recognized as a national leader in science and technology policy. She has been a member of the Academies' Board on Life Sciences (July 1, 2014, to June 30, 2017) and a member of the National Academies' Committee on Future Biotechnology Products and Opportunities to Enhance Capabilities of the Biotechnology Regulatory System (March 15, 2016, to March 31, 2017).

Suzanne Ortega became the sixth president of the Council of Graduate Schools on July 1, 2014. Prior to assuming her current position, she served as the University of North Carolina (UNC) senior vice president for Academic Affairs (2011–2014). Previous appointments include executive vice president and provost at the University of New Mexico, and vice provost and graduate dean at the University of Washington and the University of Missouri. Ortega's master's and doctoral degrees in sociology were completed at Vanderbilt University. With primary research interests in mental health epidemiology, health services, race and ethnic relations, and higher education, Ortega is the author or co-author of numerous journal articles, book chapters, and an introductory sociology text, now in its ninth edition. An award-winning teacher, Ortega has also served on a number of review panels for the National Science Foundation (NSF) and the National Institutes of Health and has been the principal investigator (PI) or co-investigator on grants totaling more than $9 million in private foundation, state, and federal funds. She currently serves as PI on a major NSF- and Andrew W. Mellon Foundation-funded study, documenting the career pathways of Ph.D. students and alumni, up to 15 years out, at more than 50 major U.S. research universities. Ortega serves or has served on a number of professional association boards and committees, including the boards of the Council of Graduate Schools, the Graduate Record Exam, the National Academies' Committee on the Assessment of the Research Doctorate, the NSF Human Resources Expert Panel, the Education and Human Resources Advisory Committee, North Carolina E-learning Commission, and the University of North Carolina Press. She currently is a member of the board of trustees of American University in the Emirates.

Christine Ortiz is the Morris Cohen Professor of Materials Science and Engineering at the Massachusetts Institute of Technology (MIT). Ortiz is the founder of a new nonprofit organization, Station1, that is building a foundation for the university of the future — a scalable model of higher education based on inclusion and equity, learning through frontier project-based inquiry and research, and the integration of science and technology with societal perspective and impact. Ortiz served as the dean for Graduate Education at MIT between 2010 and 2016, supporting approximately 7,000 graduate students from 100+ countries. With more than 25 years of experience in higher education, Ortiz has led cross-institutional initiatives in global education, technology-enabled learning, new methods of learning assessment, fostering diversity and inclusion, and postsecondary financial models. Ortiz has served on more than 50 MIT departmental and institute committees and working groups. As a professor of materials science and engineering at MIT, Ortiz is a distinguished scientist and engineer with more than 175 scholarly publications, has supervised the research projects of more than 80 students from 10 different academic disciplines, and has received 30 national and international honors, including the Presidential Early Career Award in Science and Engineering, awarded to her at the White House by President George W. Bush. She is the founder and faculty director of the MIT International Science and Technologies Initiatives—Israel program, which has given approximately 600 students global internship opportunities. Ortiz serves on numerous boards, including as a regional accreditation commissioner for the Commission on Institutions of Higher Education, New England Association of Schools and Colleges.

Melanie Roberts has worked to further benefits of science and technology for society by catalyzing and supporting collaborations between scientists and engineers in the government or civic sectors. In 2018, she became director of state and regional affairs for Pacific Northwest National Laboratory. Previously, she was an independent science and education policy consultant and founding director of Emerging Leaders in Science and Society (ELISS), a program of the American Association for the Advancement of Science (AAAS). ELISS developed collaborative leadership skills and mind-sets in graduate students through an experiential program that focused on regional challenges. She has also held positions in the federal government and academia. As an assistant director at the Biofrontiers Institute of the University of Colorado Boulder, she promoted interdisciplinary and cross-sector collaborations. She also worked in the U.S. Senate and National Science Foundation as an AAAS Science and Technology Policy Fellow. Roberts holds a Ph.D. in neuroscience from the University of Washington and has completed postdoctoral work in science and innovation policy at the University of Colorado Boulder.

Henry Sauermann is an associate professor of strategy, who joined the European School of Management and Technology Berlin in May 2017. He is the first holder of the POK Pühringer PS Chair in Entrepreneurship. Since January 2018, Sauermann has been the director of the Institute for Endowment Management and Entrepreneurial Finance. Previously he was an associate professor of strategy and innovation and the Ph.D. coordinator at the Scheller College of Business at the Georgia Institute of Technology. Sauermann explores the role of human capital in science, innovation, and entrepreneurship. Among other research areas, he studies how scientists' motives and incentives relate to important outcomes such as innovative performance in firms, patenting in academia, or career choices and entrepreneurial interests. This stream of research also explores important differences in these mechanisms across organizational contexts such as industrial versus academic science or start-ups versus large established firms. In new projects, Sauermann studies the dynamics of motives and incentives over time and explores nontraditional innovative institutions such as crowd science and innovation contests. Additional work is under way to gain deeper insights into scientific labor markets and to derive implications for junior scientists, firms, and policy makers. He is a research associate at the National Bureau of Economic Research. His work has been funded by the National Science Foundation, the Kauffman Foundation, a Sloan Foundation Research Program, as well as the Georgia Research Alliance. He has published in a wide range of journals including *Management Science, Organization Science, Research Policy, the Strategic Entrepreneurship Journal, Science,* the *Proceedings of the National Academy of Sciences,* and *Science Advances.* He has presented his work at many national and international conferences and was invited to share his research with policy makers and business executives at meetings of the National Academies and the Conference Board.

Barbara Schaal (**NAS**) is the dean of the Faculty of Arts and Sciences and the Mary Dell Chilton Distinguished Professor, Washington University in St. Louis. Schaal was born in Berlin, Germany and grew up in Chicago, Illinois. She graduated from the University of Illinois, Chicago with a degree in biology and received a Ph.D. from Yale University. She is a plant evolutionary biologist who uses DNA sequences to understand evolutionary processes such as gene flow, geographical differentiation, and the domestication of crop species. Her current research focuses on the evolutionary genomics of rice. She currently serves as chair of the Division on Earth and Life Studies at the National Research Council and was a member of President Obama's Council of Advisors for Science and Technology. She has been president of the Botanical Society of America and the Society for the Study of Evolution. She is an elected member of the American Academy of Arts & Sciences and the U.S. National Academy of Sciences where she served as vice president. She was appointed as a U.S. science envoy by former Secretary of State Hillary Clinton. In February 2016, Schaal became the president of the American Association of the Advancement of Science.

Subhash Singhal (**NAE**) is Battelle Fellow and Fuel Cells director at the Pacific Northwest National Laboratory (PNNL). He joined the Energy Science and Technology Directorate at PNNL in April 2000 after having worked at Siemens Power Generation (formerly Westinghouse Electric Corporation) for more than 29 years. At PNNL, Singhal provides senior technical, managerial, and commercialization leadership to the laboratory's extensive fuel cell program. At Siemens Westinghouse, he conducted and/or managed major research, development, and demonstration programs in the field of advanced materials for various energy conversion systems including steam and gas turbines, coal gasification, and fuel cells. From 1984 to 2000, he was manager of Fuel Cell Technology there, and was responsible for the development of high-temperature solid oxide fuel cells (SOFCs) for stationary power generation. In this role, he led an internationally recognized group in the SOFC technology and brought this technology from a few-watt laboratory curiosity to a fully integrated 200-kW power generation system. He has authored more than 75 scientific publications, edited 13 books, received 13 patents, and given more than 240 plenary, keynote, and other invited presentations worldwide. Singhal is a member of the U.S. National Academy of Engineering, a fellow of four professional societies (American Ceramic Society, the Electrochemical Society, ASM International, and the American Association for the Advancement of Science), and a senior member of the Mineral, Metals & Materials Society (TMS). He served on the Electrochemical Society's Board of Directors during 1992-1994, received its Outstanding Achievement Award in High Temperature Materials in 1994, and continues as the chairman of its International Symposium on Solid Oxide Fuel Cells held biennially since 1989. He served as president of the International Society for Solid State Ionics during 2003-2005. He received the American Ceramic Society's Edward Orton Jr. Memorial Award in 2001; an Invited Professorship Award from the Japan Ministry of Science, Education and Culture in 2002; and the Christian Friedrich Schoenbein Gold Medal from the European Fuel Cell Forum in 2006. He serves on the editorial boards of the Elsevier's Journal of *Power Sources* and the *Fuel Cell Virtual Journal*, and is an associate editor of ASME's *Journal of Fuel Cell Science and Technology*. He has also served on many national and international advisory panels including those of the National Materials Advisory Board of the National Research Council, the National Science Foundation, the Materials Properties Council, the U.S. Department of Energy, the NATO Advanced Study Institutes and Science for Peace Programs, the United Nations Development Program, the United Nations Industrial Development Organization, the International Energy Agency, and the European Commission. Singhal is also an adjunct professor in the Department of Materials Science and Engineering at the University of Utah and serves on the Visiting Advisory Board of the Department of Materials Science and Engineering at the University of Florida.

Kate Stoll is a senior policy advisor in the Massachusetts Institute of Technology (MIT) Washington, D.C., Office. She focuses on basic research funding, biomedical research policy, and space research policy. Stoll also works with MIT student and alumni advocacy communities to provide opportunities for policy engagement. She received a B.A. in biochemistry and molecular biology from Reed College in Portland, Oregon, and a Ph.D. in biochemistry from the University of Washington in Seattle. She served as an American Association for the Advancement of Science (AAAS) Science and Technology Policy Fellow at the National Science Foundation (NSF) where she worked on STEM graduate education policy and created the NSF Innovation in Graduate Education Challenge. Stoll has long been interested in the role of students in the research and innovation enterprise and was a co-founder of the former AAAS program, Emerging Leaders in Science and Society, which prepared graduate and professional students to collaborate across boundaries to tackle complex challenges in society. In 2014, she served as an American Chemical Society Congressional Fellow with the U.S. House Committee on Energy and Commerce under Ranking Member Henry Waxman.

James M. Tien (NAE) is distinguished professor and dean emeritus of the University of Miami College of Engineering. An internationally renowned researcher, he formerly served as the Yamada Corporation Professor at Rensselaer Polytechnic Institute, was founding chair of its Department of Decision Sciences and Engineering Systems, and professor in its Department of Electrical, Computer and Systems Engineering. Tien joined the Rensselaer faculty in 1977 and twice served as its acting dean of engineering. In 2001, he was elected to membership in the National Academy of Engineering, one of the highest honors accorded an engineer. His research interests include systems modeling, public policy, decision analysis, and information systems. He has served on the Institute of Electrical and Electronics Engineers Board of Directors (2000-2004) and was its vice president in charge of the Publication Services and Products Board and the Educational Activities Board. Tien earned his bachelor's degree in electrical engineering from Rensselaer and his Ph.D. in systems engineering and operations research from Massachusetts Institute of Technology.

Keith R. Yamamoto (NAS, NAM) is vice chancellor for science policy and strategy, director of precision medicine, and professor of cellular and molecular pharmacology at the University of California, San Francisco (UCSF). After earning his Ph.D. from Princeton University, Yamamoto joined the UCSF faculty in 1976, where he has been an international leader in the investigation of transcriptional regulation by nuclear receptors, which mediate the actions of essential hormones and cellular signals; he uses mechanistic and systems approaches to pursue these problems in pure molecules, cells, and whole organisms. He has led or served on numerous national committees focused on public and scientific policy, public understanding and support of biological research, and science education; he chairs the Coalition for the Life Sciences and sits on the National Research Council Governing Board Executive Committee, serves as vice chair of the National Academy of Medicine's Executive Committee and Council, and is a member of the National Academy of Sciences (NAS) Division of Earth and Life Studies Advisory Committee, the Board of Directors and Executive Committee of Research!America, and the Advisory Board for Lawrence Berkeley National Laboratory. As chair of the NAS Board on Life Sciences, he created the study committee that produced *Toward Precision Medicine: Building a Knowledge Network for Biomedical Research and a New Taxonomy of Disease*, the report that enunciated the precision medicine concept, and he has helped to lead efforts in the White House, in Congress, in Sacramento, and at UCSF to implement it. He has chaired or served on many committees that oversee training and the biomedical workforce, research funding, and the process of peer review and the policies that govern it at the National Institutes of Health. He was elected to the National Academy of Sciences, the National Academy of Medicine, the American Academy of Arts & Sciences, and the American Academy of Microbiology, and is a fellow of the American Association for the Advancement of Science.

D

Staff Biographies

Layne Scherer served as the study director for the Committee on Revitalizing Graduate STEM Education for the 21st Century and is a program officer with the Board on Higher Education and Workforce at the National Academies of Sciences, Engineering, and Medicine. Prior to joining the National Academies, Scherer was a science assistant at the National Science Foundation with the office of the Assistant Director for Education and Human Resources and served as an executive secretary under the National Science and Technology Council's Committee on STEM Education. As a part of her cross-agency work, Scherer developed an interest in performance management and completed training as a facilitator and graphic recorder with the Performance Improvement Council. Scherer earned her master's of public policy from the Gerald R. Ford School of Public Policy at the University of Michigan, with a focus on education policy, nonprofit management, and quantitative analysis. She earned her B.A. from the University of Michigan with concentrations in English literature and the history of art.

Austen Applegate is a senior program assistant with the Board on Higher Education and Workforce at the National Academies of Sciences, Engineering, and Medicine. Prior to joining the National Academies, he worked in a number of professional fields including international development, clinical research, and education. Applegate holds a B.A. from Guilford College, with a double concentration in psychology and sociology. It was during this time that he developed an interest in social science research and policy through his coursework in behavioral medicine, clinical assessment, public health, health policy, qualitative and quantitative research methodology, race and gender disparities, and social science history.

Tom Arrison is a program director in the Policy and Global Affairs Division of the National Academies of Sciences, Engineering, and Medicine. He joined NASEM in 1990 and has directed a range of studies and activities in areas such as research integrity, open science, international science and technology relations, innovation, information technology, higher education, and strengthening the U.S. research enterprise. Arrison served as executive director of the InterAcademy Partnership for Research from 2013 to 2017. IAP-R produces reports on scientific, technological, and health issues related to the great global challenges of our time, providing knowledge and advice to national governments and international organizations. He earned M.A.'s in public policy and Asian studies from the University of Michigan.

Allison L. Berger is currently a senior program assistant for the Policy and Global Affairs (PGA) Division of the National Academy of Sciences (NAS). Prior to joining PGA, she provided administrative support to the director of the Board on Global Health in the Health and Medicine Division of the NAS, and meeting planning support for the Forum on Global Violence Prevention. During her 15-year tenure with the NAS, Berger has supported other program units including the Food and Nutrition Board, the Board on Population Health and Public Health Practice, and the Innovation to Incubation program (i2I) under the National Academy of Medicine. Prior to joining the NAS, Berger served as administrative assistant at the American Psychological Association, where she worked on various activities and programs that promote psychological science in academic and scientific areas of research. Berger is currently pursuing a certification program to become a Certified Meeting Professional, which is the highest designation for meeting professionals in the meeting and convention planning industry.

Jaime Colman is an M.A. candidate in international relations and economics with a concentration in African Studies at Johns Hopkins University, School of Advanced International Studies. Colman is currently an intern at the U.S. Department of State in the Bureau of African Affairs. Prior to that, she was the senior program assistant on the Board of Higher Education and Workforce at the National Academy of Sciences (through November 2017). Colman received her B.A. in sociology and intercultural studies from Houghton College.

Adriana Navia Courembis joined the Academies in January 2012 as part of the Finance Staff for the Policy and Global Affairs Division. At this position she collaborates with the financial management for the Board on Higher Education and Workforce, the Committee on Women in Science, Engineering, and Medicine, the Science & Technology for Sustainability Program, the Committee on Human Rights, and the Board on Research Data and Information. Prior to the Academies, Courembis worked with the American Bar Association—Rule of Law Initiative as a program associate and with Bay Management, LLC as an accounts payable associate. Courembis holds a B.A. in international economics from American University.

Maria Lund Dahlberg is the study director for the Consensus Study on the Science on Effective Mentoring in STEMM (Science, Technology, Engineering, Mathematics, and Medicine) for the National Academies of Sciences, Engineering, and Medicine, and a program officer with the Board on Higher Education and Workforce and the Committee on Women in Science, Engineering, and Medicine. Her work with the National Academies spans topics ranging from science communications through health care for high-needs patients, to postdoctoral research experiences, photonics, and innovation ecosystems. She came to the National Academies by way of a Christine Mirzayan Science and Technology Policy Fellowship, which she received after completing all requirements short of finalizing the dissertation for her doctorate in physics at the Pennsylvania State University. Dahlberg holds a B.A. with high honors in physics from Vassar College and an M.S. in physics from the Pennsylvania State University.

Elizabeth Garbee has a Ph.D. in science policy from the Consortium for Science Policy and Outcomes at Arizona State University. She studies the value of a STEM Ph.D. outside of academia, and how to support students in whatever career path they choose for themselves. Garbee was a Christine Mirzayan Science and Technology Policy Fellow, Board on Higher Education and Workforce, from January to April 2018. Elizabeth earned her bachelor's degree in astrophysics and classical Greek literature from Oberlin College of Arts and Sciences.

Yasmeen Hussain is currently an American Association for the Advancement of Science (AAAS) Congressional Fellow sponsored by the Biophysical Society, working in the office of Representative Bill Foster. Previously, Hussain was an associate program officer with the Board on Higher Education and Workforce and the Committee on Women in Science, Engineering, and Medicine at the National Academies of Sciences, Engineering, and Medicine, where she completed a Mirzayan Science and Technology Policy fellowship. Hussain's previous roles have included being a civil engineering technician at the Bureau of Reclamation and extensive volunteer activities in informal science education and mentoring. She earned her Ph.D. in biology at the University of Washington in Seattle and B.S. degrees in mathematics and biology at the University of Utah.

Jay Labov served as senior advisor for Education and Communication for the National Academies of Sciences, Engineering, and Medicine until beginning phased retirement in January 2018. He directed or contributed to more than 30 reports on K-12 and undergraduate, teacher, and international education. He served as director of the Academies' Teacher Advisory Council. He directed the committee that authored *Science, Evolution, and Creationism* and oversaw the National Academies' efforts to confront challenges to teaching evolution in the nation's public schools. He coordinated efforts to work with professional societies on education issues. He also managed work on improving education in the life sciences under the Academy's Board on Life Sciences. Labov is an organismal biologist by training. Prior to accepting his position at the Academy in 1997, he spent 18 years on the biology faculty at Colby College (Maine). He is a Kellogg National Fellow, a fellow in Education of the American Association for the Advancement of Science, a Woodrow Wilson Visiting Fellow, and a recipient of the Friend of Darwin award from the National Center for Science Education. In 2013 he was elected to a 3-year term as chair-elect, chair, and past chair of the Education Section of the American Association for the Advancement of Science (AAAS) and now serves on AAAS's Council and an advisory board for AAAS's Dialog on Science, Ethics, and Religion. He has been named a Lifetime Honorary Member by the National Association of Biology Teachers, has received the National Science Teachers Association's Distinguished Service to Science Education award, and was awarded the John A. Moore Lectureship in 2016 by the Society for Integrative and Comparative Biology.

Frederic Lestina, senior program assistant, joins the Board on Higher Education and Workforce staff following 2 years with the Board on Science, Technology, and International Affairs. Lestina is involved with finalizing reports for publication, organizing logistical details for meetings and staff and committee travel, and other administrative duties. Prior to joining the National Academies, Lestina worked as a political transcriptionist, interned as a cartographer, and studied science and development policy.

Barbara Natalizio is a program officer with the Board on Higher Education and Workforce at the National Academies of Sciences, Engineering, and Medicine. Prior to joining the National Academies, she was an American Association for the Advancement of Science (AAAS) Science and Technology Policy Fellow serving in the Directorate for Education and Human Resources, Division of Graduate Education at the National Science Foundation. During her postdoctoral fellowship in the Department of Cell and Developmental Biology at Vanderbilt University Medical Center, she became very interested in career and professional development for early-career scientists. These collective experiences have provided her with a comprehensive awareness of and appreciation for effective evaluation, assessment, and policy that enables her continued support of higher education reform and STEM workforce development at the national level. Natalizio received her B.S. in biochemistry and history from Montclair State University and her Ph.D. in molecular genetics and microbiology from Duke University.

Irene Ngun is a research associate with the Board on Higher Education and

Workforce at the National Academies of Sciences, Engineering, and Medicine. She also serves as research associate for the Committee on Women in Science, Engineering, and Medicine, a standing committee of the National Academies. Before joining the National Academies she was a congressional intern for the U.S. House Committee on Science, Space, and Technology (Democratic Office) and served briefly in the office of Congresswoman Eddie Bernice Johnson of Texas (D-33). Ngun received her M.A. from Yonsei Graduate School of International Studies (Seoul, South Korea), where she developed her interest in science policy. She received her B.A. from Goshen College in biochemistry/molecular biology and global economics.

Thomas Rudin is the director of the Board on Higher Education and Workforce (BHEW) at the National Academies of Sciences, Engineering, and Medicine—a position he assumed in mid-August 2014. Prior to joining the Academies, Rudin served as senior vice president for career readiness and senior vice president for advocacy, government relations, and development at the College Board from 2006 to 2014. He was also vice president for government relations from 2004 to 2006 and executive director of grants planning and management from 1996 to 2004 at the College Board. Before joining the College Board, Rudin was a policy analyst at the National Institutes of Health in Bethesda, Maryland. In 1991, Rudin taught courses in U.S. public policy, human rights, and organizational management as a visiting instructor at the Middle East Technical University in Ankara, Turkey. In the early 1980s, he directed the work of the Governor's Task Force on Science and Technology for North Carolina Governor James B. Hunt, Jr., where he was involved in several new state initiatives, such as the North Carolina Biotechnology Center and the North Carolina School of Science and Mathematics. He received a B.A. from Purdue University, and he holds master's degrees in public administration and in social work from the University of North Carolina at Chapel Hill.

E

Open Meeting Agendas

**Committee on Revitalizing Graduate STEM
Education for the 21st Century
AGENDA**

First Committee Meeting
**National Academies of Sciences, Engineering, and Medicine
The Keck Center
500 5th Street NW, Washington, D.C.
Room 201
January 12–January 13, 2017**

Meeting Objectives

- **Introduce committee members and discuss study process.**
- **Secure input from the study sponsors about the task.**
- **Begin discussion of existing resources.** Including other efforts and national initiatives, existing data and research on graduate STEM education.
- **Discuss key questions for graduate education going forward.**

Thursday, January 12, 2017   *8:00 a.m.–5:00 p.m.*

8:00 a.m.–8:30 a.m.   ***Continental breakfast***

8:30 a.m. –10:00 a.m.   ***Closed session***

10:00 a.m. –5:00 p.m.   *Open sessions*

10:00 a.m. –10:15 a.m.   *Coffee break*

10:15 a.m. –11:45 a.m.   *Introduction and conversation with sponsors*
- Panel discussion with perspectives from the study sponsors.
  - **Thomas Brock,** Commissioner of the National Center for Education Research
  - **Joan Ferrini-Mundy,** Assistant Director for Education and Human Resources, National Science Foundation
  - **Victoria McGovern,** Senior Program Officer, Burroughs Wellcome Fund

11:45 a.m. –12:45 p.m.   *Lunch*

12:45 p.m. –2:15 p.m.   *Learning from recent initiatives in graduate education*
- Panel discussion focusing on common recommendations, themes, and lessons learned from previous efforts to reform graduate education.
  - **Chris Golde,** Assistant Director of Career Communities for Ph.D.'s & Postdocs, Stanford University
  - **Trish Labosky,** Office of Strategic Coordination, Division of Program Coordination, Planning and Strategic Initiatives, Office of the Director, National Institutes of Health
  - **Linda Strausbaugh,** Board Member and Consultant, National Professional Science Master's Association

2:15 p.m.–2:30 p.m.   *Break*

2:30 p.m. –4:00 p.m.   *The state of graduate STEM education*
- Panel discussion with a preliminary review of data on graduate students, career pathways, trends within and across disciplines, and innovations in data collection.

        o **Nimmi Kannankutty,** Deputy Division
           Director, Division on Graduate Education,
           National Science Foundation
        o **Hironao Okahana,** Assistant Vice President,
           Research and Policy, Council of Graduate
           Schools
        o **Jason Owen-Smith,** Executive Director,
           Institute for Research on Innovation and
           Science (IRIS)

4:00 p.m. –5:00 p.m.   *Open discussion with guests*
           • Committee welcomes additional input from
             audience members and guests

Friday, January 13, 2017   *9:00 a.m.–12:30 p.m.*

9:00 a.m. –12:30 p.m.   *Closed sessions*
           • Closed session for internal committee
             deliberations

12:30 p.m.   *Meeting adjourns*

**Committee on Revitalizing Graduate STEM
Education for the 21st Century**

Second Committee Meeting
**National Academies of Sciences, Engineering, and Medicine
The Keck Center
500 5th Street NW, Washington, D.C.
Room 101
March 23–March 24, 2017**

*Open sessions will also be available via webcast. Link will be available at
NAS.edu/GradEd.*

Meeting Objectives

- **Summarize recent and ongoing activities around graduate education in science.**
- **Present findings from working groups.**
- **Receive input and discuss key issues.** Including presentations from and discussions with professional societies, employers, and current and recent students.
- **Identify priorities and plan next steps.**

Thursday, March 23, 2017   *8:30 a.m.–5:00 p.m.*

8:30 a.m.–1:00 p.m.   *Closed sessions*

1:00 p.m.–5:00 p.m.   *Open sessions*

1:00 p.m.–2:45 p.m.   *Panel I: Professional societies' initiatives in
                            graduate education*
- **Amy Chang,** Education Director, American Society for Microbiology
- **Dave Harwell,** Assistant Director, Talent Pool, Science, American Geophysical Union
- **Theodore Hodapp,** Director of Project Development and Senior Advisor to Education
- **Bassam Shakhashiri,** William T. Evjue Distinguished Chair for the Wisconsin Idea and Director of the Wisconsin Initiative for Science Literacy, University of Wisconsin–Madison, and former president of the American Chemical Society

2:45 p.m.–3:00 p.m.   *Break*

3:00 p.m.–4:45 p.m.   *Panel II: Career trends for graduate STEM degree holders*
- **Dana (Keoki) Jackson,** Chief Technology Officer, Lockheed Martin
- **Cory Valente,** R&D Leader—Strategic Recruiting & Research Assignments Program Network Leader—GLAD, The Dow Chemical Company

4:45 p.m.–5:00 p.m.   *Closing comments*

Friday, March 24, 2017   *8:30 a.m.–12:30 p.m.*

8:30 a.m. –10:00 a.m.   *Open session*

8:30 a.m.–10:00 a.m.   *Panel III: Perspectives from current and recent students*
- **Jonathan Kershaw,** Postdoctoral Trainee, Purdue University and ELISS Alumnus
- **James Mathis,** Ph.D. Candidate, University of Michigan and American Physical Society Bridges Program participant
- **Barbara Natalizio,** AAAS Fellow, National Science Foundation and National Postdoctoral Association Board Member

10:00 a.m.–12:30 p.m.   *Closed sessions*

12:30 p.m.   *Meeting adjourns*

**Committee on Revitalizing Graduate STEM
Education for the 21st Century**

Third Committee Meeting
**North Carolina State University
Dorothy and Roy Park Alumni Center
2450 Alumni Drive Raleigh, NC 27606
Chancellor's Board Room and Reception Room
May 22–May 23, 2017**

Meeting Objectives

- **Discuss findings from working groups.**
- **Finalize discussion paper.**
- **Hear from stakeholders.** *Including institutional leaders and employers.*
- **Discuss project work plan.** *Identify actions to advance the project by the September meeting.*

Monday, May 22, 2017   *8:00 a.m.–5:00 p.m.*

8:00 a.m.–12:15 p.m.   *Closed sessions*

12:15 p.m.–5:00 p.m.   *Open sessions*

12:30 p.m.–1:15 p.m.   *Lunch with guests (Reception Room)*

1:15 p.m.–3:00 p.m.   *Panel I: Perspectives on implementing change in graduate education*
- The panel will begin with a review of recommendations from recent reports on graduate education, and the panelists will respond to the key themes and share their perspectives on how different parts of an institution contribute to the implementation of new programs, policies, and practices.
  - **Patrick Brennwald,** Professor, Department of Cell Biology and Physiology, University of North Carolina–Chapel Hill
  - **Yasmeen Hussain,** Associate Program Officer, National Academies of Sciences, Engineering, and Medicine

         o **Thomas Miller,** Senior Vice Provost for Academic Outreach and Entrepreneurship, North Carolina State University
         o **Debra Stewart,** President Emerita, Council of Graduate Schools
         o **Kimberly Weems,** Associate Professor, Mathematics and Physics, North Carolina Central University

3:00 p.m.–3:15 p.m. *Refreshments break (Reception Room)*

3:15 p.m.–4:45 p.m. *Panel II: Building university partnerships*
- This panel will focus on the ways in which partnerships between industry and universities and across campuses can enrich graduate STEM education.
  - o **Joseph Graves,** Professor & Associate Dean for Research and Integrative Bioinformatics for Investigating and Engineering Biomes (IBIEM), Co-Director, North Carolina A&T
  - o **Claudia Gunsch,** Theodore Kennedy Associate Professor, Civil & Environmental Engineering, and Integrative Bioinformatics for Investigating and Engineering Biomes (IBIEM), Director, Duke University
  - o **Steven Hunter,** IBM Fellow, North Carolina State University
  - o **Michael Lipps,** Managing Director, Business of Law Software Solutions, LexisNexis
  - o **Le Tang,** Vice President and Head of U.S. Corporate Research Center ABB

4:45 p.m.–5:00 p.m. *Closing comments*

Tuesday, May 23, 2017   *9:00 a.m.–3:30 p.m.*

9:00 a.m. –11:00 a.m. *Open session*

9:00 a.m.–10:45 a.m.   *Panel III: Creating institutional practices to improve support for all students*
- This panel will examine the ways in which admissions, orientation, mentoring, academic support, and other practices help ensure that students from diverse backgrounds are able to enter and persist through graduate school and into the careers that align with their interests.
    o **Dona Chikaraishi,** Professor Emeritus, Duke University
    o **Christine Grant,** Associate Dean of Faculty Development and Special Initiatives, College of Engineering, and Professor of Chemical Engineering, North Carolina State University
    o **David Shafer,** Assistant Dean for Outreach and Diversity, North Carolina State University
    o **Ayanna Boyd Williams,** Assistant Dean, The Graduate College, North Carolina A&T

10:45 a.m.–11:00 a.m.   *Refreshments break as guests depart (Reception Room)*

11:00 a.m.–3:00 p.m.   *Closed sessions*

Committee on Revitalizing Graduate STEM
Education for the 21st Century

Fourth Committee Meeting

University of California, San Francisco

Closed Sessions
Byers Hall
Room 211
550 16th Street
San Francisco, CA 94158

Open Sessions
Genentech Hall
600 16th Street
San Francisco, CA 94158
September 14-15, 2017

Meeting Objectives

- **Receive input and updates from researchers and focus groups.**
- **Discuss report outline and lay out process for drafting the final report.**
- **Review and discuss preliminary recommendations.**

Thursday, September 14, 2017

8:30 a.m.–1:30 p.m.   *Closed sessions*

1:30 p.m.–5:00 p.m.   *Open sessions (Genentech Hall Auditorium)*

1:30 p.m.–1:35 p.m.   *Welcome remarks from Keith Yamamoto*

1:35 p.m.–3:00 p.m.   *Panel I: Bold visions for the future of science*
                             Chair: Alan I. Leshner
                             - Panelists will share their vision on how changes
                               to today's system of graduate education and early
                               research careers can ensure a future research
                               enterprise that fosters innovation, promotes
                               equity and inclusion, and advances U.S. national
                               interests. Each panelist will provide remarks

(10 minutes) followed by discussion with the
Committee.
  o **David Asai,** Senior Director for Science
    Education, Howard Hughes Medical Institute
  o **Elizabeth Baca,** Senior Health Advisor, the
    California Governor's Office of Planning and
    Research
  o **Michael Richey,** Associate Technical Fellow,
    Learning Sciences and Engineering Education
    Research, The Boeing Company

3:00 p.m.–3:15 p.m.   *Break*

3:15 p.m.–4:45 p.m.   *Panel II: Perspectives from postdoctoral
                             researchers*
                             Chair: Ron Daniels

- Panelists will share their research on postdoctoral
  researchers with a focus on the implications for
  graduate education and early-career researchers.
  Each panelist will provide remarks (10 minutes)
  followed by discussion with the Committee.
  o **Samantha Hindle,** Assistant Professional
    Researcher, University of California, San
    Francisco
  o **Sean McConnell,** Postdoctoral Researcher,
    University of Chicago
  o **Marina Ramon,** STEM Project Specialist,
    Cabrillo College and National Postdoctoral
    Association Board Member
  o **Nancy Schwartz,** Professor, Biomedical
    Sciences, and Director, Joseph P. Kennedy Jr.
    Intellectual and Developmental Disabilities
    Research Center, University of Chicago

4:45 p.m.–5:15 p.m.   *Open discussion*

5:15 p.m.–5:20 p.m.   *Closing remarks from Ron Daniels*

Friday, September 15, 2017

8:30 a.m.–1:30 p.m.   *Closed sessions*

Committee on Revitalizing Graduate STEM
Education for the 21st Century

Fifth Committee Meeting

Keck Center
500 5th Street
Room 201
Washington, DC 20001

Monday, November 6
8:30 a.m.–5:00 p.m.   *Closed session*

Tuesday, November 7
8:30 a.m.–8:50 a.m.   *Closed session*

8:50 a.m.–9:00 a.m.   ***Break*** (to allow members of the public to join the open session).
For public guests, please refrain from entering the room until the doors have been opened to preserve the confidentiality of the closed session immediately preceding the panel.

9:00 a.m.–10:15 a.m.   ***Panel: Open session***
* Remarks from Earnestine Psalmonds Easter, Program Director, Division of Graduate Education, National Science Foundation
  o **David Feldon,** Professor of Instructional Technology and Learning Sciences, Utah State University
  o **Julia Lane** (virtual), Professor at Center for Urban Science + Progress and Wagner Graduate School of Public Service, New York University
  o **Bruce Weinberg,** Professor of Economics, Ohio State University

10:15 a.m.–10:30 a.m.   ***Break*** (to allow members of the public to depart).

10:30 a.m.–5:00 p.m.   *Closed session*